UNFIT TO MANAGE!

To Michael Romano,

Knowledge is Power.

Use This Book to

<u>Organize</u>.

Best Wishes
Ernest D. Lieberman
August 6, 1991

UNFIT TO MANAGE!

◇

How Mis-Management Endangers America and What Working People Can Do About It

Ernest D. Lieberman

McGRAW-HILL BOOK COMPANY

New York   St. Louis   San Francisco
Hamburg   Mexico   Toronto

1 2 3 4 5 6 7 8 9 DOC DOC 8 9 1 0 9 8

ISBN 0-07-037815-0

Library of Congress Cataloging-in-Publication Data

Lieberman, Ernest D.
  Unfit to manage: how mis-management endangers America and what working people can do about it / Ernest D. Lieberman.
    p. cm.
ISBN 0-07-037815-0
  1. Industrial management—United States. I. Title.
HD70.U5L54 1988
658′.00973—dc19   87-20891
                                     CIP

BOOK DESIGN BY EVE KIRCH

*To Chris, whose faith helped make this book possible,
and whose good judgment made it inestimably better*

Acknowledgments

Many people encouraged and supported me during the writing of this book.

Christine Summerson read every word many times and pointed out innumerable places where I could say something better or express it differently.

Judy Summerson was my first "outside" reader and made me feel, with her support and encouragement, that I had done something of real value.

My parents, Archie and Betty Lieberman, gave me their lifetimes of knowledge and experience about industrial work, union organizing, retail selling, and owning and running a small business. My father's expert knowledge of industrial unions and labor negotiations was unique and irreplaceable, amounting to the equivalent of several advanced degrees in labor relations from a union perspective.

The lessons I learned from friends and their families while growing up in the ethnic, working-class city, Bayonne, New Jersey, gave me deep respect for working people and high confidence in them.

The following people read drafts or portions of my manuscript and encouraged its publication, for which I will always be grateful: David Noble, Bayard Rustin, Lynn Williams, Seymour Melman, Edward Blakely, Michael Grisham, Jim Balanoff, Betty Balanoff, Tom Balanoff, Peter Lynch, Robert Harman, Bernard Fromartz, and Robert and Carolyn Koenig. Karen Nussbaum, Owen Bieber, Philip Sparks, and Alan Howard were most generous in expressing their support.

I would like to thank all the working people who read or listened to descriptions of my project and encouraged me with words and good cheer to persevere until it was published.

I will be forever grateful for the immediate understanding my agent, Clyde Taylor, had of my manuscript and for the work he put in to get it published. The final form of the book took shape with the intelligent vision of my editor, Leslie Meredith.

Contents

Preface

This book is about a widespread crisis that underlies many of the worst problems in America and the world. Much of American management is failing and is blaming everyone but itself for its failures. Its actions endanger us all and prevent people who could do the job better from making needed changes.

Some horror stories are so bad that they can't be hidden from the public. The space shuttle Challenger exploded. The nuclear reactor at Three Mile Island nearly melted down. General Motors Corp. still can't make competitive cars. The executives of Coca-Cola Co. didn't know the old Coke was "It!" The U.S. government under four Presidents let Russia build—and bug—America's embassy in Moscow. Recurring reports of shamefully overpriced or scarily problematic military products keep shaking the Pentagon. Bank of America and General Electric Co. were embarrassed by civil and criminal penalties, respectively, for wrongdoing. Then came the scandals on Wall Street—and the stock market crash.

Meanwhile, unemployment rates and hard-core unemployment mount with each business cycle. People who once worked for a living are made homeless. Many people are at jobs that pay less than what is needed to support a family. Highly successful career professionals are fearful that their children may be failures for life if they don't get into the right *nursery* schools! And the arms race gets justified more and more for the jobs and "prosperity" it is supposed to create—terrorizing people of all ages with fears of nuclear war.

We are paying in these and many other ways for management's failure to employ Americans productively and serve their needs. We need an economy that pays people enough so they can buy what is produced, that produces what people want and need, and that

ix

provides for a peaceful and secure future. Management has failed because it has lost touch with production and operations, market demands, and the long-term needs of America.

Management has lost touch at root because in any big business or government operation, no one knows or can know everything important that goes on. Too often those in authority don't even know that they don't know, which is the most charitable interpretation one can put on the actions of Union Carbide's management leading up to and following the disaster in Bhopal, India.

This fundamental ignorance is compounded by political, faddish, or greedy demands that run directly counter to productive realities, such as insisting that the Challenger launch on a frigid day, or ordering up a new "corporate culture" (attitudes and ways of doing things, not artwork) to be installed over the weekend, or demanding unreasonably high profits and uninterrupted quarterly profit increases even though they rob the future to do it.

Despite their own ignorance, managements distrust what employees tell them and don't want to hear what employees have to say, even though ground-level employees often know better than anyone what's really going on in the production process. Executives mostly want employees to work harder, cheaper, and scared, so they try to scatter production around the world in search of the lowest-wage, most subservient labor they can find. Or else they regard human labor as a liability or source of resistance that must be eliminated at all costs, so they spend huge sums on needlessly complex automation.

Consequently, American managements have become blind, deaf, and dumb. This has led to terribly costly disorganization within big business and government, and it has given massive aid and comfort to foreign competition.

Any effective solution to our economic problems must give employees—including professional staff and middle management—more pay for their knowledge and far more authority to determine how work gets done and what goods and services are produced. Management theories are full of ways to get more out of employees. But management doesn't want to pay employees more for it.

Even most "employee involvement," "worker owner," and

Employee Stock Ownership Plan (ESOP) schemes are little more than frauds to get something for nothing from employees. When employees realize this, they withhold what they know, they stop cooperating, and productivity suffers.

Many managements don't realize the dangers they run—as if they could forever "prevail" over foreign competition, the collapse of American productive power, and a "limited" nuclear war. Others would rather rule in hell than serve in heaven. Cheerleading and rational arguments have little effect on them. And business analysts, who owe their livelihoods to management, do not say loudly enough that the emperor has no clothes, lest management's right to do as it wishes be seriously undermined.

When management fails from the top down, individual employees, even individual managers, have little power to change it, and they often suffer abuse and economic hardships. If employees are to protect themselves and enjoy the fruits of a revitalized economy, they will have to work together. They will have to organize democratically and apply their abilities through their organizations to change how management operates. Some unions and professional associations have begun to move in these directions already.

What's needed now, and what this book attempts to provide, is a far clearer understanding of what forces are at work and a strong vision of what great good organizations of workers and professional employees could accomplish.

Boy, Was I Wrong. When I graduated from Princeton University and got a job in 1970, I thought that American managements really knew what they were doing. I also thought that, in the technical and professional areas at least, good work would be recognized and rewarded. I was wrong.

My first job was as a computer programmer with Western Electric, then the manufacturing and service arm of the Bell telephone system. I was hired for a task force to help install and support the operations of a new system of computer programs for a computer center in lower Manhattan. The programs, called "Distribution Information System," or DIS for short, had been designed and written by people in Western's national headquarters, and programmers from headquarters came and went in a steady stream. The computers and programs were run by operators who reported to management in the local plant. The task force to which I belonged reported to Western's Northeast Regional Division. And each of these three major organizations had many semiautonomous organizations within them.

Yet none of these many and diverse organizations worked together. They had different bosses, different goals, and competing interests. Whether by chance or design, the sign on one office door read "DIS Organization."

Emotional turmoil filled the computer center. Mistakes are common in complex systems, especially at the start. They have to be dealt with rationally, in a spirit of learning and cooperation, without casting blame. But when mistakes occurred at the computer center where I worked, each organization—indeed each person—feared getting blamed and tried to blame someone else rather than work together to solve the problem. The result was a never-ending series of personal conflicts and computer-system breakdowns.

For example, I belonged to a four-person group of programmers whose job was to fix anything that went wrong in running the computer programs, but we had no authority over anyone in operations or headquarters. We usually didn't even know what they were doing. So when something went wrong, an operator would come running with a mixture of panic or indignant accusation into our cubbyhole to demand that we fix it. And we would fix it, but the next day the same problem would occur all over again because our instructions to avoid it had not been heeded. At the same time, our reference files of computer cards and manuals were constantly rifled and disrupted—until we locked them up, engendering more resentment. And all these problems were made worse by empire-building and technical ignorance within management.

Once for three months, the group of programmers to which I belonged was made to work in offices in Newark, New Jersey, which were 12 miles away from the action we had to support in Manhattan. And the Newark offices were 10 blocks away from the nearest keypunch machine, which we ordinarily needed to use many times a day. The reason, we were told, for being moved to Newark was that our boss's boss's boss had a large suite of offices there and needed our presence to justify having them.

When we protested, our boss merely exhorted us to rise to the "challenge."

Another time, management tried to make my group work without desks. But we needed desks to hold the hundreds of manuals, computer printouts, and "decks" of computer cards we used daily; we couldn't function without desks. We fought to get desks and won, but the price was high: Management took the desks away from other people who needed them just as much as we did, and because I had presented the arguments for my group's desks, management told the others that I in effect had taken away their desks. So they blamed me, hated my guts, and let me know it.

And after getting the desks, we still worked for over three months without a telephone in our office—in one of the telephone company's own plants.

Computer programs come in two basic kinds: applications programs, such as DIS, which turn out reports for human use; and operating-system programs, which coordinate actions within the computer and run the applications programs as a traffic cop directs traffic. After DIS was installed, Western Electric acquired more powerful computers with a much more advanced, complex operating system called OS. Headquarters revised the DIS programs for OS and our job became that of supporting the transition to the new computers and OS.

When headquarters delivered what was supposed to be a fully operational OS version of DIS, the job-control procedures, which were essentially system programs that ran the applications programs, were full of syntax errors (errors of punctuation or form that render a program unworkable). We reported to our boss that the procedures were no good, but headquarters insisted that we were at fault for not getting the procedures to work. So we were forced to try to fix the procedures, and we had to work a graveyard shift from roughly 9 P.M. to 5 A.M., which was the only time that management made a computer available to us.

Two months later, still trying to fix the procedures, we finally convinced our bosses to arrange a meeting with people from headquarters to look at the defects. I can still see clearly in my mind the man from headquarters walking warily with his boss into the meeting. After looking at examples of errors in the version we had, he asked, "How do you know the procedures are bad?"

To any competent programmer, that was like asking what's wrong with the sentence "Des guys is assery." After our senior programmer, in shock, carefully explained a few of the errors, we got a new version the next week and it worked fine. I never learned what had gone wrong, but it seemed obvious that we had been mistakenly given a defective preliminary version of the system and then ignored, disbelieved, or overruled when we complained about it.

Poor Management, Poor Quality.   Poor management such as what I experienced at Western Electric can produce poor output even when the best employees are available. Poor management wastes employees' labor and discourages them from doing their best. This situation is a classic management failure. And it can occur even when many managers personally are first-rate, if they are poorly managed by their own bosses, or if the overall organization is ineffective or misdirected. Then, even good managers can become victims of the same conditions of responsibility without authority that humble and abuse white-collar and professional employees and hourly workers.

Being excluded from making important decisions about their jobs is painful for motivated and educated employees. And when management itself has problems, work is frustrating and demoralizing. Motivated, honest employees who want to do a good job feel terrible when they are ignored, overruled by ignorant bosses, dependent on arbitrary bosses, or have to keep their mouths shut and suffer foolish bosses gladly. They feel even worse when they are lied to or have to lie to defend themselves against blind management witch hunts, or when they have to labor to support failing organizations or bad management decisions.

And all the while management is failing, employees may get no respect or credit for their work and sacrifices. Their efforts are "expected" by a management that doesn't know the consequences of its own demands and actions, or that calls unreasonable difficulties "challenges" for workers to overcome rather than problems for management to clear away. The only solution to such problems is precisely what most managements will never allow employees without a struggle: much greater participation in management decisions with corresponding authority and remuneration for people who actually get work done.

When work is not rewarded according to its worth, or when no one knows what will happen next because of frequent changes in direction or organization, bad management can create an atmosphere of jealousy and mistrust. It can also create a host of other destructive emotions, depending on the circumstances, including anger, frustration, boredom, and paralyzing feelings of helplessness, guilt, and self-doubt.

Working amid suspicion and backstabbing, not to mention fear of losing one's job arbitrarily, is painful. But when a job requires honest communication and openly given cooperation, as all highly skilled and high-quality work does, then working in a badly managed organization can be torture. Many of the best employees will either leave, become demoralized, or will be broken if they try to stick to their principles.

The cost of such management abuse of employees never appears as an entry in a corporate report or government budget. In fact, most managements cannot account in dollars and cents, the only measure they know, for what they have lost. Nor can they add up what could be gained if they listened more and shared more with employees. But this cost is real and drastically affects the "bottom line" nonetheless.

Quality cannot be produced amid fear, distrust, or blame-casting. Nor can quality be produced amid boredom, frustration, or demoralization. Management sets the organizational standards for quality by what it orders, what it rewards, and what it penalizes. And management sets the tone for quality by how much it is willing to cooperate and share with employees, and by how much managers cooperate among themselves to improve the net success of their overall organizations.

If quality is not produced, it is management's failure. And management fails most when it shuts out and does not adequately reward people who do the work in the factory, office, laboratory, computer room, sales floor, field, and even in management itself. These white- and blue-collar employees know best what is going on and how to get things done. They have unique and valuable insights into what needs to be done. Yet a great many managements routinely reject their employees' advice—and punish them for talking back!

When management fails, it escapes responsibility for its failures by blaming working people and anyone or anything else that can't talk back. Even the business press and management analysts emphasize labor costs far more than management failures in public discussions of American competitiveness.

Low quality is bad for business, and it certainly has been bad for American business. Companies that produce low quality can survive for a while, especially if the market doesn't demand higher quality. But eventually someone somewhere will come along and produce higher quality and put the low-quality operations out of business. The same problems of employee abuse and declines in quality occur in government. So unless managements are very lucky or have enormous power, if they cannot produce quality they are dooming their businesses or government agencies to mediocrity or bankruptcy. That is bad for stockholders, taxpayers, consumers, and the general public, as well as for the employees who must suffer management's failures every day on the job.

A System Amiss. Western Electric had a reputation for being better run than many companies and most government operations. And it was sincerely trying to improve and upgrade its service. Although plenty of cronies, "dead wood," and bullies cluttered management, other managers and staff members were bright, committed, well-meaning, and hardworking. And a similar computer center that I visited west of Chicago seemed to run quite well. Yet the whole operation where I worked was a disaster for many years. It failed because management had created conflict rather than cooperation, put authority in the wrong hands, and did not respect people who were getting work done.

Unfortunately, the divisions, the political infighting and empire-building, and the ignorance that I encountered at Western Electric are endemic to private and government bureaucracies all over the world. They practically define what bureaucracies are all about. And despite talk of things like decentralization, divestiture, entrepreneurialism, and cutting the size of government, bureaucracies are growing more powerful all the time. For example, military spending has grown enormously, multibillion-dollar corporate mergers and acquisitions have become commonplace, and big companies continue to buy other companies of all sorts.

No number of management gurus who visit for a week, prescribe magic formulas, collect their fees, and then leave will ever fix the ills of bureaucracy. Too often management will use the prescriptions badly rather than give up power, credit, and rewards to more competent people. And the results are more likely to be those of the "sorcerer's apprentice"—magic gone mad—than of the sorcerer himself.

Nor will money managers, stockholders, corporate raiders, or voters ever fundamentally change management in big business and government. They know even less than the gurus about operations. They fight and compete among themselves. And they have little or no commitment to improve production. Indeed in America they make such enormous demands for short-term results that even competent managers are prevented from doing good jobs.

By early 1987, after four years of "restructuring" and deregulated financial dealing, corruption blossomed on Wall Street. The trade deficit mounted to $170 billion. Productivity growth for the period was what *Business Week* called "by far the most deplorable" of any cyclical business recovery since World War II (Economic Diary, 3–17–86). Productivity was flat for all of 1986 (*New York Times*, 5–5–87, A1), and it actually fell in the second half of the year (*Business Week*, 3–30–87, 20).

This poor economic record is not a matter of managers simply making stupid mistakes, which would be simple mismanagement. Something else, deeper, is involved that misdirects the entire system and makes it think its worst blunders are "smart." Part I of this book will show what this professional *mis*-management is and how it came about. Part II will show what people who work for a living can do about it.

PART

I

◇

HOW MIS-MANAGEMENT ENDANGERS AMERICA

1

The Madness of Subsidizing Foreign Competition

Foreign Competition, Automation, and Obsolescence

People who work for a living are in for a lot of trouble ahead. Major changes in the world economy threaten to wipe out or drastically change the jobs that most people have in the industrialized world.

Many jobs are being exported to nations in Latin America and Asia where desperately poor people work for as little as 5 percent to 20 percent of wage scales in America and Europe. And more jobs are being eliminated by the use of computers and robots. Although new jobs are being created in high tech and services, people who have lost old jobs don't readily get the new ones. And most new jobs call for low skills that pay substantially less. That means rising permanent unemployment for people with the old skills, and a lower standard of living for people who get the new jobs.

Simultaneously, shortages of people with the newest, most advanced skills cause high salaries for people with those skills. But the shortages are temporary and treacherous. Salaries could easily drop and people could easily lose their high-paying jobs as large numbers of other people spend their lives' savings and borrow to the hilt to buy educations or retrain for the new jobs. Meanwhile, technology and markets keep changing and make many experts obsolete. Both glut and obsolescence threaten to strand many who were once in the elite, leaving them with high bills for their educations, homes, and other living expenses and with much lower expectations for their futures.

As major parts of the economy have gone through a depression, a smaller, elite part has boomed. Severe unemployment means depression, and shortages of labor in a few knowledge skills means inflation. We will get—have been getting—both simultaneously: escalating "slumpflation." Slumpflation leads to and accentuates the so-called two-tier economy, where luxury items flourish and rise in price while increasing numbers of people go hungry and homeless. Two separate, divided tiers make democracy unstable. We face economic dislocation, social disruption, and political repression as growing numbers of once-solid middle-class people are squeezed out of the middle, feel their lives crumbling around them, and seek desperate solutions to save themselves. A breakdown of the middle class in Germany gave rise to fascism and Hitler.

More than just manual, unskilled, and factory jobs—and all the small businesses and communities that depend on them—are being threatened or wiped out. Many office jobs can be exported to foreign labor just like manufacturing jobs. Since the 1970s, for example, U.S. companies have shipped growing volumes of computer keypunching jobs to the Far East and the Caribbean. And satellite communications promise to replace those physical shipments with electronic transfers so that smaller, more timely, or more detailed jobs can be exported (*Business Week,* 3–15–82, 136E).

The most highly skilled, educated, and privileged working people in business and the professions—hardly what one ordinarily thinks of as "workers"—also are threatened. Foreign competition and computers are hastening the obsolescence of their knowledge skills and raising still more the enormous costs of education and retraining, if they can find and afford effective reeducation at all. Increasingly, computers can do the work of experts in many fields including law, engineering, accounting, computer programming, and health. Appropriately called "expert systems," they will take away work from experts and tighten the squeeze on even the most elite "professionals." And little or no provisions are being made for the people who are being displaced.

Business Week announced the beginning of the end for many managers in a 1983 special report, "A New Era for Management" (4–25–83). The report said many cuts in management were expected due to increasing competition, including foreign competition, and computers that will eliminate many of the information processing functions that middle managers perform for top executives. And of course fewer managers are needed when work forces are cut. Since then, management cuts have shaken such stalwart companies as IBM, AT&T, Kodak, and Exxon.

High-paying high-tech jobs also are not safe. *Business Week* (3–4–85, 20) reported an analysis by Stephen S. Roach of Morgan Stanley & Co. which found that "the import share of U.S. high-technology expenditures—for communications equipment, electronic components, computers, office machinery, scientific instruments, and the like—exploded from 26.6 percent to 43 percent" between 1982 and 1984. And much worse, imports "absorbed an astounding 80 percent to 85 percent of the rise in high-tech expenditures" during the post-1982 recovery. By 1987, grave worries were expressed about the very survival of the U.S. semiconductor industry and about the U.S. military's dependence on foreign electronics.

The problem in high tech was much more than just an overvalued dollar that made foreign imports artificially cheap. For example, Italy, long considered an industrial also-ran, emerged as a surprisingly formidable competitor—and leader. Auto maker Fiat and its robotics subsidiary Comau became world leaders in computerized manufacturing, and International Business Machines Corp. and Digital Equipment Corp. (DEC) turned "to Italians for help in designing...automated factories" (*Business Week*, 12–10–84, 57). Italy also led in developing automation for what was once a labor-intensive industry: jewelry making (*Forbes*, 7–2–84, 150).

The deterioration in American high-tech competitiveness is astonishing. Malaysians have "developed impressive know-how in semiconductor assembly. In fact, this year Intel sent several of its Malaysian managers to help start up a 'factory of the future' in Arizona" (*Business Week*, 8–6–84, 35). In other words, Malaysia was compared favorably with Taiwan, South Korea, Singapore, and Hong Kong, which were giving Japan a hard run in producing high-technology products. Intel Corp., an American leader that supplied the microprocessor chips for IBM's PC and AT lines of personal computers, had to go to Malaysia—not long ago an economically backward country—to learn more modern ways to make its computer chips!

Everyone is vulnerable. "Cheap foreign labor" is not just illegal aliens in sweatshops. Malaysian engineers earned about a third of what American engineers made in 1984. In Israel, salaries of engineers employed by U.S. semiconductor and other high-tech companies were 40 percent of those in the U.S. in the early 1980s, and research and development costs ranged from one-third to one-half of U.S. costs (*Business Week,* 2–16–81, 34H, and 4–20–81, 44). Combining low salaries with a long tradition of intellectual excellence, Israel has become a world leader in a growing number of technologies.

Malaysia and Israel of course are neither alone nor even the most important in what they have done. Japan, Western Europe, the sometimes-pirate countries of Southeast Asia, and developing countries such as Brazil are all strong and aggressive competitors. All these countries have universities that can develop their own high technologies, and they can get expertise from U.S. universities and companies that sell their knowledge to anyone who wants it.

American-based multinational companies dominate less and less of high tech, and they are going increasingly outside the U.S. for labor. This is putting pressure on even the most highly paid and privileged American high-tech engineers and will eventually wipe out large numbers of those well-paying jobs high tech was supposed to produce in the U.S.

If all you have to sell is your labor, even if it's fancy professional, intellectual, or managerial labor, you are in trouble. Big money can move anywhere around the world, set up shop, and use someone else's labor to force your income down. But here's a shock for big U.S. money: It is about to be squeezed by the very nations whose peoples it has been using to suppress American wages.

Countries such as Japan, Singapore, Hong Kong, Taiwan, and South Korea are amassing, or have the potential to amass, so much foreign exchange from their exports to the U.S. and the rest of the world that their financial institutions are or could become powerful competitors. And financial centers in Japan, Hong Kong, and Singapore are rapidly growing to challenge New York markets and institutions.

Japan's capital is enormous. In 1984 it racked up a $35 billion trade surplus with the U.S. Japanese savers socked away

"$325 billion in the government's postal savings system and $315 billion in Japanese life insurance companies" (*Business Week,* 4–8–85, 58). In 1986, its trade surplus with the U.S. was $51.5 billion and its total trade surplus was $82.7 billion (*New York Times,* 1–17–87, 33). In 1987, its trade surplus hit $101 billion (*New York Times,* 5–2–87, 39).

Japanese financial institutions use a lot of that money to gain business and market share overseas. In 1985, five of the ten biggest international banks were Japanese. In 1986, four of the top five were Japanese; the only U.S. bank, Citicorp, was second (*New York Times,* 9–8–86, D20). By the end of 1986, Citicorp was sixth and was the only U.S. company remaining among the world's top 15 banks ranked by assets (*Economist,* 7–11–87, 104). In 1986, "U.S. banks' share of the global market shrank to 18.6 percent," while "Japanese banks' share rose to 31.6 percent," according to a study by the Bank for International Settlements (*U.S. News & World Report,* 2–9–87, 66). By early 1987, foreign banks provided "over one-fifth of all loans made to U.S. businesses" (*Forbes,* 2–23–87, 94). And Japanese banks began to "dominate the high end of American mortgage financing" (*New York Times,* 5–10–87, F1). They even had 25 percent of Britain's banking market (*Forbes,* 2–9–87, 10).

Banks are not the only U.S. financial institutions threatened. By late 1984, Japan's leading brokerage house, Nomura Securities Co., was larger than Merrill Lynch (*Forbes,* 12–31–84, 46). And in mid-1987, Japanese brokerage firms, insurance companies, banks, and money-management firms began to "elbow" their way into Chicago's futures trading pits (*Business Week,* 6–1–87, 106).

If trends of the early to mid-1980s continue so that the U.S. runs a budget deficit of roughly $200 billion per year (much of it going to an endless wish-list of new military weapons), "the United States will owe the rest of the world $1 trillion [in 1990]," and "the rest of the world will owe Japan $500 billion" (*New York Times,* 3–11–85, A1).

Japanese and other Asian financial institutions acquired great financial power because their nations' industrial trade was so much better than that of the United States. That superiority will not be reversed overnight. It threatens American financial institutions with the loss of their own businesses and jobs. Then shareholders and the entire U.S. financial system will be in for as much trouble as many American industries are. And you can bet that the financial power of Japan and other nations will be used to further strengthen their superiority.

The end result of all this must surely be that whatever you do for a living, you are or will soon be in danger of losing your livelihood, directly or indirectly, to someone or some machine that will do it better or cheaper or more obediently. And that will mean the end of the American standard of living as we have known it.

American Management: Subsidizing Foreign Competition

How could so many countries that only recently were backward, poor, or war-ravaged have acquired the technology, capital, and presence in U.S. markets to threaten every American who works for a living?

The astonishing fact is that American corporations, the U.S. government, and major U.S. educational institutions have long been plowing, seeding, and fertilizing the ground for the very foreign competitors who have taken large chunks of jobs and business away from America and Western Europe.

For example, in a so-called joint venture, American Telephone & Telegraph Co. gave capital, advanced technology, and engineering training to the Lucky-Goldstar Group, a $7 billion Korean conglomerate, to make advanced semiconductors and communications equipment. Honeywell Inc. taught Lucky to make computer control systems and gave Lucky "the technology to move into factory automation. It could also help Lucky to break into the market for industrial robots" (*Business Week,* 7–9–84, 102). In all, "Lucky has 19 joint ventures, and technological cooperation agreements with 50 foreign companies." Lucky even got U.S. technology for genetic engineering. And four other Korean conglomerates as big as Lucky also got high technology in joint ventures with American companies.

Now Korean conglomerates, like Japanese companies before them, are becoming household names. Hyundai started selling low-priced cars in 1986 in the U.S. and was an instant success. Daewoo followed soon after by supplying cars to General Motors Corp., while also selling IBM-compatible personal computers under the Leading Edge label. Samsung is well known in electronics. And Kia made a deal to supply cars to Ford Motor Co.

In return, the American companies got Korea's dictatorially suppressed, low-wage work force. Still, the low wages were not an overpowering advantage in themselves.

In the past, Korea had difficulties making high-quality automotive components. Its work force and management lacked the necessary skills. But according to a GM official, "We've got to bring in a lot of investment and technical assistance, and we are doing that" ("Detroit's Korean Card," *Forbes,* 12–3–84). A Korean official expects "GM's and Chrysler's entry here will surely improve the quality of Korean auto parts and the automobile industry in general" ("Detroit's New Hunting Ground for Auto Parts," *Business Week,* 11–12–84). In other words, U.S. auto makers gave (and continue to give) Korea vital help in overcoming an otherwise fatal handicap of faulty quality.

American taxpayers and soldiers also unintentionally subsidize Korean business. The U.S. fought the Korean War and has kept armed forces in Korea ever since, all done in the name of fighting communism. And we should oppose communism. But without the U.S. defense of Korea, few if any American or European companies would have risked investing in it. Further, numerous reports have told how many Korean companies got their start from American military contracts during the Korean War. These contracts at times provided precious seed capital from which giant conglomerates grew. For instance, "Hyundai got its start fixing trucks and building barracks for the United States Army in South Korea" (*New York Times Magazine,* 12–14–86, 33).

In other words, American foreign policy, tax dollars, and lives have propped up a brutal government and huge conglomerates that oppress Korean working people and exploit their labor while taking away American jobs. That's the wrong way to fight communism.

Korea is not the only country getting help. In a letter to *Business Week* (1–28–85), the President-International of GTE Communications Systems Corp. boasted that GTE has worked for ten years to help make Taiwan a technological leader. Just in 1984, "GTE has had more than 40 senior design engineers from

Taiwan participating in the development'' of GTE's new telephone switching system. And the training was done in Phoenix, Arizona. In the words of a GTE TV ad, "Gee!"

What do these engineers do after they are trained? Some emulate the entrepreneurs of Silicon Valley: They leave the employer who trained them and start up companies of their own. Only they do it in their native lands. For example, in "High-Tech Entrepreneurs Create a Silicon Valley in Taiwan" (*Business Week,* 8–1–83), the entrepreneurs were engineers who were educated in the U.S. and first worked for such companies as Hewlett-Packard Co. and Intel Corp.

In addition to engineering training, U.S. firms trained 27,700 overseas managers in 1979 and 62,000 in 1985! (*Forbes,* 6–16–86, 12).

The "spin-off" effect explains where some of the most aggressive new foreign competition has come from. It isn't from low-wage labor. It's from American-trained engineers and managers using state-of-the-art high technology and business knowledge to finance, make, and sell superior products. They are totally foreign competitors and will increasingly sap the strength of even the American companies who gave them their starts.

Giving foreign producers advanced technology, know-how, and capital for research, development, and production are all powerful forms of subsidy. Marketing is another. By selling or planning to sell Korean cars, U.S. auto makers provided access to American markets and marketing experience, in addition to the technology and production experience they were giving Korea. This was invaluable. Otherwise, some Korean companies could not easily sell their cars in America. If they couldn't sell cars, they couldn't afford to export or even make them.

The U.S. market is also unfairly accessible to foreign producers. In "America's High-Tech Crisis" (3–11–85), *Business Week* reported that by deregulating AT&T and the U.S. telecommunications equipment business, "the U.S. provided foreign competitors with the biggest unilateral trade concession of the decade—with no quid pro quo at all for U.S. manufacturers. Most foreign markets remain safely closed to U.S. products." That deregulation took place across the Presidencies of both Jimmy Carter and Ronald Reagan, so it represented the will of a large and dominant part of American management in business and government.

As subsidized foreign competitors grew up into world-class competitors, American managements rushed to serve them. Hewlett-Packard Co. helped a Taiwanese company design an automated factory so advanced that it would "show even the Japanese how an automated factory should be built" (*Business Week,* 11–26–84, 194). Isn't it nice of Hewlett-Packard to want to teach Taiwan and Japan so much? H-P's aggressive initiative is so impressive that it deserves nomination for the first ever Benedict Arnold Award.

Educating competitors is another subsidy. American universities suffered declining enrollments after the passing of the baby-boom generation and eagerly sought out foreign students. Daewoo has boasted in major business publications that it has many engineers with American educations. Some 50 percent of U.S. Ph.D. graduates in science were foreigners in 1986. Communist China had 15,000 graduate science students in the U.S. (*Business Week,* 10–6–86, 18). Adding insult to injury, colleges even recruited and gave scholarships to foreign athletes who then competed against the U.S. in the Olympics.

The most formidable competitor of all is Japan, and it has received the greatest American subsidies. In the same way that America has protected South Korea since the 1950s, America has protected Japan ever since World War II from potential aggression by communist Russia and China. Japan benefited economically because it didn't have to waste resources or tax its people and business to support armed forces. Of course the result was a peace that helped America. But huge investments were made in Japan that would not have been made otherwise. Japan also benefited from the Korean War. American contracts "greatly accelerated Japan's recovery by pumping billions of dollars into the Japanese economy for war supplies" (Donald S. Zagoria, reviewer, *New York Times Book Review,* 10–27–85, 9). And according to occasional but infrequent reports, Japan got substantial military contracts during the Vietnam War and got the bulk of the growing business and trade in the entire region of East and Southeast Asia.

As in Western Europe with the Marshall Plan, the U.S. also gave large amounts of money to Japan explicitly for rebuilding. That capital helped Japan finance steel mills and auto plants. Those same plants have since bankrupted or threatened the solvency of many American companies and their jobs, and their foreign-trade earnings continue to help bankroll Japan's growing power. What's more, U.S. subsidies to Japan continue even as it widens its productive supremacy over the U.S.

For example, rather than working with American robot makers, who were acknowledged world leaders in technology, General Motors formed a joint venture with Japan's Fanuc to provide robots for GM's new factories. That's an enormous transfer of business and opportunity from America to Japan. No wonder GMFanuc Robotics Corp. "bounded past Cincinnati Milacron and Unimation [U.S. leaders] to become No. 1 in the $380 million U.S. robotics market" (*Business Week,* 1–14–85, 126C).

Pittsburgh-based Mellon Bank "poured more than $25 million into Sumitomo Industries of Japan," which then sold equipment to U.S. steel companies ("Eminent Domain & Bank Boycotts: The Tri-State Strategy in Pittsburgh," Mike Stout, *Labor Research Review,* Summer, 1983). And Mellon participated in foreclosing on Mesta Machine Company, which was also Pittsburgh-based and until the 1980s was a major producer of steel-mill equipment and had the same product line as Sumitomo. Mellon Bank is not alone. As of 1980, "15 American banks...had invested more than $2 billion overseas modernizing and building foreign steel mills" and denying credit to American steel companies at the same time.

By licensing—selling—technology, American universities give Japan an inside "line" on the most advanced American high tech. And Japanese interest in research "is concentrated heavily in those technologies in which Japan is challenging America's competitive lead in the market place" (*Business Week,* 9–24–84, 72).

The one weakness Japan has demonstrated in world trade has been an inability—to date—to create genuinely new technology. Innovation has been the greatest strength of the U.S. and what most people say—foolishly—will keep the U.S. ahead of Japan. But now Japan has been given cheap, easy, and, above all, timely access to everything U.S. scientists create.

Maybe that's why, in the race to make a revolutionary, superfast type of computer chip, based on a "ballistic" transistor called

HEMT and using gallium arsenide instead of silicon, "nobody in the U.S. comes close" to Japan's prowess, according to Bell Lab's head of gallium arsenide research (*Business Week,* 3–4–85, 104).

And all this happened and was reported in plain view by major U.S. publications!

The U.S. military also subsidizes Japanese technology, but reports are rare and stingy with information. We must assume they are subject to censorship, both official and implicit, "in the interests of national security." But since foreign recipients know what they are getting, only the American people are kept in the dark. If that's in the interests of national security, then the interests of the U.S. government and the U.S. businesses that dominate the government are certainly not the interests of American working people.

For example, the Pentagon spends huge amounts of American taxpayers' dollars perfecting highly automated methods to produce its most advanced high-tech weapons. Yet according to *Let's Rebuild America,* a book published in 1983 by the International Association of Machinists and Aerospace Workers (IAM), the Pentagon licensed Japanese manufacturers to make these products and gave them the information and technologies to do it. Such agreements are called military "co-production."

But the Japanese manufacturers then take these technologies and production processes and apply them when appropriate in their civilian businesses. And they consistently beat American manufacturers, who don't have access to the U.S. military technologies or who don't apply them well to civilian production when they do have access.

The IAM should know about these things. Many of its members work for military contractors. But this kind of information has rarely been reported in the business press or anywhere else, despite military spending being the largest "industry" in the world. So most people are not informed and may doubt the IAM's charges.

After the IAM published its book and tried to promote a "Rebuilding America Act," *Newsweek* confirmed that the Pentagon exported its advanced technologies to Japan ("Japan's Arms Industry," 1–2–84). And soon thereafter National Public Radio aired a similar confirmation ("Morning Edition," 1–3–84).

The *Newsweek* report said that Mitsubishi makes "F-15 fighters under license from McDonnell Douglas Corp.," and Fujitsu Ltd., Japan's leading mainframe computer company, "ships 70 percent of its gallium arsenide chips [military computer chips] to the United States." Further, "Mitsubishi, for instance, has transformed what it has learned from its F-15 production into cost savings on its commercial products such as its new Diamond One jet." Let's not forget that Mitsubishi also sells autos in the U.S., supplies parts to Hyundai, and undoubtedly applies some of what it learned from military production to make cars. And Fujitsu took over the lead from IBM in selling computers in Japan in the early 1980s.

There's a disturbing lesson here for American military producers as well as for American working people. Japan has embarked on a program to build a new jet fighter, the Fighter Support Experimental, or FSX. And Mitsubishi Heavy Industries Ltd. pushed powerfully to build the FSX alone, keeping out American aircraft companies. At the time of this writing, a compromise was reported possible in which an American company, either McDonnell Douglas Corp. or General Dynamics Corp., would get a small share of the business (*Wall Street Journal*, 5–21–87, 25). But Congress and American companies, naturally, had been hoping Japan would "buy an off-the-shelf" U.S. fighter to fill Japan's defense needs.

It would be farcical if it weren't so tragic. The Pentagon taught Japanese manufacturers technologies and advanced production processes that the Japanese then used, or could use, to bankrupt American companies and destroy American jobs. Even U.S. arms makers and their associated jobs have lost out.

Sometimes the Pentagon justifies itself by saying it gives contracts to the low-cost producer. As if Americans' money and technological effort, which we intend to defend and improve America, should be allowed to undermine America if the price is right! But *Newsweek* also said that it cost Mitsubishi 50 percent more to make F-15 fighters than it cost McDonnell Douglas, even at the dollar's then-inflated exchange rate compared to the yen. That's because Japan's low-volume production was inherently inefficient and costly. After the dollar's fall, *Forbes* reported that Mitsubishi's F-15s cost twice as much as McDonnell Douglas's (1–26–87, 33).

American managers in industry share blame with U.S. government officials by failing to take advantage of, or failing to demand more control over, America's own technologies. *Newsweek* summed it up: "'When an American company works up a joint deal with a Japanese company, the Japanese always learn more,' says an American aerospace executive." By now everyone has admitted that. Many people also feel that Japanese electronic technologies are in many ways better than America's. The Japanese are of course highly capable, but they have been allowed—encouraged—to stand on the shoulders of U.S. technology while many an American management has stuck its head in the sand.

In a story on military co-production agreements, the *New York Times* reported, "Last year a Defense Science Board task force found that much of the flow of technology has been from the United States [to] Japan in these and other agreements" ("In a Trade War, U.S. Is Well-Armed," 4–5–85). That quote was buried near the end of a report that was itself buried on page 14 of the business section of the newspaper. And the headline hid still further how co-production is undermining America.

The story of military co-production subsidies was repeated ominously in Brazil. Secretary of State George P. Shultz signed a military co-production deal giving Brazil advanced military technology (WCBS Radio, New York, 2–3–84). Yet despite the fact that Brazil is a major arms exporter and has been aggressively pursuing nuclear energy (*New York Times,* 2–7–84, A3), neither CBS nor the *Times* explained what military co-production would do.

Brazil is often run by a military dictatorship. Its workers are suppressed and work for low wages. Many American companies produce there for export. And Brazil wants to become a world leader in every way from military power to advanced technology. So Brazil protected its domestic markets from foreign competition and forced U.S. companies to reveal their technologies.

Moreover, Brazil owed $108 billion to foreign creditors as of early 1987, and it struggled at best to pay just the interest on its debt. Giving Brazil so much money was a fantastic, mind-boggling subsidy. Here's an example of what that money did.

In "The Death of Mining," *Business Week* reported that Brazil "will be the world's premier iron-ore producer when its giant Carajás mine comes on stream next year" (12–17–84). That mine of course would devastate U.S. mining. Yet the $5.1 billion mine "was underwritten with a $500 million loan from the World Bank," which is backed by the U.S. Note the multiplier effect. An international loan can act as a foundation, an imprimatur, for economic activity valued at a much higher amount. So the literal amount of $108 billion lent to Brazil by foreign creditors may understate the actual effect. Other examples are equally alarming.

Forbes reported that a $29 million loan by the World Bank in 1979 started the Korean semiconductor industry and resulted by 1985 in $600 million being invested, with more to come from the World Bank (11–4–85, 33). According to John Young of Hewlett-Packard, these plants alone could supply over half the world demand for memory chips in 1985.

By the mid-1980s, the Third World reportedly owed a total of over $700 billion. These massive subsidies have produced global overcapacities in mining, electronics, autos, steel, and a host of other industries. Overcapacity plagues the world and is the classic precursor to depression.

Even the loans made by the U.S. banks were subsidized. They were backed by a widely believed guarantee that the U.S. government would step in to bail them out if Brazil or other big debtor nations repudiated their debts or otherwise failed to pay. That belief was well founded. Federal Reserve Chairman Paul Volcker lead the effort to bail out Brazil with more loans (*Forbes,* 3–26–84, 83), as he reportedly pumped up the U.S. money supply in 1982 to create liquidity for foreign debtors such as Brazil, Mexico, and Argentina.

Being owed so much, U.S. banks have a powerful interest in doing everything they can to help Brazil and other debtors boost their exports to the U.S. That way, countries acquire the foreign currency to pay interest on their huge debts. But Brazil struggled to pay its interest even when exports boomed to the U.S. in 1985. In early 1987, a new crisis forced Brazil to suspend debt payments entirely.

One might think that all these subsidies should have been enough, but many countries, including Brazil and Taiwan, also illegally copy U.S. products—it's called counterfeiting and piracy—and have been allowed to do so by the U.S. government. *Forbes* reported that illegal foreign sales were $60 billion in 1985 and U.S. companies were robbed of $25 billion in sales (11–17–86, 40). In part, the laws were weak, but they were not enforced either. And talk of stronger laws and enforcement never got followed up. With business and government so committed to supporting foreign production, it's hardly surprising that efforts to fight even illegal actions would be weak or nonexistent.

Finally, here are a few brief examples of more subsidies:

Forbes concluded that the U.S. pharmaceuticals industry was "actually helping the Japanese gain entry into the $21 billion-a-year U.S. prescription drug market" through joint ventures (3–24–86, 178).

In 1983, *High Technology* said "Japan is riding U.S. technology to the forefront of space exploration and development" (May 1983, 27). Four years later it said, "What the Japanese have learned [in a joint production partnership] from Boeing could land them a slice of the world's airliner market" (March 1987, 42). It also added that "Japan's aircraft industry grew and developed largely through U.S. military co-production programs."

With the U.S. crippled in space after the explosions of Challenger and the Delta, Atlas, and Titan rockets, Japan could very well repeat in air and space (and pharmaceuticals for that matter) what it did in steel, cars, computer chips, and consumer electronics.

Taiwan, South Korea, Brazil, Mexico, Hong Kong, and Singapore got duty-free benefits that amounted to $9.3 billion annually under the General System of Preference (GSP), according to Nicholas Targ in *Multinational Monitor* (February 1987, 12). And the Overseas Private Investment Corporation (OPIC) gave multinational corporations billions of dollars in political risk insurance, loans, and loan guarantees to invest in these and other countries. Congress created and funded GSP and OPIC.

It just doesn't matter what reason banks, universities, companies, the U.S. government, and the Pentagon give for what they have done. The simple fact is that Japanese and many other foreign producers got supports that have been of great value or would have been totally unattainable otherwise. In return, they paid very little or got it all for free. These practices amount to a gigantic subsidy in real life for foreign producers at America's expense—with great peril to America and the rest of the world, including those countries being subsidized.

U.S. foreign policy is dominated by fear of communism. We

should be at least as concerned about who is giving away—betraying—America to economic competitors.

The Worldwide, "Four-Dragon" Squeeze

The global nature and relentless tightening of the squeezes on working people are much more serious than most people realize. World peace itself is threatened.

South Korea, Taiwan, Hong Kong, and Singapore, which were called the four "little dragons" of Asia and later renamed "tigers," have themselves been squeezed by "cheap labor" (*Business Week,* 3–28–83, 64).

Multinational corporations that once invested in the four dragons are now either automating in advanced industrial countries or investing in countries that have lower-wage labor than the four dragons. Hong Kong's hourly wages were reported to have *risen* by 1983 to $1.15; and Korea's, to $1.40. So they could then be undercut by countries such as Malaysia, the Philippines, Indonesia, Sri Lanka, and China. Indonesia's average hourly wage rate was less than 40 cents! Sound familiar?

The four dragons undercut the Japanese who undercut the U.S., and yet the four dragons themselves are squeezed by even lower-wage labor. According to the report, "the four economies will thrive only if they...step up...to high-tech and capital intensive manufacturing." According to a Taiwanese official, "It is a life-and-death struggle."

The four dragons won't die quietly without a fight. And they appear to have fought back vigorously. High tech took a beating as the job savior of America when Atari closed its factory in California and moved assembly to Hong Kong and Taiwan. By October 3, 1983, *Business Week* (124D) told us of "The Four Dragons That Threaten U.S. and Japanese Chipmakers." And in its June 25, 1984, issue, *Business Week* (42) reported "The U.S. Recovery Has Four Asian Nations Roaring Back."

The four dragons fought back by automating furiously, leaving the most simple assembly work to the lower-wage countries, and squeezing right back the high-tech, higher-wage companies in Japan and the U.S.

Bad as they are, these squeezes and struggles haven't stopped with the four dragons. Countries around the world with populations involving billions of poor people are becoming involved and more than a few will succeed, if for no other reason than that the most advanced corporations will—traitorously to their "home" countries—invest in the lowest-wage labor countries to make them succeed, if only temporarily.

For example, Americans are trying like gangbusters to get China involved in making products for the U.S. So avid is the effort to make China legitimate and get at its one billion potential workers that after his tour of China, President Reagan even objected to calling it "communist."

But Hong Kong, which has extremely close ties to China, may beat the U.S. to China's labor. "Hong Kong provides China with investment, technology, services and management expertise," boasted a Hong Kong special advertising section in *Business Week* (6–3–85). "In return, China provides the low-cost labor Hong Kong lacks." Others have called Hong Kong the "gateway into China" and predicted "Hong Kong could very well become the New York of China—its financial and trading center" (*New York Times*, 2–2–87, D1).

And India, despite its many well-known problems, may beat out Hong Kong *and* China. India has both low-wage labor and a much more Westernized economy than China. India is estimated to have an urban consumer society of from 100 million to 200 million people—and large markets can support large producers. India also has skilled workers and engineering and management talent, and a large number of them speak English. Both *Business Week* and *Forbes* report "profound" changes under the leadership of Prime Minister Rajiv Gandhi (*Business Week*, 11–19–84, 52; "India's Good News Is Good for Us, Too," M. S. Forbes, Jr., *Forbes*, 4–22–85, 31). And India is getting help from Japan in auto making (*U.S. News & World Report*, 5–6–85, 48).

Last but not least, India, like Japan and Brazil, has its own military co-production agreement with the U.S., "permitting the use of sophisticated American technology for Indian business and military ventures" (*New York Times*, 5–18–85, 36). Malcolm Baldrige, U.S. Secretary of Commerce, emphasized that American business would help India in its thrust "to develop its own high-tech industry." Doesn't that determination stir your heart? The U.S.

Department of Commerce too has earned a nomination for the Benedict Arnold Award.

There is no end to the four-dragon squeeze. When management sends jobs to the lowest wage labor in the world, American workers cannot possibly compete no matter what they give back. To paraphrase what an Ohio industrial worker said on National Public Radio in mid-March, 1983: "If you're going to get paid like a coolie, you're going to live like a coolie." Then most Americans will live like coolies too. Few small businesses or professionals who do business with coolies can earn much more than coolies themselves. And many small businesses or professionals will not earn anything at all as demand disappears for their suddenly unaffordable products or services. During the Great Depression, Ph.D.s had hard times getting work, and lawyers and doctors got paid very little—that's why doctors made house calls. Those days could easily return if the standard of living for the average American working person declines dramatically.

America needs a much wider and deeper debate over what is happening. Native industries—the millions of smaller businesses whose profits and losses are based on what happens in their own localities—are being squeezed in a life-or-death struggle just like American workers.

Organized American workers could add much to that debate. It is in their interest to preserve their jobs. They have union organizations that could give strong voice to their thoughts. Contrary to the image of dumb or benumbed and deskilled assembly-line automatons, they know a great deal about how foreign competition is undermining America's vitality. Many of them are in fact far more sophisticated than the level of public discussion that has occurred to date.

For example, in 1983 a 63-year-old Bucyrus-Erie assembler and member of the United Steelworkers from Erie, Pennsylvania, educated me about imports from Korea and Brazil. For years he had seen machine parts coming into his shop from Brazil and other countries and was disturbed about how that was taking away American jobs. He ended with a rising note of anger in his voice: "What do they think they are doing?" He added that they were hurting themselves as well as him. And he was right. The plant, which made power shovels, closed two years later. He had been way ahead of me and had already long been waiting for someone to make a public case for what he knew from daily experience to be true and terribly important.

Like that worker, millions of industrial workers see jobs disappearing and see components being imported from a growing list of Third World countries. They see and suffer the squeeze firsthand and think a lot about it. But without national organs to express and amplify their perceptions and to debate and formulate positive economic proposals, they are divided by silence, hamstrung by disunity, and unable to defend themselves or help America.

Business journals, whose audience is employers who wish to reduce American wages and weaken unions, tell this story quietly or not at all. They don't want to wake and arm their opposition. But by censoring or muting the story to keep it from the American public, they keep its true extent and danger from themselves too, and thereby fail to understand it or take adequate measures. They too need the freewheeling, open debate that can be produced only by extending the discussion to working people. Even the American-based multinationals, whose largest single portion of business is still in America, need such a debate to preserve their American base in the long run.

As the global squeeze on jobs and wages tightens, it will reduce the living standards of most of the industrial world toward grinding poverty while raising wages only a little in the poorest countries. But it will increase profits for the rich and powerful a great deal in the short run. The four-dragon squeeze reveals the true meaning of the American government's "deregulation" and "free-trade" policies: Multinationals are free—and feel compelled—to seek the lowest-wage labor they can find anywhere in the world, and any working person who doesn't "agree" to lower wages and benefits is free to starve.

But it may not be long before everyone is threatened. What will happen when no one can buy many products even if they are made cheaply? If markets disappear in industrialized countries for Third World goods because working people in industrialized countries are impoverished, then Third World jobs will disappear too. Global depression or inflation, terrorism, civil wars or revolutions, dictatorships, and wars will become ever more likely and dangerous.

If world trade collapses, or if terrorists or nations use—or merely threaten to use—nuclear weapons against highly vulnerable civilian targets, then modern economies could easily collapse. But most survivors couldn't go back to earlier methods of agriculture and manufacturing because once-easily available resources have been used up or polluted, the knowledge to use them in old ways is practically gone, and the nuclear wars that could bring down civilization would contaminate what remains. Even if the human race is not wiped out, modern civilization might never recover. Then all the profits, money, and luxuries—and the people who depend on modern civilization for their wealth and power—will be wiped out too.

2

The High Cost of Fighting Unions

Leaders in American business and government are subsidizing foreign competition that both destroys American jobs and threatens American business itself in the long run. This is surely madness, but there is a method to it: They are engaging in a strategy to flee high-wage and union labor at all costs and, at the same time, reduce wages and weaken the unions that remain in the U.S.

Seeking low-wage, nonunion foreign labor seems to make perfect sense in the context of American management's obsession with reducing labor costs. However, the movement of jobs overseas was not nearly as preordained by lower foreign wages as some people would like us to believe. It and other steps that management took within the U.S. to reduce labor costs raised other costs and reduced overall business competitiveness immensely.

A Costly Business Decision to Weaken Unions. After the long recession that began in 1980, many basic American industries faced serious losses and began trying to find every possible way to survive. Some business reporters finally reported or implied that manufacturers, in their quest to avoid unions, had made bad business decisions.

The auto industry is a prime example. To create new efficiencies of production in the early part of this century, Ford Motor Company had pioneered the concept of concentrated, integrated mass production at River Rouge, near Detroit, Michigan. Yet after World War II, American auto makers defied efficiency and spread production all around the U.S. "Ford Chairman Caldwell speculates that 30 years ago auto executives may have deliberately spread their plants around the country to keep their newly unionized workers dispersed as much as possible" (*Business Week,* 6–21–82, 88). American auto makers stayed spread out until they were threatened by Japanese competition. Then they reshaped to concentrate production in the unionized Midwest.

Low Wages Are Not Always "Cheap"

It may seem that an employer with lower wages will always have a competitive advantage. But low-wage labor is not necessarily "cheap" labor. Getting low-wage labor can be costly in plenty of ways.

Dispersing factories and spreading out operations over large distances increases transportation costs, increases problems of communication and coordination, increases the chances for errors and disorganization, and thereby lowers quality and reduces flexibility.

Scattering Production. Low-wage foreign labor can be uncompetitive even in the apparel industry. The problem is poor response to complex and changing markets. For example, a garment typically took 66 weeks in 1986 to reach retailers' shelves. According to Peter Harding, manager of textile industry services at Kurt Salmon Associates Inc., a garment would spend 55 of those weeks waiting between processes or to be processed (*Inc.,* May 1986, 20). Significantly, imports made up half of the $55 billion U.S. apparel market in 1987 (*Business Week,* 1–12–87, 122D, and 8–3–87, 80). And garments imported from low-wage countries are generally the slowest to be delivered. It just takes longer to ship garment parts and designs from the U.S., send them to and fro among Asian or other nations as they are assembled into products, and then returned to the U.S. for final sale.

Apparel makers who need 66 weeks to deliver a garment cannot be leaders in supplying fashionable clothing, where sales volumes change rapidly and where, not incidentally, hot items bring high profit margins. A lot of business and profits can be lost in being slow to market or in having little fashionable clothing to sell. Making garments in the U.S. can speed up the process considerably, increase sales of trendy items, and reduce inventory costs for retailers, who then don't have to carry unwanted clothing. Unfortunately, that option is precluded when foreign labor is employed to cut wage costs.

Inc. magazine reported that slow turnaround and poor response to customers also afflicted overseas production of advanced semiconductor computer chips (May 1986, 20). Perhaps it was just coincidence that when Texas Instruments Inc. supplied improperly tested computer chips to the Pentagon and got bad national publicity for it (Dan Rather, CBS Evening News, 9–11–84), the chips had not come from Texas, but from Taiwan (*Newsweek*, 9–24–84, 30). Fortunately the chips were not found to be defective (*New York Times*, 4–16–85, D1). Still, the improper tests suggest the problems that can arise when production is scattered to the four winds—or to the four dragons.

Auto parts also can be made in low-wage countries. But while Japanese suppliers followed Japanese auto companies into the U.S. and threatened the $100 billion American auto parts industry (*Fortune*, 9–1–86, 72), Echlin Inc. was reportedly doing just fine selling its own U.S.-made parts with high-quality service and responsiveness to customers (*Forbes*, 4–6–87, 48). Saying that in a service industry "pricing is often secondary," *Forbes* concluded that "there's a lot more to international competitiveness than U.S. versus Taiwan wage rates."

The high costs of the wage-cutting approach are staggering (not to mention the implications for U.S. national security in depending on foreign computer chips). *Business Week* reported the apparel industry annually "squanders an estimated $25 billion, much of it lost to markdowns because apparel makers and retailers have trouble matching their inventories to consumer demand" (1–12–87, 122D). And attempts by the industry to eliminate waste involved producing in the U.S. to improve the match between supply and demand.

Imagine for a minute that the wasted $25 billion were somehow recovered by efforts to produce most apparel in the U.S. If only half went for wages, that would be one million more jobs at $12,500 per year—not a high wage, but unfortunately not uncommon in the garment industry and much of the South, where many of the jobs would go. And another one million or two million jobs might possibly be supported as the full $25 billion was spent and taxed. That would be two million to three million jobs lost through management waste in one industry alone! Of course, there's no way to say this would happen, but it does give some feeling for how costly the wage-cutting approach might be in money and jobs to the U.S.

Quality. Other industries also waste a great deal. Eastman Kodak Co., for example, estimated that in 1985 "about 32 percent of all photo products coming off the production line were defective" (*Business Week*, 2–23–87, 138). According to *BYTE*, in 1983 Hewlett-Packard estimated that "as much as 25 percent of its manufacturing assets were tied up in solving quality problems" (November 1983, 4). And W. Edwards Deming, the American expert widely credited with teaching Japan about quality, said that 15 percent to 40 percent of the cost of most American products consisted of embedded waste (*U.S. News & World Report*, 2–2–87, 20).

When products are defective, labor is wasted and management complains of "high labor costs." Reducing waste by improving quality would automatically reduce "labor costs" without reducing wages.

The Japanese learned this lesson, aimed for "zero defects," and reaped "low labor costs" in addition to high quality. While U.S. makers of 256K computer memory chips were able to keep only 17 percent of every batch of chips they made, the Japanese, with fewer defects, kept 54 percent. That's over three times the productivity, or less than one-third the unit "labor" cost (labor per chip), although of course it has nothing to do with wage costs at all (*Business Week*, 8–18–86, 66). Since defects in chips can cost a great deal to buyers of products such as computers that use chips, the quality/cost advantage is decisive. As a direct result, Japanese companies came to dominate important parts of the vital semiconductor industry.

Unfortunately, American management sought to reduce wages rather than its own waste. Failing to design and produce high-quality products, it sought pitifully low foreign wages to make up for its own inadequacies. As a result, management continued to produce inferior products, became increasingly uncompetitive, and drained the U.S. of jobs and prosperity.

If American management had learned to use skilled or well-situated (close to market) U.S. labor, it would have been much more successful and would have served America much better. A growing number of Japanese and other foreign companies have built plants in the U.S. or have taken over failing U.S. plants and reported success with U.S. workers. Several reports in 1986 said that Honda cars built in the U.S. were as good as and cost as little to make as those built in Japan. Y.C. Wang, a Taiwanese billionaire, bought 13 chemical plants in the U.S. and made profits using U.S. employees where U.S. managements couldn't. "American employees were excellent," he told *Forbes* (7–15–85, 92). On its cover, *Forbes* summed up his attitude toward American management in a word: "Scorn."

Japanese-managed factories in the U.S. produced $155,000 per worker in 1984 versus only $87,000 for U.S.-owned plants (*Business Week*, 1–19–87, 66). For the same wage rate, the Japanese-managed unit labor cost was only 56 percent of the U.S.-managed unit labor cost. Let's assume for the sake of argument that Japanese companies got equally great productivity in Japan. Let's also adjust for a currency exchange rate that inflated the dollar by as much as 70 percent and correspondingly deflated the yen by 41 percent (255 yen to the dollar at one point versus 150 yen to the dollar later). This means that in making cost comparisons, Japanese wages were converted at only 59 percent of their proper value. Multiplying the productivity factor of .56 times the currency factor of .59, the Japanese actually got unit labor costs that were only one-third of U.S. labor costs—even if wages, when computed at the more equitable currency exchange rate of 150 yen, had been the same in both countries!

Just in Time. When companies seek the lowest-wage foreign labor, they scatter production around the world and raise nonwage production costs. Besides transportation costs, large stockpiles of inventories must be kept on hand to buffer supplies that could be delayed for any number of reasons when they come from far away. But large inventories are expensive to finance, are expensive to house, and get in the way when they are stored next to the assembly line. Worse, they encourage sloppy and expensive management practices, since spare parts can be easily secured if the original part is defective or is installed improperly.

While Ford and GM scattered production around the nation and later around the world (producing a so-called world car), Japanese auto makers, especially Toyota, copied Ford's original River Rouge concept in the 1950s and developed it until they dominated auto production. They call their system *kanban,* which means parts are delivered by suppliers "just in time" as they are needed to be assembled. *Kanban* puts great pressure on doing things right the first time and on involving workers strongly in running production. That means much less inventory to be financed, higher quality because faulty parts are detected immediately, smaller and less complicated—thus less costly—assembly factories, and closely knit industrial complexes that increase responsiveness and reduce transportation costs and mistakes.

By reversing the inefficiencies of scattered production, *kanban* is credited with increasing productivity, raising quality, reducing costs, and disciplining the management of production operations (*New York Times,* 3–25–83, A1). The cost savings alone from *kanban* were estimated by consultant James E. Harbour at $500 per car in 1983—a full 25 percent of the so-called $2,000 labor-cost gap American auto makers complained of.

To put it another way, American auto makers raised manufacturing costs at least $500 per car when they scattered factories to fight unions. And that doesn't count the lost jobs and lost sales as consumers turned to higher-quality Japanese cars.

To produce "just in time," Japanese auto makers had to make peace with their unions. Concentrated production depends more on workers' voluntary initiatives to clear up bottlenecks. Simultaneously, it is more vulnerable to strikes since there are fewer places to shift production. Judging by several reports, working in Japanese auto plants can be plenty hard. Japanese unions are practically captives of their companies and often enforce company discipline more thoroughly than any management could. But numerous reports suggest that management convinced its workers—at least until Japanese workers began to get squeezed in the late 1980s—that they were in business together. There appears to have been a sense that workers would get a fair share of prosperity—as embodied in "lifetime employment," efforts to retrain and keep displaced workers, and relatively modest management salaries. This had the paradoxical side effect of actually lowering wage demands, lowering labor costs, reducing strikes and their costs, and raising productivity and quality.

In short, with the proper management of business (and government, which influences currency exchange rates), U.S. wages could be both low-cost and high-quality. There is simply no good excuse for sending so many jobs out of the U.S.

Concentrating for Survival

U.S. auto makers and other U.S. manufacturers did not acknowledge the lessons of *kanban* until they were faced with possible bankruptcy. Then in 1984 they began to pull back toward their main centers of production and distribution (*Business Week*, 5–14–84, 176D; "Kanban, American-style," *Forbes*, 10–8–84).

The dispersal of production after World War II was an expensive antiunion luxury. "To take advantage of lower labor and energy costs, [manufacturers] spent huge sums building new plants hundreds and sometimes thousands of miles from their existing facilities" ("Now It Pays to Stay Closer to Home," *Business Week*, 5–9–83, 132B). But in the 1982 recession, which was a depression for heavy industry, "all corporate decisions are now driven by cost-cutting and survival," according to economist Jerry Jasinowski of the National Association of Manufacturers.

When a deep recession threatened bankruptcies and made cutting costs the most important consideration, U.S. auto makers and other manufacturers found the unionized, U.S. industrial heartland was the low-cost place to be. That's because U.S. manufacturers could take advantage of a skilled labor force, advanced American technology, short lines of transportation and communication, and quicker, easier adaptations to changes in marketing and operating conditions. They could reduce costs, increase quality, and create premium prices—hence premium profits—for premium products.

For example, in the same *Business Week* report mentioned above showing it pays to stay closer to home, we are told that "the increasing sophistication of many manufacturing operations makes highly skilled labor a necessity," which is "more important than wages or even unionization.'' Kulicke & Soffa Industries, a maker of semiconductor manufacturing devices, decided to stay at its base in Philadelphia because it wanted "to maintain the labor force and expand on it.'' And Lear Siegler Inc., a Santa Monica, California, aerospace and auto parts company, found that "the quality of machine-tool labor it had in Detroit could not be matched elsewhere.''

When Japanese auto companies began to build plants in the U.S., they too concentrated in the heart of the largest auto market, the eastern one-third of the country, with plants built or scheduled in Ohio, Illinois, Indiana, Kentucky, Tennessee, and Michigan. And their suppliers began to follow them.

Just as some manufacturers found advantages concentrating in the industrial Midwest, others found advantages pulling back to the U.S. from foreign plants. Some employed highly trained, better-paid technical people in America and used automation to beat out foreign or labor-intensive production, especially for high-quality or high-tech products. Others benefited from stable markets and proximity to suppliers and buyers.

GM's Delco division (electronics), Motorola (semiconductors), RCA and North American Philips Corp. (TVs), Ford (transmissions), Kayser-Roth's Catalina (apparel), and Textron's Gorham division (stainless-steel flatware) all moved at least some production back to the U.S. after 1982 (*New York Times,* 6–20–83, D1; *Forbes,* 5–23–83, 35).

As a consequence of these belated efforts to concentrate production, many of the far-flung U.S. auto and steel plants fell into trouble, especially in the Sunbelt, where labor rates and transportation costs had risen (*Business Week,* 11–7–83, 43; 5–9–83, 132B).

Unfortunately, the trend toward concentration doesn't necessarily mean an increase in manufacturing jobs in the U.S. Large numbers of jobs are still being exported. And the jobs that are being concentrated are increasingly being automated: Management is designing skilled labor out of the production process.

An official with ITT Information Systems told *Business Week,* "The price differential between the Far East and U.S. manufacturing has less and less to do with labor rates. There is little labor content left [in manufacturing]" (9–24–84, 110E). "After studying the hidden costs of off-shore assembly operations,'' Apple Computer Inc. decided to produce its Macintosh computer "entirely in the U.S. with a new, highly automated, just-in-time factory" (*Business Week*, 5–14–84, 176D).

So most of the factory jobs that have already been lost will not be returned to the U.S.

Subsidizing High-Cost Automation

Even automation and concentration have been pursued in costly ways to "control" or eliminate human labor entirely rather than seek the greatest productivity and lowest total costs.

Trying to replace all skilled human labor is so difficult and costly that efforts to do so cannot be justified easily—if at all—economically. In his book *Forces of Production* (Knopf, 1984), David Noble, professor of history, Drexel University, showed in great depth that excessive automation can be very costly and that there are no unambiguous statements of cost savings from most efforts at automation in the American machine tool industry.

In other words, large-scale automation is usually incorporated with many other changes that themselves cut costs or are very beneficial to business, such as quality control, "just-in-time" inventory control, new products with higher profit margins, and more flexible response to market demand.

Reports in the news media usually make the claim that labor-saving automation cuts costs, but they rarely give figures for actual cost savings or separate the effect of automation from all the other changes that might have been made. In such cases, savings that are attributed to automation just may have come from the other changes. They may even mask higher automation costs—when the machinery actually works.

According to Seymour Melman, professor of industrial engineering at Columbia University, no papers existed as of September 1984 on the economic justification of an advanced form of automation, "flexible manufacturing systems" (FMS), because it was failing badly. FMS, as implemented by American management, was so messed up that the machinery was "down"—unusable—50 percent to 60 percent of the time. Since then, many reports have acknowledged that FMS and even more extensive, full-factory automation systems, such as computer-integrated manufacturing (CIM), have had serious reliability and cost problems in the U.S.

To show why capital spending began to decline in 1986, *Forbes* told the story of H.R. Krueger Machine Tool, a company in Farmington, Minnesota, with sales of $12 million to $20 million a year. Krueger invested $1.5 million in the most advanced machinery and watched productivity go "through the floor" (11–17–86, 33). Four years and a total of $4 million later, it finally cut 20 percent from design man-hours, but the total cost was still higher than normal hand drafting, and the company's break-even point (how much it has to sell to cover costs) more than doubled from $4 million to $8.5 million in sales a year.

Many companies in the machine tool industry have historically been too small to spend $4 million on anything, and most that could wouldn't do it to raise their break-even points to $8 million! In such cases labor-eliminating automation was so expensive and trouble-prone that it hurt much of the capital equipment industry in the U.S.

Krueger survived only because it began to make higher-quality products and get higher profit margins. Yet Krueger's customers, U.S. auto companies, had not previously demanded higher quality. And evidence from Japan suggests that the older system might have been modified at less cost, in a shorter time, to produce as well or better.

Some of the most successful Japanese companies, notably Toyota, automated primarily by using relatively simple machines and integrating them with their skilled work force. This method was cheaper, less prone to breakdowns, and produced high quality (*Economist*, Survey, 5–30–87). And David Noble argued forcefully that better forms of automation could be achieved in the machine tool industry simply by starting with skilled machinists and designing tools for them instead of trying to eliminate the machinists altogether.

Why is U.S. automation overly complicated and expensive for companies of Krueger's size or smaller? And from where did the money come to try such faulty automation schemes?

Since the 1950s the U.S. Air Force has been spending tax dollars to devise factory systems that can indeed eliminate all human workers. In so doing, the military subsidized a highly inefficient form of automation (as well as subsidizing foreign competition) to break unions. In addition, large manufacturing companies such as General Electric Co. and General Motors are themselves military contractors, have large amounts of money to invest, and want to eliminate labor. They work hand in glove with the military on these subsidized projects. And if the result of expensive machinery is to keep out small competitors or make them dependent on the big companies, so much the better.

The U.S. financial system also encourages excessive automation. Banks and other lenders make profits by lending to companies that borrow capital to finance expensive machinery. Through their control of capital in general, lenders have enormous influence over what manufacturers do. And that influence is biased heavily for machinery and against people.

The result is that automation has been much more costly and less effective in America than in Japan. That's a terrible competitive disadvantage for the U.S.

Confirmation of this hit the headlines late in 1986. While spending as much as $40 billion on automation, GM had gone in three years from being the low-cost to being the high-cost U.S. car maker. Its profits fell below those of Ford for the first time in 60 years. And it lost market share. According to management analysts inside and outside GM, including H. Ross Perot, whom GM later paid $700 million for his silence, all that money spent on automation had been wasted.

The clincher was that a GM-Toyota factory, which Toyota managed in Fremont, California, had by late 1986 achieved the highest productivity and quality of all GM plants. It was done through simple management and work changes. And it was done with what GM had thought were "troublesome" union workers in a relatively unautomated, old plant. Consequently, GM scaled back its automation plans greatly at the end of 1986.

Where had GM gone wrong? In the opinion of auto analyst Maryann Keller, "The goal of all the technology push has been to get rid of hourly workers" (*Wall Street Journal,* 5–13–86, 1). And apparently not just GM had that objective. Tom Peters, the management consultant and author, said American management systematically developed automation "with the avowed purpose of driving workers out of the system."

Some Japanese companies also followed the labor-elimination route, and they paid a high price. According to a study by Michael Cusumano of MIT, as reported by *Fortune*, "Toyota pulled away from Nissan in the 1960s and 1970s because it concentrated on managing workers, while Nissan poured money into computers and robots" (12–22–86, 78). Like GM, Nissan later adopted many Toyota techniques.

David Noble had been right all along about the motives, costs, and weaknesses of U.S.-style automation.

Union Labor Can Be Cheap

The costs of excessive automation and scattering production are not the only ones incurred when union labor is avoided at all costs. Seeking nonunion labor can substitute unskilled or inexperienced labor for skilled union labor.

Construction. My father, who worked in a unionized iron-working shop in northern New Jersey, told me many times how his boss would try to subcontract work to the nonunion South, where wages were much lower. But much of that work was welded badly and failed safety inspections. So the work had to be done over again and cost his boss much more than doing it originally in his own shop. His boss would even complain on occasion that he didn't know what he would do without my father and other skilled welders, even though they were a "pain in the butt" as active unionists. They were the only ones he could trust to get work done well and fast.

Union workers tend to be more highly skilled for several reasons. Higher union wages attract the best job applicants. In addition, industry-wide union-negotiated benefits, especially in seasonal industries such as construction with many small employers, create systems of seniority and unemployment benefits that support workers during slack times. Rather than leaving the industry or the area, they remain available for employers when work picks up. And an employer can get those skilled workers easily by working through the union.

A 1986 study for the National Bureau of Economic Research concluded that union labor was cheaper in commercial construction because union hiring halls supplied large numbers of skilled workers on short notice, which nonunion contractors couldn't do, and unions screened workers to keep up quality (*Forbes*, 11–17–86, 10).

Inc. magazine reported how unions "helped clean up the company's bottom line and straighten out its management mess" when Jim Ansara, a Boston building contractor, invited the union in (March 1987, 60). Why did he do it? Previously a nonunion subcontractor had told Ansara he "could always tell when he was on a union job: it was cleaner and better organized." And Ansara himself had had experience with a union subcontractor. "He did astounding work, and I was amazed at how organized and knowledgeable his people were on the job." Furthermore, Ansara was impressed how the union workers, aged 35 to 45, greatly outperformed Ansara's nonunion 25-year-olds. After Ansara went union, supervisors' jobs became much easier because they spent "almost no time now mediating spats among workers." And jobs were done much faster. According to the company's controller, "while the company's hourly labor rate went up...its labor costs on many jobs have gone down."

Offices. The value of providing a skilled work force can be easily seen in occupations where unions are weak or nonexistent. "Manpower" employment agencies make a good business providing skilled office employees for temporary work. Kelly Services advertises that it trains and provides skilled labor. And new agencies are appearing that supply skilled professionals and managers on a temporary basis (*New York Times*, 3–22–87, Careers section, 5; *Forbes*, 3–9–87, 90). In other words, where unions don't exist, some of their services have to be reinvented. And at considerable cost. "Temp" agencies charge an arm and a leg for the people they provide—far more than is usually paid full-time employees—and yet the temporary employees themselves get paid much less than full-time employees. The "temp" agency pockets the difference.

There is no reason why temporary office work can't be likened to seasonal construction work. The image is certainly different, but the realities of uncertain work and skilled labor are the same. "Hiring halls" are an old practice in some unions, as is providing and enforcing a series of tests to certify competence in various skills. A union "hiring office," or some other organization of office employees, could conceivably send people to fill temporary jobs and negotiate a contract that splits the difference of what "temp" companies now pocket.

An enormous and growing number of people are involved. While some people choose to work part-time or as temporaries, many have no choice. Large companies are increasingly filling office slots with such "contingent" labor. Smaller companies are beginning to "lease" employees from employment services that sever completely the bond between manager and employee. And a growing number of people work for companies from their homes. Audrey Freedman of the Conference Board estimated in 1986 that these contingent workers totaled 25 million people, or 25 percent of the work force (*Business Week,* 12–15–86, 52).

At the same time that use of contingent—or "disposable"—office labor has grown, office and service productivity has flattened or even dropped. That connection hardly seems a chance coincidence, considering how much productivity depends on close, long-time cooperation and teamwork among employees. Except in the most permanent of situations, contingent employees are unlikely to know or care about each other. But union workers, or members of professional employee associations such as teachers and airline pilots, are much more likely to know each other and look out for each other. They belong to their own team and understand better how to work together.

Reducing Costs. When unions create and preserve a large job pool of experienced skilled workers from which employers can pick when they need them, unions can raise productivity, quality, and teamwork—three crucial business advantages. And employers can lay off workers in slack times without fear of losing them forever. That minimizes costs when business drops—another absolutely vital business advantage.

By comparison, advanced automated machinery—even "good stuff"—can be very expensive to buy and use. Money must be borrowed to pay for it and interest must be paid right from the start. Yet a mechanized workplace is often full of "bugs"—malfunctions—at the start because it is so complicated. Initial bugs may delay production and lose business and customers, but interest payments must still be made.

Complex and expensive machinery must also be run at or near capacity to turn a profit, but that can't be done all the time. When sales fall during recessions, incomes drop, interest rates rise, and the debt burden of the machinery rises accordingly. That makes an employer who single-mindedly replaces people with machines highly vulnerable to bankruptcy during recessions. That's not the way to create a strong and growing business.

Small companies just can't afford the expense and dangers of U.S.-style automation. Even the largest, "best" U.S. companies, including General Electric, IBM, and John Deere & Company (along with General Motors) got hurt badly "by weak sales after putting huge sums into modernization projects that rank as major engineering achievements" ("GE's Costly Locomotive Gamble," *New York Times,* 1–25–87, F4).

Productivity. There is still another advantage to union labor. Many unions have traditionally negotiated productivity increases in return for pay increases. The expression is "To get, you have to give." In such cases unions either identify productivity increases or prod management to find them, and they get the cooperation of the work force.

Overall American productivity has long been the highest in the world. The *Economist* reported that Japanese productivity in 1985, as measured by real gross domestic product (GDP) per worker, was only 75 percent of America's (8–23–86, Survey, 3). For much of the 1980s at least, that advantage applied, to a smaller degree, even in the steel industry. And productivity growth has long been highest in the U.S. in the manufacturing sector, which has been most heavily unionized. But in the overwhelmingly nonunion service sector, productivity grew much more slowly, only one-fifth as fast from 1970 through 1984, and not at all from mid-1984 through early 1986 (*Business Week,* 12–24–84, 13; *U.S. News & World Report,* 6–16–86, 51).

And in services, one of the most profitable and successful companies, United Parcel Service, was unionized—by the Teamsters. UPS earned twice as much per sales dollar in 1985 as Federal Express. It earned over seven times as much overall ($568 million) (*Business Week,* 6–16–86, 78). And it paid wages of $15 an hour plus benefits (*Business Week,* 12–29–86, 37).

In sum, having unions can create a highly flexible, skilled, productive, and low-cost work force. Even though individual workers get paid more, unions can in many cases reduce business costs, raise sales, and contribute to a business's health. And that's only natural, because unless unions become complacent or corrupted—which ultimately weakens them fatally—unions have little self-interest in putting employers out of business. That's something that can't be said for banks, Wall Street raiders, and "vulture" capitalists.

When employers seek nonunion labor just for the lower wages it represents and ignore questions of skill, productivity, quality, and nonwage costs, they create hidden costs and dangers to their business. Yet those hidden costs and dangers are rarely computed in comparisons of nonunion with union wages. Nor are the hidden costs and dangers of excessive automation sufficiently computed. They are often-overlooked reasons why the quality of American products has declined and many businesses and government services lurch toward bankruptcy.

Implacable Antiunion Bias

Unfortunately for U.S. competitiveness, the trend toward maximizing productivity through concentration is most pronounced during recession. Once profits are made again, they can be spent again on running away from unions.

Just how badly employers seek to avoid or defeat unions is revealed in several news reports. Buried deep in a report on construction unions was a reference to an "almost missionary zeal by antiunion employers" in the construction industry (*Business Week,* 2–4–85, 54).

National Public Radio reported a "paranoia of unionization" (the words are those of a management consultant) that kept companies from locating in Louisville, Kentucky (NPR—WNYC, 10:45 A.M., 2–21–86).

Forbes magazine has said on more than one occasion that "hard times have their uses," a principal one being to increase the number of unemployed workers and thereby lower wages and weaken unions.

In 1981, *Business Week* (4–13–81, 116) reported "the start of an antiunion drive." Four years later it reported that "arch-conservatives" are worried that the U.S. Labor Department, their "command post in the battle against unionism," may become more "accommodative" toward labor under its new secretary, William Brock (7–15–85, 45).

The *New York Times* calmly reported that financial analysts felt United Airlines "could endure a prolonged strike" by pilots "without serious harm" because it had "half a billion dollars in cash and short-term securities and a strong line of credit," despite losing "between $5 million and $7 million for every day of the strike" (5–28–85, D1). In labor disputes, "prolonged" can easily mean months. According to this report, a strike of 100 days would have cost United Airlines $500 million to $700 million. Even a short strike of 10 days would have cost $50 million to $70 million. Yet that was not deemed "serious harm." It's not hard to infer that the financial community of the U.S. put a price of half a billion dollars on beating the pilots' strike and union.

If that seems an excessive conclusion, consider the case of USX Corp., formerly U.S. Steel Corp. It locked out members of the United Steelworkers of America for nearly six months beginning in August 1986, lost an estimated $700 million to $1 billion, and won pay cuts estimated at between $75 million and $85 million annually (*Business Week,* 1–19–87, 56; *New York Times,* 2–2–87, A14; *U.S. News & World Report,* 2–2–87, 46; NBC Nightly News, 1–31–87). At $850 million for losses and $80 million in annual pay cuts, USX would need 10.6 years just to get back what it lost. This makes no sense at all except in the context of war money to defeat a union. Not one dollar in "tribute" to unions, but hundreds of millions of dollars to beat them!

A major *Business Week* report on "The New Corporate Elite," which is "changing the face of U.S. business," contained the observation that "with the exception of corporate rejuvenators who have inherited unions, virtually everyone else in the service and high-tech areas will do anything to keep organized labor out" (1–21–85, 70). In other words, the leaders and movers of the U.S. economy will do "anything"—including, we now know, selling out the U.S. to foreign competition and spending vast sums of money—to defeat unions.

The "battle against unions" is global. In "Europe's Tougher

Labor Policies,'' the *New York Times* (4–28–85) reported that for a year in advance of the 1985 economic summit of world leaders, the Reagan Administration had ''missed no opportunity to berate its European allies'' for not fighting unions enough. The subheading of the story read, ''Unions have lost some control over jobs and wages. But the Summit will call for faster action.''

Even where manufacturers have abandoned the U.S. for low-wage foreign labor, they still want nothing to do with unions. A report entitled ''Malaysia: Unions Have U.S. Electronics Makers Scared'' is most revealing (*Business Week,* 6–13–83, 58). ''The Malaysian government recently shocked the industry by permitting 600 workers to unionize at an ITT Corp. electronics subsidiary.'' The shock was so bad that ''one electronics plant in Penang has threatened to pull out if unionization succeeds, and Motorola Inc. says it is anxiously watching the ITT outcome.'' Hewlett-Packard too was ''very concerned.'' The article began by emphasizing Malaysia's former advantage of a ''largely docile, nonunion work force.'' And it ended by quoting the managing director of Hewlett-Packard that if unionization proved successful, ''corporate officials would hesitate to invest further in Penang.''

Malaysia sported low wages, a skilled work force, and high-technology capabilities: a full set of reasons that manufacturers have claimed why they had to move production and jobs out of the U.S. Malaysian unions would surely raise wages somewhat, but they would still be terribly low by U.S. standards. Yet American companies would abandon even Malaysia just because its workers wanted to form a union!

No matter how much manufacturers claim they are making decisions based solely on hard economic considerations, they are not. They set out to break unions, and it backfired. They raised their costs and they lost their markets.

3

The Squeeze "Made in America"

U.S. subsidies of foreign competition actually got their start in America. When American corporations first began after World War II to move factories to places in the South and West where unions had made few inroads, they managed to weaken unions in the North and put downward pressure on wages. But to do so, they had to build up the nonunion economy initially with subsidies from the union economy—just as they later subsidized foreign production at the expense of America in general.

Now that unions are being beaten, subsidies to the nonunion Sunbelt and rural areas are beginning to produce less antiunion effect per buck, and the subsidies are being withdrawn: The Sunbelt and rural areas are getting pressured to reduce wages by foreign competitors and by American corporations that have exported jobs to low-wage foreign countries. This method is called divide and conquer: Working people are being divided; and American big business with the aid of government is doing the conquering—at the price of making American business mortally vulnerable to foreign competition and making America much weaker and poorer.

Subsidies to Bleed and Squeeze the Union Economy

After World War II the unionized parts of the economy were by far the most productive and efficient. Businesses had grown the most where business had been the most profitable. They were located centrally in their markets, nearest to natural resources such as iron and coal, and had abundant water to use and travel on. And the industrial unions followed the biggest and most efficient producers.

When manufacturers spread production to nonunion areas, they needed subsidies to make their scattered, nonunion production economically attractive and "competitive," and the subsidies could come only from the richest—unionized—parts of the economy. The vast water and highway projects that spread through the U.S. after World War II were certainly not paid for by the sparsely populated, often-poor states where many were built.

Besides interstate highway and water projects, subsidies for the Sunbelt, suburbia, and rural areas have included a wider network of roads in sparsely traveled regions, cheap and available rail and air fares (enforced by government regulation) to small or scattered communities, cheap water, sewage treatment and drainage systems, and equal rates for telephones, mail, and electricity (more government regulations).

These were all subsidies because low use and large distances in rural and sparsely populated regions mean high real costs— above the rates actually charged. They were made up by charging urban residents more than the cost of their services. Cheap gasoline also subsidized traveling large distances in the dispersed economy, and military spending was disproportionately heavy in the nonunion economy. The subsidies were paid by taxing and overcharging the unionized economy and spending the money in the nonunion economy. Here are more details:

1. A gigantic subsidy for the agricultural South began at the expense of the Northeast after World War II when millions of rural poor white and black people were moved off small plots of sharecropped or tenanted land and, in effect, sent North. This enabled the size of farms to increase and their efficiency to soar because of the larger machines that large farms could support. It also relieved the South of the burden of caring for much of its own poor.

The North could not exclude the people who were displaced— they were American citizens. Many found work in the post-World War II industrial boom, but many did not. The cities and states that had public welfare laws were forced by the U.S. Supreme Court to put unemployed newcomers on welfare regardless of their length of residency. The cities and northern communities that had been prosperous and more generous toward their own poor were made to shoulder the burden of supporting millions of people displaced by the modernization and industrialization of

Southern agriculture. Many cities still carry that inequitable burden in the descendants of the people who were displaced. The people who were displaced but never employed have suffered greatly, and the cities that have to support them have been bankrupted and wasted by that unfair burden.

2. The price of gasoline in America has stayed well below world levels. Some conservative economists say the government kept gasoline prices artificially low. Cheap gasoline and large federal and state road-building programs supported an immense dispersal of industry and population into the Sunbelt, as well as into suburban and rural areas.

Because of the large distances traveled all over this country and among dispersed populations, and the waste of energy and resources that occurs in dispersed single homes, America uses too much energy. America has long been and still is dependent on OPEC and other foreign oil producers. Hundreds of billions of dollars were paid to OPEC and the oil-coal-gas-uranium companies. The total expense has amounted to a gigantic drag on the economy that has been ruinous for America.

3. The American auto industry built the best large cars in the world—because large distances and cheap gasoline in the American market demanded them. But other countries could not afford to buy significant numbers of America's large gas-guzzlers. When gasoline prices skyrocketed, American car makers couldn't sell those cars even in America, and all the capital invested in them was in effect wiped out by obsolescence overnight.

U.S. auto makers had to invest a reported $80 billion, and plan to invest another $80 billion by 1990, to make newer, smaller cars (*Business Week,* 9–12–83, 72). That investment cost plenty in a period of unprecedentedly high interest rates; and the cars, being untried and unproven, could not keep up with improvements in Japanese cars. So the U.S. auto industry was beaten and would have been destroyed—except for protectionist legislation. The Japanese won because they made cars for the larger world market in small cars, which gave them more experience, larger production runs, and greater production efficiencies.

The large distances that Americans travel, plus gasoline that is still cheap compared to the rest of the world, continue to demand and keep American cars at the large-car end of the world market, permanently hampering U.S. auto makers' market size, production runs, and competitiveness in small cars. Lower American quality is also blamed, but quality could easily be an indirect casualty of the gasoline subsidy: The first way American managers tried to make profits on small cars was to lower their quality. And along with the sinking auto industry went many other industries, businesses, and communities dependent on auto making or artificially cheap energy.

4. Equal or "universal" rates are huge subsidies. They are paid by customers to utilities or other providers of services regardless of a customer's location or cost of service. That makes scattered users in less-populated regions pay a price that is less than the cost of delivery of the utility or service. Equal taxes, which are paid for public services regardless of location within a geographical area, are a huge subsidy too.

Take the case of postal delivery. It costs more to send a letter from Los Angeles to Boston than it costs to deliver a letter within the same city. Yet every first-class letter has the same price, no matter what its cost of delivery. In an apartment building, a postal carrier can stand in one spot and distribute mail to as many as 200 or more apartments. But in rural areas, mail delivery requires a car or truck to drive between *each* mailbox, and naturally it takes longer. That means higher labor costs as well as equipment and operation costs. The same is true for most services: Concentration of population means more service can often be delivered easier, faster, and cheaper.

But people in concentrated areas usually haven't paid cheaper rates. They pay the same as people who are more difficult or expensive to serve. Or they even pay more. "The average [telephone] bill for local service still runs only $15.70 a month in the city and $10.59 in the country (rural rates are subsidized by city dwellers)" (Jane Bryant Quinn, *Newsweek*, 1–21–85).

People in concentrated areas pay more than the cost of delivery, and people in dispersed areas generally pay less. Universal rates and uniform taxes are an immense subsidy paid to the dispersed parts of the population and the economy at the expense of the concentrated.

5. Federal and state governments tax the concentrated parts of the economy, and government—especially the Pentagon—spends more of that money in the less concentrated parts. Since the con-

centrated parts of the economy are the most unionized and industrialized, the unequal distribution of tax dollars amounts to bleeding the union economy dry.

Federal statistics sometimes mask how much blood is shed. Senator Daniel Patrick Moynihan (D., N.Y.) reported that in 1976, although New York was credited with getting more from the federal government than it paid in taxes, $14 billion of that credit never reached New York State (*New York Times,* Op Ed, 8–4–77). That money was actually spent on foreign aid and to pay interest on the national debt. It was credited to New York only because the transactions took place on Wall Street! What's more, because the federal government spends more than it takes in taxes, each state received in 1976 on average "some 129 percent of their ascribed tax payments. If New York had received that average in fiscal 1976, we would have got $17.1 billion more than we did get." That's a $31 billion deficit—in one year! Further, "if New York got the proportionate amount California got, we should have received $32.3 billion more than we did," Moynihan said.

A study by State Policy Research Inc., a private research company, showed that with only a few exceptions, states in the Northeast and Midwest paid much more in taxes per person to the federal government in 1984 than they got back in federal spending, while states in the South and West got more back than they paid (*New York Times,* 6–19–85, D27).

At the bottom of the list were Illinois and New Jersey, which lost $1,161 and $1,013 per person respectively. Seven of the bottom ten were from the Northeast and Midwest. But eleven of the top thirteen were from the South, West, or sparsely populated and remote states. New York lost $232 per person and was thirty-sixth on the list; California gained $395 per person and was seventeenth on the list.

Is it any wonder that New York nearly went bankrupt in the mid-1970s, or that the entire Northeast and industrial Midwest fell on such hard times? Or that the Sunbelt grew so miraculously? But that kind of bloodletting can't go on forever. And it hasn't.

Sunburn in the Sunbelt

Losing the Subsidies. The subsidies to the Sunbelt gave uneconomic nonunion businesses unfair advantages and made them artificially profitable. Simultaneously, the subsidies made the unionized parts of the American economy more expensive and increasingly "uncompetitive." The nonunion economy grew at the expense of the union economy, and the union economy deteriorated. The process gathered momentum like an avalanche until large parts of American industry were destroyed. Now American national security and the nonunion economy itself are threatened by that collapse.

As the unionized, industrialized parts of the economy finally became crippled, the subsidies to the Sunbelt and nonunion parts could not continue in the same way. Ironically, the very union wages that some people blame for the unions' decline also made those higher subsidies possible through greater purchasing power, a more dynamic economy, and higher income taxes. With industries failing in the Northeast and Midwest, the Rust Belt, unionized workers and the communities based on them could no longer pay the taxes or the regulated-service rates they once paid. The industrialized, unionized economy became like the golden goose that was killed. The decline of the old-line industrial states meant that less tax subsidies went to the Sunbelt just as more displaced people flocked to it from the North and Midwest.

Working Americans in the Sunbelt have plenty to worry about. Their industrial jobs, which have moved there within the last 20 years and which seemed like gifts from heaven, have begun to disappear. Sunbelt growth is getting slammed as capital and jobs are exported and low-wage labor is imported.

Capital investors who sought out the lower-wage labor, low taxes, and then-cheap land of the South and West have profited enormously. But they were also free to take their money and run anywhere in the world they could find lower-wage and nonunion labor. And they did. Companies such as Atari left the U.S. and took Sunbelt jobs with it. They began to drain investment capital out of the U.S. South and West even faster than they had built it up. But working people sink roots in communities and cannot run quickly to new areas of prosperity. They are stuck when their local economies turn sour.

Here Comes Mexico. In Los Angeles, Miami, and throughout the South and West (reaching pretty far north to places like New York City), American and international employers brought the four-dragon squeeze to and across the doorstep of America's border: illegal labor flooded into the U.S.; and capital fled to build plants in Mexico, Central America, and the Caribbean. These places have millions of people who rank among the poorest and most desperate people on earth, and their populations are increasing rapidly to keep them poor and desperate for American employers.

Why should a manufacturer send auto parts, garment cuttings, computer parts and keypunching, or anything else needing hard manual labor, to Hong Kong or Indonesia when terrified and desperate low-wage labor can be found much closer—in the Americas or in the U.S. itself? Why invest capital and build plants in Argentina, South Africa, and Asia when they can be built south of the Rio Grande? And the goods that are assembled, which include many things besides auto parts, are "brought back to the United States under special low tariff rates" ("U.S. Auto Makers Using More Mexico Plants," *New York Times,* 7–25–82, 1). Who wrote that law?

By mid-1987, jobs in *maquiladora* plants in Mexico just south of the U.S. border had grown to 300,000, double the number in 1982 and rising rapidly (*Economist,* 5–23–87, 25). Indonesia, look out, here comes Mexico!

Ironically, American companies will also have to look out. Although Americans developed northern Mexico as a low-wage manufacturing area, Japanese companies began to move there in a big way in 1986. Without major improvements in U.S. management, superior Japanese managements could use Mexican or other low-wage labor for themselves and defeat the very American companies that fled to Mexico to escape U.S. workers. Those American companies may then have to retreat to the U.S. and would need strong local-content laws to defend *themselves* against the combination of Japanese management and Mexican labor. And South Korean companies are already "prowling Tijuana" to put pressure on the Japanese (*Newsweek,* 6–22–87, 46). In trying to beat American labor, American managements have set in motion a squeeze play on their own cheap-labor squeeze that could ultimately bankrupt themselves and impoverish America.

Rural South. The squeeze is tightening as it works its way up from the dirtiest, most dangerous, hardest manual labor. And it hits the rural South most of all, where labor-intensive manufacturing had first run to escape unions in the North, and where labor-intensive manufacturing is now leaving for still lower-wage labor. According to a town councilman in one depressed mountain town in North Carolina, "if [investors] do come in and develop this town, we'll roll over backwards" ("Rural Southern Towns Find Manufacturing Boom Fading," *New York Times*, 3–21–85, 1). Meanwhile, two U.S. senators from North Carolina, Jesse Helms and John East, were among the most vigorous supporters of U.S. intervention in Central America, even though it served to maintain the low-wage, slave-like conditions that robbed rural North Carolina of jobs.

That's just what employers were hoping for from the four-dragon squeeze: desperate and willing labor that's even cheaper than slaves—because employers have no obligations to support "free" labor. And above all, they get employees who would be too desperate, thankful, and frightened to join unions!

The squeeze must tighten because many American managers continue to think the best—and sometimes only—way to get high profits is to cut wages, break unions, and push workers as hard as possible, or else abandon America entirely. They say it lowers prices and is good for the consumer. But is it?

Bad for Consumers. Working people in the South and elsewhere who lose their jobs also lose their ability to consume. Calling that good for consumers is cruel.

Further, low foreign wages certainly don't always translate into lower prices. To the arguable extent that low foreign wages really reduce costs, companies often mark up prices an extra amount and pocket extra profits rather than pass on lower prices to consumers. Top-priced "designer" clothing is often made in Hong Kong or Costa Rica, for example. Mid-range Shetland wool sweaters retailed in 1985 at $28 at the Gap, a retail chain, although some were made in high-wage Scotland and some were made in low-wage Hong Kong. And mass-market softballs retailed in 1985 at $5 apiece although they were stitched in Haiti with labor costs of 8 cents apiece ("The Big Money in Amateur Softball," *Forbes*, 7–15–85).

Worst of all, any lower prices the consumer gets can only be temporary. The more goods the U.S. imports, the more the dollar must eventually fall and raise the price of imported items. It happened in 1986 with Japanese products. At the same time, pressure began to build on Hong Kong, Taiwan, and Korea to raise their currencies' values and their products' prices. And domestic producers began to raise their own prices as import prices rose. (One wonders if this monopoly-like rise in prices and profits was one of the "new perceived values" that was sending the stock market higher.)

Deregulation. Government policies have also been fashioned to tighten the squeeze. During the Carter Administration, which began the process of deregulation that the Reagan Administration continued, there came to power in government a group of rich business interests with the special interest of "getting the government off our backs." They meant to remove from their backs all the safeguard regulations that protect working people, consumers, and communities from harm and abuse by business. They will certainly not try to increase safeguards for working people, and they won't help most people who are already endangered or suffering. In the process, many poor and middle-class people are losing the *shirts* off *their* backs: It must be no small measure of comfort to them to know that they are doing their part for the glory and profit of an unregulated "free market" that leaves them "free" to pay or starve and leaves a few free to profit hugely.

Gasoline and heating oil prices have been deregulated and are far higher than they were throughout the entire post-World War II period until 1978. Local telephone bills have risen sharply. Despite widely advertised (and sometimes deceptive) low fares for a few heavily traveled airline routes, deregulation of airlines, railroads, and buses raised prices or cut service for millions of rural Americans and businesses. They had been lured to the seemingly cheaper areas, seduced by unfounded growth, and depended on those subsidies. Then they were left high and dry with nowhere to go. And after many low-priced companies such as People Express went bankrupt or were bought up, prices began to rise again.

Less service and higher prices: That is the meaning of "deregulation" to the Sunbelt and suburbs. The union economy was bled dry and couldn't keep paying the subsidies, and military spending kept demanding *more*! So the Sunbelt and nonunion economy had to pay. Increasingly, that's where the money is.

Deregulation was pursued in a way that gouged working people the most and gave away the nation's natural treasures to private interests. Little effort was made to protect working people while the nation's economy adjusted. And not coincidentally, the temporary bout of "competition" that deregulation fostered was used to weaken or break the associated unions, especially in trucking and air travel.

Meanwhile, government deficits and cutbacks have hit the Sunbelt. And where subsidies have dried up, enormous bills have taken their place. In an ongoing, long-term crisis, roads, dams, water supplies, aqueducts, bridges, tunnels, and sewage "infrastructures" are deteriorating or lie uncompleted, with future money for them increasingly in doubt ("State and Local Government in Trouble," *Business Week,* 10–26–81; also, "The Crumbling of America: A New Crisis in Public Works," *Business Week,* 12–1–86).

Raising Interest Rates.   Since many subsidies were spent in ways that have become uneconomic, they in effect consumed large amounts of the nation's capital. That, along with greatly increased military spending, helped raise interest rates by making less capital available to be lent.

"Real" interest rates—interest rates compared to inflation—have been high since 1979 and promise to remain high as a result. In the Sunbelt, that translates into homes and land that do not rise in price enough, or can't be sold in many places fast enough—where they can be sold at all—to pay off mortgages. Many working people have lost their homes or farms through no fault of their own. Many more can't afford homes at all. Even oil states have been hurt from falling oil prices induced by high interest rates. Farms and high technology have also been devastated, as high interest rates helped raise the value of the dollar.

The most obvious government actions contributing to sunburn in the Sunbelt have been deregulation, cutbacks in spending, and encouraging imports through one-way "free trade." But just as important have been monetary and fiscal policies of President Reagan and Federal Reserve Board Chairman Paul Volcker.

By keeping money tight, they raised nominal and real interest rates, caused a deep recession—actually a depression for agriculture, mining, energy, and manufacturing—raised unemployment, and permitted only a sluggish recovery in the U.S.

Strengthening the Dollar and Imports. By running huge budget deficits and funding the military buildup, the government supplied money to pay for foreign goods and mask the pain of lost jobs in the U.S. And by borrowing dollars abroad, they created a foreign demand for dollars that kept the dollar expensive and imports cheap. This encouraged more imports, more job losses, and reduced underlying U.S. production and purchasing power even further.

Senator Daniel Patrick Moynihan and others have already shown that the budget deficits were a deliberate strategy to squeeze social spending. For years the high dollar was treated in the press and in official statements as something devoutly to be wished—and they got it. Finally, in September 1985, the U.S. engineered a major drop in the value of the dollar compared to the Japanese yen and the German mark. But at the same time, the dollar remained stable against currencies for such countries as Korea, Taiwan, and Brazil where U.S. multinationals manufactured and U.S. banks had large loans (with interest that must be paid by exports sold to the U.S.), even though these countries ran high trade surpluses with the U.S.

In short, the budget deficit paid for the trade deficit, which made ever more Americans poor and desperate to work, but paid banks and multinationals handsomely. The value of the dollar was managed at its maximum possible level to encourage imports for at least eight years, from 1979 well into 1987. That was another powerful subsidy to foreign production and hurt U.S. jobs immensely. And it was government policy.

Now the squeeze on the Sunbelt has begun to take away jobs and may destroy the cities of the very people who thought that their prosperity would never end. It has taken a long time, but all working people are increasingly in the same boat being hurt by the same squeeze, first of the unionized economy, and then of the subsidized economy. Unless all working people act together and avoid regional rivalries and other divisions, they will sink together. Only the big businesses and rich investors will have profited by building, selling, and moving on to new areas to exploit and then abandon all over again.

The Farm Depression

The antilabor forces that laid low industrial workers and high tech also sent the farming community into a deep depression. The pattern is startlingly familiar:

The *New York Times* (8–3–86, F1) reported that U.S. companies are investing extensively in foreign growers and processors, especially in Mexico, Brazil, and other Latin American countries. Banks and the U.S. government encouraged exports from these countries to pay their debts, and they kept these currencies undervalued to help do it—the same subsidies squeezing high-tech and heavy industry.

Banks, chemical makers, equipment makers, and academic agricultural experts developed highly expensive automated ways of farming (machines and chemicals) and encouraged farmers to go deeply into debt to do it. Then the U.S. government pursued high-interest-rate policies that made that debt impossible to repay—the same folly of favoring capital over labor.

At the same time, small farms were ruthlessly foreclosed, and the automated methods of farming increasingly enabled "professional" managers to take over those farms for lenders and investors (*New York Times*, 3–17–86, A1; *Inc.*, December 1986, 14; *Business Week*, 9–8–86, 66). In addition, the government paid huge subsidies to the largest growers, who are also the most capital intensive and automated—the same squeeze of subsidized automation that hit industrial workers.

These capital intensive methods destroy soil fertility, as their counterparts destroyed General Motors' industrial productivity. Pest damage was as high in 1986 as in 1945, before pesticides were widely used (*Newsweek*, 7–14–86, 73). Meanwhile, other reports show that "pioneering" farmers such as the Amish and others who avoid pesticides get profits or even higher yields by older, more labor-intensive methods of farming (*New York Times*, 8–28–86, A10).

Finally, chemical companies sell dangerous pesticides that are forbidden in the U.S. to the Third World, especially Mexico. Contaminated food is coming back into the U.S. unchecked and unspotted to poison U.S. consumers ("Poison Produce," *Wall Street Journal,* 3–26–87, 1)—as chemical and industrial pollution poisons workers, communities, and the environment in the U.S.

The U.S. risks becoming dependent on foreign food just as it is increasingly dependent on foreign steel, autos, electronics, money, machine parts, and shoes, to name but a few. And parts of the Sunbelt and Midwest are devastated as family farms disappear and the businesses built on them collapse.

Coincidence or Collusion?

Leaders of American business and government have undermined American production efficiencies, abandoned industries, subsidized foreign competitors, and given away dangerous military technologies that other nations could use to make and launch nuclear weapons of their own.

This would all be insanity except for the one consistent effect of weakening or breaking American unions and lowering living standards for most people who work for a living. That cannot be coincidence, though it needn't be a grand conspiracy either.

Subsidy of the nonunion economy, making low-wage labor available at the expense of the unionized economy, was and is the one direction on which most businesses and their representatives in national and state government could always agree. The subsidy acquired extra strength from the extra representation that rural areas get in the U.S. Senate, in Presidential elections from the electoral college, and from state legislatures before the "one-man one-vote" ruling. Some states have had such low populations that they could send only one representative to Congress, but they still had two senators representing them in Washington.

In 1985, after a lot of population changes had occurred, ten states with populations under one million had a combined population of only 7.2 million, and seven more with populations between one million and two million had a total of 9.9 million, while the U.S. had 238 million in all (excluding D.C.) (*U.S. News & World Report,* 1–13–86, 10). That meant 3 percent of the population had 20 percent of the Senate, and 7 percent of the population had 34 percent of the senators. That's an enormous power to shape legislation, channel economic subsidies, and tilt Presidential elections against the union-supported economy.

No conspiracy is needed among like-minded business people because they come to the same conclusions naturally about seeking low wages and docile, nonunion labor. But getting together to negotiate policy must happen in private business institutions such as the Business Roundtable, which is composed of the chief executive officers of 180 top business giants and can push forward the agenda of squeezing unions.

Whether by design or common intent, the squeeze on unions could proceed undisturbed and widely supported by many powerful business interests and government. It is no accident that squeezing unions results in squeezing all working people. Especially since the Great Depression, unions have defended all working people by forcing the rich and powerful in both capitalism and communism to restrain their otherwise limitless greed and to share more of their wealth with all working people. By squeezing unions, the rich and powerful become more so, and the rest of us grow weaker and poorer.

How Organized Workers Defend All Working People

People sometimes forget that capitalism can be just as brutal, dictatorial, and terrorizing as communism. And it can behave even more dangerously—witness Nazi Germany, Argentina's warmaking generals, and the death squads of some Latin American countries.

Every company or government employer is implicitly, and often explicitly, a totalitarian dictatorship that has nearly arbitrary power to hire, fire, and assign tasks among workers. If employers appear more humane than this, it is usually because workers in the past fought long, hard, and bloodily and forced civilized behavior on many a would-be dictator. Unions fought with strikes, bargaining collectively, and pushing for laws to protect average working people. The labor movements of Western Europe did these things successfully, and Solidarity in Poland and the black labor movement in South Africa tried to do them.

In the 1930s and 1940s, American workers won the right to organize and represent themselves and gained unemployment insurance, workers' compensation, the minimum wage, and dollops of respect and security on the job. President Franklin D. Roosevelt got credit for writing the civilized employment laws and creating the social safety nets that we take for granted, but organized workers were the main force pushing for them.

To President Reagan, these were the principal "mistakes of the past 50 years" that he worked so hard to undo. It's as if he had never heard of the Great Depression, a "mistake" of the very "unregulated free-market system" that he dedicated his long political career to restore. Of course, mistakes were made in the past 50 years, but what organized workers fought for were not mistakes. They benefited every person in society and shored up capitalism as a whole.

What unions won created higher wages and social benefits, a wider distribution of wealth, greater purchasing power for consumers, and consequently more sales and profits for business. In short, unions helped stabilize capitalist economies by lessening the effects of unemployment and depression. People born after the Great Depression have little experience to imagine how dangerous, destitute, and grindingly destructive life was then. It wasn't called "crushing deflation" for nothing.

The benefits unions won still buoy the consumer part of our economy. Many small businesses, professionals, consultants, salespeople, and white-collar employees unknowingly owe their livelihoods ultimately to the social stability, increased buying power, and civilized freedoms from dictatorship that organized industrial workers forced, in their own self-defense, on an otherwise unbridled capitalism. And the consumer-driven part of our economy still employs by far the most people.

Even nonunionized workers, unorganized white-collar employees, and middle management and professional staffs in corporate and government bureaucracies benefit from unions. Many employers have carried union-won gains into the pay and benefits of their nonunion employees to discourage them from wanting to join unions. And employers that are not unionized feel pressures to offer competitive rates to their employees.

Many people have come to call American unions narrow "special interest" groups. That's highly unfair to unions—and detrimental to many nonunion working people. In 1987, the AFL-CIO

proposed a broad range of laws that would protect far more nonunion people than union workers (*Business Week*, 2–23–87, 140).
Of seven major goals, six were for worker retraining and advance
notice of plant closings, tracking exposure to toxic materials, a
higher minimum wage, parental leave, protection from lie-detector
abuse, and retaliation against countries with big U.S. trade imbal-
ances. These were in the public's highest general interest. To scorn
rather than praise and support unions for their legislative efforts does
the public a great deal of harm.

How to Restore the Great Depression. Unfortunately, the antiunion warriors, with President Reagan most prominent, have broken down many union-built defenses of working people. With
support of lenders and Wall Street, employers have cut wages,
benefits, social programs, and the broad purchasing power that
union wages created and that still buoys our economy. They are
taking that wealth for themselves. But first they had to humble
or break the unions that defended working people and social programs. That's why a war against unions amounts to a war against
all working people. That's why the Sunbelt and nonunion parts
of the U.S. have gotten squeezed as unions have been weakened
or broken.

In reversing "the mistakes of the past 50 years," employers
and lawmakers have restored many conditions that helped create the Great Depression. By suppressing wages, they reduced
demand for goods and services. By subsidizing foreign production with hundreds of billions of dollars of loans, they wrote bad
loans, created dangerous global overcapacities, exported jobs, and
reduced demand still more. By borrowing heavily, they made the
U.S. the world's biggest debtor and dependent on both foreign lenders and foreign producers. And they deregulated financial markets
so "anything goes." This has put the financial system at risk to bad
debts, increased speculation, fraud and corruption, and wild fluctuations. The stock market has already crashed. And other bub-
bles could also burst explosively.

These were all far greater, more dangerous mistakes than any
real or imagined abuses unions have been accused of. Yet business
and government leaders ignore or deny that they have caused these

conditions or that the social programs and regulations unions created guard against the return of depression.

Unions' Maginot Line. Many working people have grown up during America's prosperity and don't know what a great debt they owe unions. They don't know what terrible suffering they are being exposed to for the first time in their lives. And if they are now feeling squeezed, they don't know what's behind it, don't know what to do about it, and don't know how much worse it could get.

Today, the old protections unions built are about as useful and will be no more successful than the Maginot Line was effective in defending France against the flood tide of Hitler and Nazi Germany. Unions will not remain strong—some will be destroyed—and the benefits accruing to all working people from unions' activities will be wiped out if unions try to defend only the past and fail to defend against the present and future attacks on them and on all working people.

Such traditional union tactics as strikes just don't work anymore, and traditional liberal tactics of government regulation just don't work, when companies and capital are free to move anywhere in the world and when government helps them do it. Unless working people organize to take a direct hand themselves in running the economy—and especially resisting the mad subsidies of foreign competition—they will have nothing to bargain with, there will be nothing to bargain for, and we all will get squeezed tighter and tighter.

Waging War on Working People: Central America, the Arms Race, and Dictatorship

U.S. business people reportedly view the Caribbean basin and Central America as the Far East of 30 years ago ("Trade Winds in the Caribbean," *Newsweek*, 11–14–83, 89). Some have noted that the Grenada invasion cleared away concern about Marxist regimes that was deterring investment, just as the Korean and Vietnam wars protected and encouraged investments in Japan, Korea, Singapore, Thailand, Malaysia, and the Philippines. American business people especially like the basin's nearness to the U.S. and its labor force willing to work for as little as 20 cents to one dollar per hour.

Haiti, for instance, was said to be "emerging as the low-wage capital of the world, the Taiwan of the 80's" ("Haiti's Allure for U.S. Business," *New York Times*, 6–17–84). According to Clyde Farnsworth, "Some 300 companies, nearly all of them American, have set up factory operations here in recent years. They are companies that once would have been drawn to Taiwan, South Korea, Hong Kong, or Singapore—but that was before wages in those countries rose sharply." How sharply had Far Eastern wages risen? To "$5 a day or more in many countries," while Haitian wages were $2.65 a day.

Consider: Many American business leaders felt wages of $5 a day were too high!

Low wages were not the only "advantage." Shipping costs were much lower because of the shorter distance, companies got a U.S. tax exemption, and President Reagan's 1983 Caribbean Basin Initiative allowed products to enter the U.S. duty-free. Last but not least, says Farnsworth, "Labor unrest is also a rarity in a country that has been ruled for 30 years by the authoritarian Duvaliers."

How would you like to work for $2.65 per day, or sell goods or services to people who earn $2.65 per day, under a dictatorship that killed people who asked for more? That's the direction in which working people in the U.S. will be pushed if Central America and the Caribbean basin are developed as a low-wage resource for U.S. business.

The Reagan Administration and Congress have done a lot to make the Caribbean more like the Far East of 30 years ago. President Reagan proposed and won large-scale economic aid for the "development" of labor-intensive manufacturing in the Caribbean basin. Despite talk in early 1987 of a drop in Caribbean trade, the drop was in raw materials and agriculture, reflecting the global oversupply and low prices in commodities generally, but imports of labor-intensive manufactured goods continued to rise (*New York Times*, 2–1–87, F6).

In addition to the action in Grenada, President Reagan supported military force throughout Central America and justified his actions as fighting communism. Would he were really fighting communism!

The Iran-Contra scandal revealed so much profiteering by middlemen, and associated reports revealed so much wealth being accumulated by leaders of the Contras, that American moneys, both overt and covert, appear to have gone much more to enrich a few individuals than to fight communism. And the very arguments in favor of fighting in Central America appear to have been cooked up by people who wanted to pocket those moneys in the first place. Further, powerful factions of the anticommunists in El Salvador and Nicaragua were supporters of former dictators, killers of three U.S. nuns, and murderers of tens of thousands of people. Their presence in the anticommunist forces gave rebels in El Salvador and the Nicaraguan government the powerful justification that they were still fighting the forces of hated and murderous dictatorships. And to top it all off, if communism were really purged from Central America, the region would be developed to take jobs away from working Americans! As in Korea and Vietnam, that's the wrong way to fight communism.

If anticommunism were really a burning issue to U.S. leaders, and if they really felt that "you can't trust the communists" enough to be able to work successfully with them, why did Presidents Nixon and Reagan go all the way to China to curry favor with a huge, brutal, and potentially very powerful communist government? The Chinese people are just too poor to be good markets for U.S. goods. Could it possibly be a coincidence that China offers the U.S. plentiful, low-wage labor? Or that south of the Rio Grande, American companies and allies already control low-wage, nonunion labor and are fighting to get more of it?

In Latin America and the Caribbean, as in other parts of the world, American business and government leaders have used anticommunism as a smoke screen to hide their real goals and justify their antilabor policies. They want to secure slave-like labor markets that are 8,000 miles closer to the U.S. than the labor markets of Southeast Asia.

There is, fortunately, another way to fight communism, a way that helps rather than hurts working people: Strengthen independent unions throughout the world. Communism has not come to power in any country with independent, democratic trade unions (except in East European countries conquered by the Russian Army). The victories of communism in China, Cuba, Vietnam, even Russia, and the ascendency of communism in Nicaragua, all came about where a brutal and corrupt dictatorship first ruled, and often where the U.S. backed that dictatorship. Independent, democratic unions defend workers' interests and society against any form of oppression.

Many U.S. unionists advocate such a policy. But it is totally opposed by business interests that simply cannot support unions in any shape, manner, or form, and it's effectively castrated by the added resistance of business and government interests that can support only pro-government company unions, and then only grudgingly, as a last resort.

If workers in Central America, the Philippines, and many other countries really had independent, democratic unions, they would act as a bulwark against the dictatorships of both right and left as they have in Japan, Western Europe, and the U.S. Governments that acted with the support of their working people would attract strong support instead of literally pushing large numbers of people into the arms of communist rebels. The appeal of communism would be greatly weakened, and the need to use armed force and wage wars would be greatly reduced. At the same time, unions would raise wages for many of the most oppressed workers and would reduce pressures to lower wages in industrialized countries. That's the right way to fight communism: Strengthen independent unions around the world.

Instead, the harder the U.S. has fought communism, the more it has hurt working people. If *those* failed policies of the past, not the list President Reagan complained of, are continued in the future, how many more soldiers' lives and taxpayers' dollars will be spent to take away jobs, ruin lives, and bankrupt communities in the U.S.?

Taken as a whole, something has gone terribly wrong with American economic, political, and military policies. Companies export jobs to the poorest labor on earth, reduce living standards in the U.S., undermine the economies of other nations, and increase world tensions. Together with the government, they support murderous dictatorships and make military conflicts more likely and prevalent. And the Pentagon subsidizes more job exports with gifts of American technology to foreign producers.

The arms race is fueled by misguided attempts to "create" jobs. And it is further fueled by understandable attempts of frightened citizens to seek security in a world that is made dangerous by economic, social, and military unrest.

In effect, corporate, government, and military managements have been waging war on working people at least since 1950. That war has spread into some very brutal governments and dangerous conflicts—El Salvador, Nicaragua, and Grenada recently—that threaten even nuclear war in the tensions they create under the excuse of "anticommunism." At the same time, that war strengthens oppressive forces within the U.S.

As subsidized foreign production weakens the American economy, pressures grow to make Americans work harder and longer for less pay and benefits. Many people who defend political freedoms find themselves powerless to oppose these economic pressures. Quite a few even agree, however reluctantly, with laws and practices that lower living standards and restrict such freedoms as collective bargaining rights. They think there is no viable alternative.

When the Polish communist government crushed the trade union Solidarity, President Reagan lit candles in public for Poland. But in private American bankers applauded the suppression of Solidarity (*Business Week,* 12–28–81, 48; *New York Times,* editorial Topics, 1–5–82; *Wall Street Journal,* editorial, 12–23–81). By their own logic, they had every reason to. Leaders of American big business, government, and finance have long supported dictatorships and suppressed labor in Brazil, Chile, Haiti, Nicaragua, Korea, Vietnam, the Philippines, Taiwan, and many other countries. President Reagan himself had crushed the air traffic controllers' union PATCO in 1981 for doing essentially the same thing as Solidarity. The Reagan Administration even knew martial law was coming but did not warn Solidarity (*New York Times,* 4–17–87, A9).

If unions are rendered powerless, the forces that applaud and abet foreign dictatorships will be greatly strengthened in the U.S. They will no doubt be strongly inclined to seek a dictatorship to suppress working people in America. Who then will remain with sufficient power and desire to stop them?

4

The Super-Liquidity Trap, and Other Ways Management Corrupts Itself and Endangers America by Making Unions Public Enemy No. 1

The Super-Liquidity Trap

Financial and industrial managers can move production anywhere they wish anytime they wish. They can buy and sell companies like chips in a poker game or get into and out of industries like someone trying on new suits of clothing. But before they could do that, they had to create highly liquid national and world markets: markets where anything could be bought and sold and anything could be gotten or shipped anywhere at any time around the world. In other words, they had to make it easy and quick to get into or out of any economic activity. They have done so by making super-liquid markets, and they are proud of it.

But in creating super-liquid markets, where they could buy, sell, and profit at any time, American policymakers also created the very short-term pressures of instant money movements that force even the best managers to plan for the short term. Whether they have to defend themselves against corporate raiders or want to make the most money they can in the shortest time, they cannot or do not want to plan for the long term or make investments that are locked up for many years. Something important will always happen in the near future to change what they will do.

Many management observers complain bitterly of management's short-term focus. Many managers complain equally bitterly that the economic markets force them to keep a short-term focus. Yet they don't question management's use of super-liquid markets to abandon America and make war on working people. What do they expect? To play with fire and not get burned?

I'd better mention now that super-liquidity is very different from the "liquidity trap" of the 1930s with which John Maynard Keynes was concerned. That was a condition of depression, falling prices, and almost zero interest rates in which the government couldn't stimulate the economy by printing money. Liquidity—money—was trapped as cash because interest rates were too low to save and consumers waited for price cuts. Consequently, demand had to be created.

The super-liquidity trap of the 1970s and 1980s is very different. It biases financial markets toward consumption rather than creation of productive assets. In financial terms, the difference between short term and long term is approximately the difference between money and capital. Financial markets dealing in long-term obligations such as stocks and bonds are called "capital markets." Capital is wealth that is used to make more wealth. It is an investment meant to take time before it yields profits because any productive activity requires a time of preparation, and that preparation must be paid for in advance, before it can be put into operation. Normally wealth that is not committed to long-term goals cannot be productive. Factories must be built and paid for (or the money borrowed and repaid with interest) before they can start producing. Successful market research and financial planning must also be paid for before a company will invest in a product or a bank will lend to a business.

On the other hand, financial markets dealing with short-term obligations are called "money markets," which include the day-of-deposit to day-of-withdrawal money market funds. Money is wealth that can be spent at any time—consumed—and it is usually spent on items that are consumed rather than on items that produce.

Some degree of liquidity in financial markets is essential to recycle investments that turn out to be unproductive. Their salvage value is liquidated—sold for money—and then the money can be reinvested. Even productive assets can lose their value and need to be liquidated if the products they make lose value or if better ways of making them are invented. But the process can be productive only if the money is reinvested in capital.

The root of the problem facing America is that American management is quickly losing the ability to manage the production of goods and services. This was explained in great depth in a major report by *Business Week* entitled "The Hollow Corporation" (3–3–86). It warned that as growing numbers of U.S. companies abandon manufacturing in the U.S. and seek foreign partners to do the manufacturing, they lose the capacity to manufacture anything at all and will eventually weaken the entire economy, including technology and services.

Because management often can't invest money productively in the U.S., it looks for more and more ways to make short-term profits and amass personal wealth and power. Seymour Melman wrote of management's nonproductive activities in his aptly titled book, *Profits Without Production* (Knopf, 1983).

Excessively liquid markets greatly expand management's ability to "make" money instead of goods and services. Since no one can manage physical productive assets very well without having an intimate working knowledge of them, managers who get into and out of companies and industries every few years cannot build up or update their productive knowledge. So management deteriorates, productive assets are managed ever more badly, and the decline feeds on itself as short-term profits are chased with increasing intensity.

In short, liquidity is an essential part of economic markets, but the minute-to-minute liquidations or potentials for liquidation of capital, factories, companies, and even industries that have been created in America go far beyond the productive purposes of liquidity. They have made liquidity itself a goal. Money isn't recycled into long-term, productive assets, so productive assets are diminished or destroyed. Then liquidity consumes—"liquidates"—capital.

An indicator of how financial markets have been converted to short-term liquidators of capital is that the managers of hundreds of billions of dollars in pension and mutual funds, banks, and the like are called "money managers." No one except David Roderick, head of USX, seems to talk of "capital managers." Yet Roderick presided over the liquidation of U.S. Steel into an energy company, with its stock market symbol, "X," for its name.

Forbes felt the perfect metaphor for the new economic activities was right out of *Star Trek*: "Beam me up, Scotty." Meaning: "[Business] will be zapping around the world for plants, parts, markets, ideas, staying where things look good, leaving fast where things look dicey" (5–5–86, 6).

Rather than producing new capital and wealth, many American managements are producing money and profits by liquidating (selling) what other people built in the past and by borrowing—stealing—from what we need to build in the future. It's a gigantic run at the nation's "piggy bank" and gives new meaning to the old expression "eating into capital."

Profits are also made—and "new values" are seen—by gaining anticompetitive, monopoly-like influence over prices, products, and labor. For example, companies pay inflated prices to buy up competitors. The seller makes a profit because competition kept his profits and stock market price low, and the buyer hopes that reduced competition will allow prices to be raised. The buyer may also be a management that hopes to entrench itself by reducing competition regardless of profit. Opportunities for monopoly-like profits abound as deregulation and large numbers of mergers have increased concentration in many industries. Buyers also look for companies where they think they can defeat a union and knock down wages. That kind of monopoly-like profit has grown as unions have been weakened throughout business. And the arms and medical industries have never operated with much competition. Government expenditures in these areas in the hundreds of billions of dollars annually create enormous potential for monopoly-like profits.

Raiders, investment bankers, and leveraged-buyout specialists often seem to be first to realize when new monopoly-like profits become possible, or at least they convince some buyer that "new values" have appeared. They play the middlemen in deals and make huge amounts of money through investment fees, greenmail, or buying low and selling high. Their success stories in turn entice far more money to join the search for "new values." And corporate managements get involved by buying up their own stock to raise its price and fend off raiders. Collectively, they have driven up the stock market at the same time that productive competence and living standards in America have declined, which is to be expected since anticompetitive situations reduce productivity.

These raids on the nation's resources and freedom (in the case of monopoly-like control) can go on for a long time because the U.S. has immense resources and freedoms. But eventually they must run out. And superior foreign producers such as the Japanese are already grabbing a large share for themselves, raising stock prices further as they buy up American companies. As long as American policymakers insist on liquidating American jobs to weaken unions, they will have to liquidate American capital, productive capacity, and freedom too.

Super-liquidity can be as disastrous to society as runaway inflation or crushing deflation. Each breaks the connections that hold a complex society together. Each destroys long-term capital investments, for no one but the most desperate person will gamble substantial wealth or human energy and emotion on what are at best doubtful futures.

When money zaps around the world, it betrays and destroys people and institutions in society every time it moves. Under such conditions people lose faith in themselves and in the future. They suffer from deprivation, betrayal, and abandonment of deep human feelings. And they seek quick gains and gratification rather than investing and building for longer-term rewards.

Management itself suffers as the people who own, move, or "make" money betray people themselves. According to Robert Swain, an outplacement expert, "50 percent of managers use some sort of drugs" ("Managers and Drug Abuse," *New York Times,* 8–5–86, D20). "The Strange Agony of Success" tells how "tens of thousands of young people are finding that in achieving business success today, they have distorted their lives and fallen into emotional turmoil" (*New York Times,* 8–24–86, F1). Based on interviews with psychotherapists and troubled individuals, the report adds that the "relentless pursuit of power and wealth can make people lose all perspective." The results range "from drug addiction and cynicism to depression and intense self-doubt. Sometimes the result is outright criminal activity." In such circumstances, it's little wonder that greed and corruption that exceeded the bounds of rationality spread through Wall Street, as executives with million-dollar incomes broke the law to get even more.

The more that money liquidates capital and people, the more rises the complaint that precious productive skills are being lost or not being developed. Could it be otherwise?

Human skills and the people who possess them are the essence of capital: They are the most long-term, most creative, most productive investments of all. People must be supported and educated from birth so that they can become contributing members of society. Doctors, managers, engineers, and a host of skilled professionals and trades people represent upward of 30 years of investment by parents, employers, and society in their development. It has taken decades, centuries, or millennia to create the language, customs, religions, laws, and above all the social and economic organizations we take for granted today. But where the continuous link of civilizing and investing is broken, individuals cease to be productive, civilizations sink toward barbarity, and the entire investment may be lost.

Capital, continuity, and people are inseparable. The more that U.S. prosperity needs to develop high-tech and other high-information abilities, the more it needs to create and support education, skills, and hope for the future in people.

Yet the U.S. consumes people even faster than it consumes financial capital. Most U.S. businesses make little or no investments in their own employees. The Reagan Revolution cut back on much of government's commitment to people. Mentally ill or physically disabled people were put out on the streets and left to fend for themselves or starve. Even productive employees can be discarded the instant they cease to be highly productive, and some are discarded for no economic reason at all, such as when they are fired just for disagreeing with the boss. And it can't be a coincidence that drug use is widespread and growing. The more the U.S. consumes people, the more it will consume its financial capital too.

America will never regain long-term economic competitiveness until it regenerates a commitment to long-term investments. That means renewing a commitment to serving the interests of people: of employees the country needs to be productive; of consumers it needs to buy what is produced; and of all citizens, who become productive employees and financially endowed consumers in totally unpredictable ways.

As it is presently constituted, management is incapable of providing America with such long-term commitments and leadership. But organized workers have long fought the liquidation of American jobs and productive capacity. They need to update their tactics to meet the new challenges, but their efforts to keep America employed preserve this nation's most productive, long-term capital: its skilled work force. They present the most realistic defense we can have against the super-liquidity trap. We need to support and help them in our own best interests.

The Super-Liquidity Trap and Real Labor Costs

When the super-liquidity trap biases economic activity in favor of money and against long-term capital investments, it also biases managers, analysts, and the business press against employees. This hostility distorts their views of real labor costs and convinces them that they are making good business decisions when they are not.

Manufacturers reportedly felt that Michigan was the worst state in which to locate a factory because of "its heavy labor costs and union membership" (*U.S. News & World Report*, 6–17–85, 66). But U.S. labor costs in manufacturing represented "as little as 5 percent and usually no more than 15 percent of total costs" (*Business Week*, 3–3–86, 74). If unions raise wages by, let us say, 20 percent, that creates a wage-cost differential of only 1 percent to 3 percent. Yet because Michigan is identified with the United Auto Workers Union, manufacturers' minds are so prejudiced and poisoned that they reportedly would locate anywhere else before locating in Michigan, despite its powerful advantages of central location and large pool of skilled labor.

Similarly, labor is a small part of construction costs in New York City and yet is blamed for high costs. In the story "Labor Factor Confounds Cost-Cutters," the chairman of the 600-strong Building Trades Employers Association was reported to have called labor a "minor portion of the job." He estimated labor cost at no more than "15 percent of total development cost," and disputed work rules were only a small portion of that 15 percent (*New York Times*, 7–20–86, R1). A researcher at the Real Estate Board speculated that a 10 percent reduction in labor costs might amount to only 2 percent in savings. That doesn't seem like something important enough to "confound cost-cutters." Not coincidentally, these figures were buried deep in the long article.

Land, materials, borrowed money, insurance, taxes, and compliance with regulations greatly outweigh the cost of labor in construction. And the buyer pays additional costs for mortgage interest, insurance, and bank and broker fees.

As for the labor itself, some New York construction workers, crane operators for example, are considered to be by far the best and fastest in the world (*New York Times*, 12–7–86, R1). Speed and accuracy are so important because even small delays, whether due to slow work or accidents and disorganization, can cause enormous expenses.

Just how special these construction workers are was revealed for all to see when, in Manhattan on July 21, 1982, the 137-foot, 11-ton boom of a construction crane collapsed atop a 44-story building nearing completion of construction. After debris from the collapse had killed one man and injured 16 people, the boom stretched way out over the edge of the building and threatened to fall on the street below, near the corner of East Fifty-third Street and Madison Avenue. Worse, a 30-foot section at the tip of the boom was nearly broken off and dangled downward precariously. Traffic and business in that busy part of Manhattan were totally closed off.

According to the next day's *New York Times*, before city officials and builders could act, three workers who were on a totally different building nearby rushed over on their own initiative to help. With the aid of William Jessup and William Stewart, Louis Carroll climbed out onto the boom, lowered himself down through midair, with the towers of Manhattan as a backdrop, and secured the tip. The picture of Carroll, the boom, and his friends filled a large part of the newspaper's front page. Later he said, "I just did a job. I'm good at it. I did it because I was there."

While this was clearly a case of heroism, construction and industrial accidents occur all the time and workers frequently respond just as well and just as modestly, although with less notice. It's that kind of initiative, acting without management direction, that makes American workers so skilled and productive. Yet many in American management—especially financial investors and MBAs, who increasingly dominate investment decisions but know nothing about production—say this kind of labor is America's biggest problem! ("A Times Poll of MBAs," *New York Times*, 12–7–86).

By providing skilled labor when and where it is needed, unions help speed up work and create cost savings. Indeed, when there is a shortage of highly skilled labor, such as in New York City in the 1980s, builders in effect pay what the market bears.

Beyond construction costs, the prices a buyer pays are also affected by profit markup, price-fixing, other forms of business collusion, and payoffs to government officials and organized crime. *Fortune* reported for example that collusion, such as bid-rigging by a Mafia concrete cartel, added as much as 20 percent to Manhattan construction costs (11–10–86, 28). That money went to companies, not labor. The report also estimated that "sweetheart" labor contracts with organized crime pushed up costs between 0.5 percent and 2 percent. Even for this relatively small percentage, it is money that builders pay—bribes—to prevent workers from striking, and not just in construction. The President's Commission on Organized Crime, in a March 1986, 455-page report, said legitimate business people often willingly collude with organized crime to win, among other things, lower labor costs (*New York Times,* 3-17-86, D1). Finally, payoffs, corruption, and delay-causing incompetence in New York City government were revealed on a vast scale in 1986 (a sad fact not unique to New York). Labor got none of that either.

What was it about labor then that really confounded the cost-cutters? Perhaps they were frustrated at having so little labor left to cut. In any case, talking about it made good headlines.

Anticipating the bloodletting of dismissals and strikes in the news divisions of CBS and the other networks, *Forbes* went beyond the news to show how "the real fat is in...programming costs" (8–25–86, 92). Using the words "flagrant featherbedding" and "the clearly corpulent catalog of union costs," *Forbes* made unions and union wages seem to be killing the networks. Yet in the only specific example it gave of how nonunion production was cheaper, 75 percent of the cost cuts actually came from cutting out management "overhead," which was a 30 percent surcharge added by Hollywood studios on top of actual program production costs. While that 30 percent overhead was mentioned three times in the story, it was generally included in the phrase "other costs" as if it were relatively minor, although it was in fact three times as great as all the other excess costs combined. *Forbes* should be commended for being so openly honest in its bias!

No major publication in the business press is more objective, far-sighted, and honest than *Business Week,* yet even its reports have been badly unbalanced by antilabor thinking, although it doesn't appear that way at first reading. For example, in its excellent report "The Hollow Corporation," it pounded away at the idea that lower foreign wages were the dominant reason Americans couldn't manufacture at home.

During the long report, approximately twenty-five factors were given as contributing to the advantages of foreign production. But most of them were mentioned only once, in passing, and then dropped. These factors included superior Japanese management and production techniques, superior foreign technology, cheaper foreign capital, tax and government policies, and foreign barriers to U.S. goods. Many problems with the U.S. financial system were also noted, especially the lack of "patient capital." But mostly they were not directly connected to foreign cost-competitiveness, even though Japan's cheaper capital (half the cost of U.S. capital, according to the report) is a decisive cost advantage, especially in capital-intensive industries such as autos, steel, and semiconductors.

Low foreign wages, however, were mentioned 13 times, and low foreign costs, which in context meant primarily low foreign wages, were mentioned 7 times, for a total of 20 times. In addition, low foreign wages were mentioned on the cover and "Asia's labor-cost advantage" was pinpointed in the tables of contents of the magazine and of the special report itself. That's an overwhelming emphasis on low foreign wages of 23 repetitions and 3 prominent placements.

Absent from the entire report was recognition that Japan's autos beat American cars on quality and technology (in the forms of fewer repairs and higher fuel economy) and often have sold at premium prices well above the official sticker prices. Nowhere was there a simple statement that quality, innovation, technology, design, more efficient production processes, and marketing are often more important than wages in foreign competitiveness.

In other words, many Japanese and other foreign products do more, do it better and nicer, and may even be higher priced. So, lower Japanese labor costs, if they really were lower, are not even relevant. That's why Japanese companies can expect to make profits on the manufacturing plants they are rapidly building in the U.S. *Business Week* mentioned the Japanese presence in the U.S. twice but totally ignored its significance in debunking the myth that foreign wages are an insurmountable obstacle to manufacturing in the U.S.

Also absent, except for the barest oblique reference, was recognition of the plague of management breakdowns running through American business and government, as if management were equal everywhere and were not one of Japan's most decisive superiorities. And the high direct costs of transportation and lack of quality control inherent in far-flung operations were only lightly touched upon.

Finally, the idea of the advantage of foreign wages was actually contradicted in the report itself. It said "lax government regulations and favorable tax policies" were the "chief criteria" of U.S. manufacturers in "searching the world for the best factory site." Yet even that was not stated directly: The key phrase about regulations and taxes was inserted parenthetically, between dashes, and not followed up at all.

The evidence is overpowering that factory wages, while important, are only one of at least the 25 factors the report gave that affect manufacturing. Nevertheless, the writers treated "cheap foreign labor" as if it were a fact of nature like good weather in Southern California rather than a man-made advantage given by American management to foreign producers.

Most of that foreign labor, especially in Third World countries where wages and skills are very low, wouldn't be competitive if U.S. companies and government hadn't freely given away technology, financing, protection, education and training, assured access and aid in selling to American markets, and the long list of other subsidies described in the previous chapters. What's more, without U.S. subsidies, foreign labor often is not cheaper.

Astonishingly, Japanese labor costs have not necessarily been lower! And West German labor costs have been higher. In June 1984, when the dollar was much higher in value than in 1987, a study by West Germany's Dresdner Bank reported that Japan's unit labor costs were almost identical to those of the U.S. (*U.S. News & World Report*, 1–21–85, 50). That's because while U.S. wages were higher, so was productivity—by 59 percent. That is, U.S. labor was much more productive than Japan's. (Much more is said in the following chapter on Japan about the productivity of Japanese and American workers.) And the subsequent rise in the value of the yen (almost 50 percent, from roughly 230 yen to the dollar in June 1984 to 155 yen to the dollar in February 1987) meant that U.S. labor costs as of early 1987 were substantially lower than Japan's. Meanwhile, West Germany enjoyed huge trade surpluses with the U.S. despite having substantially higher labor costs, according to Dresdner Bank.

The single-minded and often misguided concentration on "low wages" leads to excessive efforts to eliminate the so-called disadvantage of U.S. labor. For example, "even though labor costs have been under control, business is increasingly gearing its capital-spending plans to labor-saving investment rather than expansion of capacity" (*Business Week*, 7–15–85, 57).

The only remedy to the hollow corporation that *Business Week* explored in depth was for U.S. manufacturers to build totally manless factories where "labor costs would be virtually zero." Once more, the report identified many powerful reasons "how automation could save the day," including high quality, flexibility, quick responses, low inventories, and achieving large economies of scale on low quantities of production. It even said "these intangibles provide the most concrete reasons for automating." But that statement was buried, while "slashing labor costs" was highlighted in bold print as a subheader. This bias against human labor is why American automation systems have often been designed to eliminate rather than supplement human labor, and also why they cost so much that few American companies can afford them.

Management and the Press. Management's antilabor bias strongly influences the press. For a long time, *Forbes* argued against "reindustrialization," saying that the decline in manufacturing (heavily union) and the growth of the service economy (mostly nonunion) were good for the U.S. Fingering labor as the main or sole factor in competitiveness, *U.S. News & World Report* (9–2–85) asked on its cover, "Can American Workers Win the Battle" against Japan? And *Newsweek* (2–10–86) speculated that if only Japanese workers "relaxed...Japanese products may become somewhat less competitive."

Four full years before the "Hollow Corporation" report, *Busi-*

ness Week reported that due to automation in electronics, "cheap labor is no longer the competitive advantage" it was in the 1970s for Hong Kong, Taiwan, Korea, Singapore, and Malaysia ("Asia: Automation Is Hitting a Low-wage Bastion," 3–15–82, 38). And some U.S. companies found it was "just as economical to produce at home in the U.S. or Japan."

The obvious intent of the fixation on labor is to push American workers to work harder for less pay. And the message is getting across. For example, "many American workers concede that the Japanese do better work" (*New York Times*, 9–1–85, 36). But the unintended price is that the most private thoughts of American executives and business analysts are also biased toward making bad business decisions concerning labor.

So strong is the unspoken nature of the hostility toward unions that reporters and analysts can't devote their jobs to exploring it in depth. That means their own thoughts go undeveloped, and ideas and facts are forgotten, which is catastrophic for their mental integrity.

When people can't talk or write about important events, especially if doing so can cripple a career or lose a job by offending management, they are not likely to think about it either. Then the external censor becomes an internal censor and understanding is degraded. Even honest analysts become uneven, one-sided, and corrupted. A person can come to wonder why he or she doesn't understand things anymore. Consequently, the implications of the antiunion war are not explored adequately even by people who know it exists.

And some who should know better write as if they don't. They sound sympathetic to working people yet take at face value management's talk about cooperation, as if management were just waiting to be wooed by "cooperative" unions. The talk is of equal partnership, but the reality is that management almost always wants to break unions or get them to force concessions from the work force. These writers have no power to make management cooperate and their assurances to labor are empty. But by repeating management's talk with their own conviction, they can lull working people and union officials into a false sense of security. For example, when William Brock became the new Secretary of Labor, much was made of his more friendly attitude toward unions, even though no fundamental change was made in the Reagan Administration or American business.

The bias against U.S. labor and unions has become so deep in the press and business thinking that it can only be described as a mania. While superficially "smart" to compare the numerical values of wages and take a cheap, quick profit, it is out of touch with deeper realities of economic survival.

The people who seek the poorest labor on earth are cheating and stealing from the American people just as a marathon runner might cheat and steal a prize by cutting across a loop in the course or hitching a ride. If challenged, they claim victory on the grounds of superior "enterprise." If they believe that, then they are lying to themselves as well as to the rest of us. They don't know how to employ skilled U.S. labor profitably, but they insist on taking huge salaries for themselves and getting quick, big profits anyway. At the same time, they want the benefits of living and spending their profits in a country, the U.S., that can remain prosperous and strong only by finding ways to employ its highly skilled and educated work force at high wage levels. That's trying to have it both ways. But they can't undermine the U.S. and leave it strong at the same time.

Professional Mis-Management

Management's consumption of people and its bias against unions are not fundamentally matters of mean personalities or individual failings. Those would be simple mismanagement: the failure to use generally accepted procedures, or malfunctions or aberrations within the system. The whole system of American management, working especially through the super-liquidity trap, has driven managers to take actions that hurt their own organizations in the long run. It is a system rooted deeply in an insatiable greed for wealth and power coupled with the belief that wealth and power can be gotten only by forcibly extracting them from the labor of others.

On the theory that the less they pay to "labor" and the harder they make "labor" work, the more they can pocket themselves, top managers, stockholders, lenders, and government officials who represent them begrudge every penny and every ounce of authority they have to share with employees. They even try to eliminate human labor entirely through automation so they won't have to share any power at all with "labor." The result is a mistrust of and hostility toward working people that is returned by employees.

This extractive or brute management is very old and can work in primitive circumstances. The most severe form of it—compelling effort—is called slavery. But it is economically inferior; it is better at producing quantity than quality. And it is increasingly counterproductive in modern production.

Information, cooperation, and creativity are needed to create quality. They are produced much more effectively with carrots than with sticks. And they must be induced and nurtured to produce optimally. The system that does that is called freedom, and its most advanced expression is called democracy.

Anyone who doubts the superior productivity and intelligence of democracy can look to the bankruptcies of Brazil and Argentina under military dictatorship, the destruction of Nazi Germany and Imperial Japan, and the deteriorating communist economies. The more that elements of freedom and democracy are brought into the workplace, within the context of a coherently structured organization, the more the workplace becomes productive and effective.

Unfortunately, despite talk and a lot of evidence that working with employees contributes to excellence in management, most managers, stockholders, and lenders continue to try to force concessions from "labor." And they continue to support and enlarge a huge management bureaucracy to police all employees. But then stockholders—who cannot manage business themselves—must pay their police bureaucracy huge salaries and bonuses, and must cede virtual autonomy to management in running the corporation. The same pattern of a police bureaucracy is repeated in government operations, except that voters and taxpayers have less control over "public" management bureaucracies than stockholders have over "private" management bureaucracies.

Treating working people like dumb beasts of burden or obstacles to be removed excludes the information that they possess about what is really happening in production, marketing, and public acceptance of the business or government unit. The result reduces competitiveness, reduces profitability, and winds up costing more than whatever might have been shared with "labor." Ultimately, the entire stockholders' and bondholders' investments or citizens' taxes can be wiped out by bankruptcy due to bad management. And bankruptcy is precisely what is threatening more and more businesses and governments.

Subsidizing and then losing out to Japan and other competitors is an enormous example of how greed and resulting management practices have severely hurt American competitiveness and cost stockholders, taxpayers, and the nation far more than they would ever have had to pay to win their employees' willing cooperation. In fact, *Business Week, Inc.,* Louis Kelso, father of the Employee Stock Ownership Plan (ESOP), and Corey Rosen, founder of the National Center for Employee Ownership, have reported many times that where employees get even a small share in ownership or participation in management, they work harder, smarter, *and* for less pay. Common sense confirms this conclusion: People will accept lower pay in return for a job they feel better about.

Some American managements realize this. However, most try to use talk of cooperation with employees to gain power and compel wage concessions from the work force. At the same time, they blame their failures on "high wages" and "troublesome" labor. Many employee participation or "ownership" plans have been designed much more to pay off or bail out failing managements, stockholders, and lenders than to raise productivity ("ESOPs: Revolution or Ripoff?" *Business Week,* 4–15–85). Often, employees get a bad deal. They exchange a lot of pay and protection and maybe their lives' savings for inferior working conditions; yet management still retains power or gets even more power. And employees may still get laid off, or the plant or office closes and they lose their jobs anyway. When this happens, employees resent being cheated and resist more than ever giving up wages or cooperating with management.

By not genuinely sharing with its work force, management suppresses information and cuts itself off from many facts in the reality of operations. Cut off from reality, management is blind and deaf. Highly paid, it grows fat and lazy. Unaccountable to anyone, except in a vague and general way to stockholders, it is smug, arrogant, and complacent.

The better that managers do their jobs by making profits without producing, the more they are rewarded, and the worse is the result for the economy, the nation, and their own institutions in the long run. That's not simple mismanagement. It is *mis*conceived management, *mis*guided management, *mis*organized management, and *mis*paid management. It is "professional *mis*-management."

Mis-management is the greatest single reason why major U.S. industries are failing and why many government operations are either going bankrupt or are bankrupting us to pay for them. It arises out of management's fundamentally hostile attitude toward employees. And it leads to the super-liquidity trap that makes the system destroy itself.

Productivity of Sharing Information. Many important factors affecting business and government operations cannot be easily quantified. But that doesn't mean they don't exist. Indeed, the most important items in business, such as consumer acceptance, labor cooperation, and the state of competition, can never be fully quantified. Yet they must be dealt with. Any effort to reduce business to an accountant's spreadsheet by considering only what can be given dollar values will work in the short run, but it will run afoul of deeper business currents in the long run.

Many of these factors involve subtle qualities of information and group cooperation. But managers often take cooperation and information for granted and don't calculate them as economic quantities as they calculate wages, raw materials, and costs of capital. They just don't calculate that to get top-quality cooperation or information, they must give it first.

When it comes to building top-quality information and cooperation, it *is* better to give than to receive, at least in a reasonable way. When employees are convinced of the necessity of management's actions, they go along peacefully. But to be convinced, they must have access to the same information that management has, or else they will distrust and resist everything management does and says. Sharing information is also good business on basic operational grounds.

One of the best ways to solve troubling problems is to explain them to someone else. Sometimes this procedure is called "talking out a problem." This procedure forces one to examine all assumptions for the listener's benefit. Frequently, solutions are discovered during the explanation itself, for only then are the full or implicit consequences of many assumptions and conditions really examined and thought out. Of course, one can only talk out a problem with friends, trusted associates, or other respected individuals.

Losses in Not Sharing Information. Managements that are suspicious of employees or treat them like enemies cannot talk out problems freely. When management suppresses, punishes, or excludes working people, including middle and lower managers, from full participation in the talking-out process, then it shuts out valuable information and blocks the even more valuable free flow of thoughts that frequently create the best solutions.

Once working people are excluded and treated like animals or enemies, then middle and lower management will be treated with doubt and suspicion too. Then upper management's refusals to share cause distrust, fear, and internal conflicts and disarray throughout management itself. Top management will even intentionally create rivalries and internal conflicts in the name of "keeping everyone on their toes" to keep subordinates from developing independent power centers.

Also, such managements demand "hard" work from employees. They want employees to work hard at difficult tasks. But hard work is often dumb work. It substitutes brute strength for skill and intelligence. Union workers complain, and business reports confirm, that American managements often demand highly skilled American workers to work *harder* but not necessarily smarter. In the auto and steel industries especially, management has long demanded "Do as I tell you and don't talk back!" That is a stupid demand.

By questioning management orders, employees can often improve them. Sometimes the boss's orders are so vague—amounting to mere demands because he doesn't really know what to do—that workers have to figure out their own ways to get work done. That is even more likely to happen in an office or field job than in a factory. Then work gets done better without the boss's involvement. Consequently, worker skills are just as important as wage costs, and American workers' skills are exceptionally high.

In the words of James Cook, executive editor of *Forbes*, "The U.S. still boasts the best-educated work force in the world. The U.S. enrolls more of its young people in its high schools, sends more of them on to college and still boasts the highest industrial productivity in the world" (3–24–86, 62).

That superior productivity is hard evidence that many American workers—*especially* unionized workers in heavy industry—work harder or better than their European or Japanese counterparts. According to a survey by the U.S. Commerce Department, a majority of managers of U.S. subsidiaries of foreign companies agreed. They said U.S. workers were as good or better than foreign workers. That opinion was held by five German managers in another survey too (*Forbes,* 12–5–83, 10).

Yet that highly educated and skilled work force is routinely abused, excluded, and repressed at work by American management. It's enough to shatter the spirit or create great anger and resistance in the hearts of the most able workers. Indeed, many workers who give management "trouble" are actually trying to fix problems. They get into trouble principally because they go outside or fight the very things that are going wrong in management's system. Their productivity would zoom if they had more pay and authority for getting work done and deciding on how the employer's resources should be used.

"A Little Knowledge Is a Dangerous Thing." Being unable to share with or trust employees' opinions, upper managers make decisions and exercise power by relying heavily on quantifiable data: accountants' reports of things that can be counted and verified. So reports proliferate. Office work becomes a huge expense. Layers of extra management get added to oversee office work and turn out the reports. The process becomes increasingly debilitating as people churn up more and more of the company's resources in massaging reports and fighting over them. And the likelihood grows astronomically that the reports are useless at best and terribly misleading or dangerous at worst. For errors of omission and commission can creep into a report in a thousand ways when information is withheld and cooperation is poisoned.

Worse, many managers, politicians, and bureaucrats have some kind of "expert" training or credentials and really think they know what they are doing, especially if they have MBAs and come from the financial community. But when weather forecasters *see* the weather coming with satellites and measure it every step along the way on the ground and in the air, when the weather is an unconscious quantity that doesn't deliberately try to confound forecasts, and when forecasters still can't predict the weather reliably five days in advance, then how can a handful of elitist managers and bureaucrats know the consequences of their investments for many years to come when they invest hundreds of billions of dollars annually affecting billions of conscious, secretive, and willfully contrary people in businesses and locations around the world?

Sometimes financial managers actually demand accurate predictions of the weather! Banks reportedly demand that farmers make five-year business plans before extending credit ("Computers: How Ya Gonna Sell 'em Down on the Farm?" *Business Week,* 2–18–85).

But for a farmer's five-year plan to be accurate, it would have to predict not only his own weather but the weather of all other farmers in the world. It would have to predict how much they will plant, because farm prices are now set by liquid world markets that depend on supply and demand all over the world. And it would have to predict foreign currency exchange rates for five years in advance. That's because the depression in farming in the U.S. in the 1980s was due in good part to the high-valued dollar that priced U.S. food out of international markets. Then there are other factors such as infestations, new fertilizers and pesticides, emergence of resistance to pesticides, and ever-shifting prices for fertilizers. Anyone who could predict all that would be spending his or her time making billions of dollars on investments instead of trying to stave off bankruptcy on a family farm.

Malcolm S. Forbes, editor-in-chief of *Forbes,* says he has contempt for such ridiculous reports and plans. "Anyone who says businessmen deal only in facts, not fiction, has never read old five-year projections" (*Forbes,* 7–1–85, 18).

When money managers in banks, mutual funds, and investment and brokerage firms apply their little bit of knowledge and force us with their financial power to jump to their tune, they waste a great deal of our nation's resources and weaken America immeasurably. In particular, when they invest America's wealth outside America on the simple-minded justification of seeking lower wages, they are extremely dangerous and do enormous damage.

Wage Myopia. Some managers understand the long-term folly of current management practices. But few can resist the short-term market illusion or the economic, political, and legal pressures to try to raise profits by lowering labor wages. And most don't know how to produce competitively in America with highly skilled, highly productive, but higher-paid workers.

Even many unions, and some of the most militant union dissidents, implicitly ratify management's myopic focus on wage costs. They accept management's claim that what it does is good for business and assume that when management "screws" workers, *that's* good for business too. So they complain of management's ruthless brutality as if everything it did really were economically justified and were indefensible only on moral or humanitarian grounds.

In many cases, however, management's efforts to get the lowest wages and impose the hardest working conditions are indefensible on both moral *and* economic grounds. Besides failing to utilize employees' full skills, a preoccupation with extracting the most from labor interferes with many other important business considerations.

Capital, technology, creativity, marketing (everything from identifying what the market wants to providing and selling it), total organizational effectiveness, and currency exchange rates are vitally important to business success and have nothing to do with wages or labor. The first five factors are totally management's responsibilities. And management in business and government formulates fiscal and monetary policies that heavily influence the value of the dollar. The high value of the dollar, overpriced by as much as 70 percent at one point, was the most effective single weapon management had in strengthening imports and in weakening unions.

Innovation, market size, social peace, and military and foreign policies are also important and have nothing to do with wage costs. And the more that quality is a prized value in products and services, the less that cost and price themselves are decisive.

In short, labor costs are often just a minority fraction of total costs, and wages are even a smaller factor in the long-term success of business and government operations. Yet management affects 100 percent of operations. Bad management can sink any business no matter how efficient or low-cost its workers are. Any analysis that does not put the prime responsibility on management is simply not honest. Any analysis that fails to probe the depths of mis-management is incomplete and will likely be ineffective. But management will also continue to welcome that omission because it protects management and justifies the single-focus attacks on wages and unions.

More Nonwage Business Costs. Leading economists, business people, and government policymakers argue that America must not subsidize "inefficient"—by which they mean high wage— American industries by "protection" from foreign competition. But they don't count all the nonwage business costs to themselves and to this nation that are raised by dispersing production to foreign lands and becoming dependent on foreign producers. And they insist on protecting their own huge "assets."

Many denounce "subsidies" for "overpriced" American union wages. But President Reagan's tax "simplification" plan of 1985, and the actual law passed in 1986, passed over the business-loan tax deductions that subsidized many nonproductive corporate raids and mergers, even though the borrowing drove up interest rates and the dollar and contributed to farm bankruptcies and America's trade deficit. And agricultural subsidies for "agribusiness" were continued while family farms were foreclosed.

Despite a lot of noise, little has been done to punish sometimes-flagrant abuses and reduce superhigh costs in military contracts. Even where the government wins, the punishment is still light. For example, when General Electric Co. was indicted in March 1985 for defrauding the federal government by altering time cards on contracts for the Air Force, it was barred for only 21 days from bidding on Air Force contracts, with bid restrictions kept only on the offending Space Systems division. And all restrictions were lifted less than six months later, after GE pleaded guilty, paid $800,000 in restitution of the fraudulent claims, and was fined $1.04 million, the maximum, by a federal judge in Philadelphia (*Business Week,* 5–27–85, 46; GE spokesman). In a much more troubled case, General Dynamics Corp. has remained one of the nation's largest military contractors despite years of accusations and (small) penalties for abuses, which included billing the U.S. government $155 for boarding a GD executive's dog (*New York Times,* 8–15–85, D1).

The U.S. spends hundreds of billions of dollars for arms and economic assistance so that multinational corporations can have secure sea-trade lanes, secure host governments, and dictatorships to protect their investments against labor or civil unrest, which naturally wells up in resentment to oppression and becomes fertile ground for communist insurgency.

No wonder the Japanese and other manufacturers from Asia to Latin America long showed little fear of a protectionist backlash: The U.S.'s "free trade" protects *them.* They were openly— but quietly—paid and encouraged to invade the U.S. economy as antiunion shock troops. But in the process, they increased their own strength at American expense and wiped out many jobs, including those of American managers who so short-sightedly invited them in.

If American strength is weakened enough, numerous countries will challenge America and start fighting among themselves—not a pleasant prospect in this nuclear era. The next time a country like Argentina goes to war, it may have nuclear weapons.

If the U.S. government gets its way to dramatically increase Japan's military production, American military producers will face the same foreign competition that beat General Motors. If Japan's military industrial complex is revived to its 1930s vigor, a new and dangerously aggressive military force will enter the world. Many Asian nations will form new and unpredictable alliances, some certainly with Russia or China, against Japan. And if China is frightened back into Russia's arms, the entire U.S. foreign policy since the early 1970s of rapprochement with China will have been shattered and the U.S. greatly threatened.

These are all huge and uncounted costs passed on to the American people by allowing employers to seek the most slavelike labor in the world.

More and More Wage and Job Cuts. Rather than letting up, the attack on wages and jobs is intensifying, despite the small role wages and labor play in business competitiveness. As employers push unions back and wages down, they talk more—not less—of narrowing the wage gap with foreign countries by reducing American wages still more.

According to Louis Uchitelle, reporting in the *New York Times* (6–26–87, D2), "For the first time, American manufacturers are talking openly about a new and startling wage goal: They want to greatly narrow the gap between what they pay their factory workers and the earnings of workers in South Korea, Brazil, and a handful of other Third World countries." After the apparently obligatory disclaimer, "that does not mean that businessmen want wages to plunge" from the U.S. factory average of $13.09 in total compensation, Uchitelle gives some disturbing examples of employer thinking.

Walter Joelson, chief economist at General Electric, is quoted as saying, "What in the Bible says we should have a better living standard than others? We have to give back a bit of it." It's notable that economist Joelson almost surely did not mean that *his* standard of living should be lowered to that of a Third World country. According to reporter Uchitelle, "a common view is emerging" and is expressed by chief economist Jerry Jasinowski of the National Association of Manufacturers: "Many manufacturers now feel that we are not going to be able to afford the wage difference." This despite the fact that wages are a small and shrinking cost of manufacturing!

Every person who works for a living should understand clearly what these business economists really mean. The "wage difference" manufacturers are talking about is with "South Korea, Brazil, Mexico, Hong Kong, Taiwan, and Singapore" (with others to be added to the list), where wages are rarely more than $3 an hour and frequently are much less. American employers seek to close that gap rapidly. And their principal way to close it, other than exporting jobs, is to lower American wages greatly—with pay in services to drop as manufacturing wages fall. Unions, most Americans, and foreign workers would be far better off if the gap were closed, to the extent it is really a competitive problem, by allowing foreign workers to organize unions and raise *their* wages.

What, Me Worry? Because they continue to lower wages and weaken unions, dominant policymakers seem unworried—they in fact seem overjoyed—about the growing weaknesses in the American economy. To be sure, some leaders began to sound a bit worried early in 1987 and political talk emerged about making the U.S. "competitive." But the key policies will not—and in fact, cannot—really change until major changes are made in how American and world markets operate.

Big business and rich individuals are still able to move their money around the world with impunity and act as if they will lose neither it nor the power that goes with it. That liquidity is least likely to change. It is the driving force of the ruinous super-liquidity trap. Accordingly, even weak protectionist trade measures still face tough sledding. And the "competitiveness" craze of criticizing "corpocracy" in American management faded quickly from public view. Although such criticism could be resurrected by a candidate in the 1988 Presidential election, "competitiveness" seems to have done little but to put more downward pressure on American wages while leaving management powers intact.

Leaders in business and government seem to envision a "two-tier" world economy in which a rich upper class from many nations administers high profit "services" and the rest of the world's peoples—including many American working people—labor in poverty. That's a peculiar kind of "international socialism." And if the United States' stability is undermined, the rich can retire in comfort and luxury to Costa Rica or the Bahamas.

Unfortunately for noble dreams of ruling a two-tier world, nations exist and world events are carried out through national powers. What is the American dollar worth without American industrial power to back up American military power to back up the dollar? Nothing.

"Those Whom the Gods Would Destroy, They First Make Mad." Information is the leading component of business or government success. It is contained in quality, technology, production processes, effective organizations, financial analyses, all aspects of marketing, and countless other activities that require judgment, skill, knowledge, and sensitivity. It is possessed by large numbers of employees. And to be created and used well, it requires cooperation and honesty among large numbers of people. Indeed, social cooperation is necessary on virtually a global scale to support free markets and conduct world trade.

Yet when management makes war on unions and working people, it creates conflict rather than cooperation, it loses access to vast amounts of information, and it uses badly what information it manages to retain. Then management becomes out of touch with reality, harms business and government, and corrupts the individuals who work within it.

By attacking labor costs obsessively and neglecting the other components of productivity and high quality, until low-wage non-union labor appears to be an insurmountable advantage, "smart" American managers are undermining America's economy, the military, the nation, the dollar, and the companies for which they work. Many a "smart" manager will lose his job by complete fault of his own. Not even Benedict Arnold was so treacherous, for he at least sold out to a major world power that supported him. But no one will support a falling America.

Fighting American unions at the expense of the entire nation is at best "penny-wise, pound-foolish." At worst, it is stupid, incompetent, criminal, and a brutal betrayal of America. "Smart money" and the managers who invest it commit the most terrible crime of mis-management: They are bringing down the system that supports them.

5

Myths of Cheaper and Better Japanese Labor

The decline in U.S. standards of living has to be stopped. As the preceding chapters have shown, labor costs are not the sole determinant, nor even the dominant determinant, of economic competitiveness in many industries.

A good example of this is Japan. Japanese labor is widely believed to be an overwhelming advantage in Japan-U.S. competition. However, a closer analysis of much that has been written about Japan in the business press shows that cheaper and better Japanese labor is a myth. But failures of American management are very real.

The Myth of the $2,000 Labor-Cost Gap

For years the press reported claims that cars cost $2,000 less to make in Japan than they did in the U.S., chiefly because of cheaper and harder-working Japanese labor. But the facts contradict those claims.

The *New York Times* (2–16–83, D1) published a table of data from Harbour and Associates estimating the cost advantage Japanese auto makers had per subcompact car. Excluding an American advantage due to shipping costs of $485, the costs broke down into:

Better Management Systems	$1,398
Union-Management Relations	182
(Absenteeism, Flexibility,	
Union Representation)	
Lower Wages and Benefits	550
Superior Technology	73
Total Cost Advantage to Japanese	2,203

In this analysis, only 25 percent of the Japanese auto makers' production cost advantage was due to American labor costs! And that advantage was nearly canceled out by shipping costs from Japan. But 63 percent of the advantage was attributed directly to management. The remaining 12 percent intimately involved management, since management chooses technology and management style usually determines the tone of "labor relations." And no account was apparently taken of the undervalued yen, which artificially lowered Japanese labor costs.

The report by John Holusha accompanying the table added, "The key advantage enjoyed by Japanese manufacturers is an efficiency of production...fewer man-hours per vehicle, greater flexibility in using labor, lower inventories and assembly techniques that reduce repair costs."

Earlier, *Business Week* (9–14–81, 92) had explored the same question. It too reported a "U.S.-Japanese wage differential amounting to several hundred dollars per car" out of a total differential after shipping ranging from $1,300 to $1,700.

Business Week also reported, "Auto makers are surprisingly willing to concede that the problems are largely their own doing. Studies...lay much of the blame for Detroit's predicament on sloppy management methods, not labor costs....Adds William J. Harahan, director of technical planning for Ford's Manufacturing Staff, 'The resolution of the problem is 80 percent a management responsibility and 20 percent production worker responsibility.'"

Just as labor was only 20 percent to 25 percent of the so-called cost gap with Japan, *Business Week* reported it was only 25 percent of total costs in 1984 (10–1–84, 37). In 1982 it reported that all costs in assembling a small car, consisting of labor and materials, were only 36 percent of the sticker price. Corporate overhead and dealer markup took the rest (3–1–82, 111).

Labor's relatively small component in production explains why, according to many reports, Japanese companies operating in the U.S. whittled that $2,000 cost gap down to $500 or less by early 1986, excluding transportation (and excluding subsequent further upward revaluations of the yen). But adding in $500 per car for shipment from Japan to the U.S., costs in the U.S. were the same—there was no gap!

Putting together similar estimates from the *Economist, Forbes, Business Week,* and the *New York Times,* it was cheaper to make cars in the U.S. with the yen at 150 than in Japan or perhaps even South Korea and Taiwan. That explains why, according to *Newsweek,* Honda felt Accords were made so cheaply in Ohio that it considered exporting them to Taiwan in 1988 (1–19–87, 42). But as late as September 1986, Detroit still couldn't compete even in the U.S. and *Business Week* had to ask, "Now What's the Problem?" (9–1–86, 72).

Significantly, Japanese auto companies got low costs in the U.S. with wages close to union scale. Honda, for example, paid an average hourly wage of $12.25; while Toyota at the NUMMI plant in Fremont, California, paid United Auto Workers wages. And Japanese companies succeeded with both union and non-union workers: Toyota was unionized, and Mazda and Mitsubishi planned to employ union labor in factories they were building.

It is true that Honda and other Japanese auto companies started in the U.S. by assembling cars from parts made in Japan. Their cars were perhaps 50 percent imported from Japan. But more and more of "American" cars are imported too—from Korea, Taiwan, and Brazil for example. Japan isn't a cheap labor country compared to them. Further, the most valuable imported Japanese parts, such as engines and transmissions (drivetrains), require skilled labor or advanced technology and automation. That labor is Japan's most expensive, and the costs of automation and technology are not labor costs—"cheap" or otherwise—at all. Yet these parts are so competitive that they are going increasingly into cars made everywhere, even in "cheap labor" countries like Korea and Taiwan (*Business Week,* 6–16–86, 96D). Finally, Japanese suppliers began flocking into the U.S. to supply Japanese assembly plants in the U.S. That reduced the "cheap Japanese labor" factor of imports even more.

Other nonlabor factors also affect costs—and profits. Many of the cost-advantage estimates seem to leave out the crucial question of design. European companies sell high-priced, highly profitable cars by selling "superior design," both style and technology. Japanese companies generally mastered the practice of designing low cost into products: They reduced the number of parts needing assembly, and they designed simpler, faster, more reliable ways to assemble. This resulted in superior quality, which was also a design target. And higher quality reduced costs.

For example, *Fortune* reported in early 1987 that Japanese cars averaged an estimated $55 in warranty costs in the first year of operation, but U.S. cars averaged from $100 to $400 (2–2–87, 96). Considering that U.S. cars had been improving in quality, the upper figure of $400 probably represents a fair minimum estimate of warranty costs in the early 1980s when the "$2,000 gap" was being debated. Assuming that Japanese warranty costs were $100 then, that's a $300 gap in costs after the cars were sold.

European and Japanese companies offered cars with few options. That greatly reduced costs too. *Forbes* (9–24–84, 54) reported that there were 69,120 possible option combinations on a 1982 Ford Thunderbird but the 1982 Honda Accord offered only 32. That's right, 32. And the U.S. makers offered many more models than their foreign counterparts. This meant lower volume—and higher costs—per U.S. car. The greater complexity of models and options also meant much greater office costs. In the same story, consultant Paul Branstad of Booz, Allen & Hamilton estimated that greater complexity raised costs per model as much as $2,100 between 1968 and 1982. Branstad estimated that low volume and complexity alone accounted for a full $800 of what he estimated was a $1,500 cost gap with Japan (which would be a $2,000 gap if shipping had been factored in).

In another view of the "$2,000 gap," John Holusha of the *New York Times* (5–28–83) reported that auto executives felt that Japan had a $735 advantage on a $6,000 car because of tax advantages. Japanese companies effectively paid no home tax on exported cars and paid low tariffs to enter the U.S., but U.S. companies paid a high income tax on all cars they sold. Philip Caldwell, then chairman of Ford, estimated that only $700 of the gap was related to manufacturing. If we estimate 20 percent of that to be labor, then labor contributed only $140 to the "$2,000 gap"!

The *New York Times* report also estimated that the undervalued yen added another $600 to $700 to Japan's advantage, based on the difference between 235 yen and 200 yen to the dollar on a $7,000 car. Since then, of course, the yen has dropped well below 200. With the yen around 150 in mid-1987, that difference would be more like $1,200 to $1,500.

It's difficult to make exact or lasting cost comparisons, but these reports are surprisingly consistent. For much of the 1980s, according to the most knowledgeable and confidential management sources, labor was no more than 20 percent of any cost gap with Japan, while management of business and government (which affects taxes and currency exchange rates) was at least 80 percent.

Yet Detroit kept trying to cut labor costs and even added to overhead (in automation) as if labor costs were the whole and only problem. The result was failure, because it was trying to do exactly the wrong thing. And the Japanese succeeded in the U.S. as well as in Japan because they attacked the whole problem and didn't try to take the solution out of labor's hide.

America will never again be competitive as long as "public opinion" blames workers for the entire mess and allows management free rein to conduct business as it wishes.

Real Labor Costs: No Gap

There is something startling about the above estimates that seems like the story of the blind men trying to figure out the true shape of an elephant. Adding the many nonlabor costs in the U.S. from the preceding reports,

$1,500	manufacturing inefficiencies (Harbour)
800	complexity (Branstad)
300	quality/warranty (*Fortune*)
700	tax (Caldwell)
600	yen at 200 instead of 235 (or $1,500 at 150 yen) (Holusha)

one gets a total nonlabor gap of $3,900 for a $7,000 car before the yen dropped and a whopping $4,800 after the yen fell.

How then did U.S. companies have only a $2,000 cost gap?

Where did the efficiencies come to reduce the gap by a minimum of $1,900?

Could mostly unionized (UAW) U.S. workers have made up the difference through superior and cheaper-than-believed labor? If so, U.S. union workers must have been creating a cost advantage of at least $1,900 per car! Perhaps that's really why the Japanese could produce competitively *in* the U.S. and even think of exporting *from* the U.S. Although foreign and unfamiliar with how UAW workers work, Japanese managers could still win enough greater cooperation to get lower costs than U.S. managers. Imagine how much costs could be cut if the workers really were free to figure out their own best ways to get work done.

There may no doubt be some overlap and double counting in adding up the above estimates. Still, the various costs don't overlap that much, and they add up to too large a figure. Even subtracting for reasonable overlaps and double counting, the $1,900 to $2,800 U.S. labor cost advantage can't reasonably be reduced to a $500 disadvantage, much less the implied $2,000 "labor cost" disadvantage that U.S. managements broadly complained of. The result must be that according to figures in the most respected business journals, U.S. union workers were cheaper, not more expensive, in terms of what they produced per car.

A great deal of data has been published about hidden Japanese labor costs, productivity, artificial currency exchange rates, actual Japanese wages, and management practices that support the conclusion that American labor is cheaper. The evidence shows that:

- Japanese labor was not nearly as cheap or good as management would have us believe.

- Japanese management, aided by enormous subsidies from U.S. business and government, and stimulated by costly, inferior labor, greatly outperformed American management.

- American union labor was—or could have been—a major competitive advantage at existing pay rates.

- American companies could still be competitive if management made peace and shared with unions and labor generally instead of making war on them.

Hidden Costs. Japan's true labor costs were raised by bonuses and hidden company subsidies to many workers, such as housing, education and training, and lifetime employment guarantees. These are difficult to evaluate because they are not bought and sold in an open market, but they can be considerable.

Land and housing in Japan are very expensive because it's a most crowded country. When housing prices jumped enormously in the 1980s in major U.S. cities—some quadrupled in New York City—they gave a taste of how valuable a housing subsidy can be in Japan. If the subsidy is only a dormitory bed for a young worker, it could still be very valuable. The worker might not otherwise be able to live near—and hold—the job at all. According to data from the United Auto Workers in the early 1980s, housing for married Japanese auto workers rented for $23.60 to $41.90 per month, and 5 percent mortgages were offered when the market rate was 8.5 percent. Meanwhile a U.S. auto worker paid $300 a month for a single bedroom apartment, and mortgage rates were 15 percent to 18 percent.

College bills in the U.S. are enormous—and the educations they provide are often useless on the job. Japanese companies prefer to train workers in what they really need for the job. Perhaps that's why consultant James Abegglen said that Japanese workers were the best educated in the world (*Business Week,* 3–17–86, 92D). That doesn't necessarily mean their education is broad or fosters creativity and independent initiative—quite the contrary—but it is useful, productive, and highly cost effective. A U.S. worker could easily spend $20,000 to $40,000 to acquire the same education—and then not get a job.

Many Japanese workers also get annual or semiannual bonuses amounting to major proportions, perhaps 30 percent or more, of yearly pay. When Japanese wages are quoted in hourly rates, they can leave out these bonuses and understate Japanese wages considerably.

Simultaneously, American companies grossly exaggerate U.S. wages by adding in "benefits," for example saying a steel worker got $22.50 an hour when wages alone were $12 to $13 (*New York Times,* 1–17–86, A10). Yet the benefits primarily enrich insurers, the medical industry, pension managers, and whoever else ultimately gets paid. And one must wonder if the companies really spend that much on benefits in the first place.

The promises made by pension plans often border on fraud. Many workers have gotten little or no pensions because companies terminated their pension plans or "terminated" their employees. And still more employees are forced to change jobs before they acquire any—or only meager—rights in a pension.

The benefits of medical "benefits" are also dubious. Prices and expenses for medical services have skyrocketed, but few of them have actually helped improve health. The real heroes in improving health have been more and better food, housing, clothing, sanitation, and clean water as well as relatively cheap antibiotics and cheap public health measures such as vaccinations, avoidance of toxic materials, and safe working conditions. For the enormous funds the U.S. spends on medical bills—more than 10 percent of the entire gross national product—indicators of health such as infant mortality and longevity trail those of many other industrialized countries.

It's easy to see that an hourly Japanese wage of $6 could be double in value to an employee, or $12, after bonuses and the hidden subsidies are added in. And a so-called $23 an hour labor cost in the U.S. could also be just $12 in value paid, as wages, to a U.S. union worker. No difference.

Productivity. According to U.S. Department of Labor statistics cited in the *Economist* (8–23–86), average Japanese productivity (real Gross Domestic Product per worker) in 1960 was only 25 percent of that in the U.S.

This means that if a Japanese worker got paid 25 percent of the U.S. rate for 25 percent of the output, American management could have distorted it to say that U.S. labor was four times as costly as Japanese labor—in raw wages. But the truth would have been that the unit labor costs in the U.S. and Japan would have been equal: 25 percent of the pay for 25 percent of the output!

Worse, most Japanese products were shoddy in 1960 and sold poorly in the U.S. Even if wages had been just 25 percent, they would have been expensive because what they produced couldn't be sold. Japanese productivity rose after 1960, but so did wages.

For example, *U.S. News & World Report* (World Business, 5–14–79) reported that in 1978, Japanese hourly labor costs averaged $6.65, while in the U.S. they were $9.35. That's the way they are usually reported, to make American labor sound more expensive. What they don't say is that while Japanese labor costs were 71 percent of those in the U.S., Japanese productivity was only 60 percent. These statistics came from Gus Tyler, an official of the International Ladies Garment Workers Union (ILGWU), interviewed on the *MacNeil/Lehrer Report* (4–26–79). Tyler's statistics are confirmed by the *Economist*'s statistics. And as late as 1986, *Forbes* was still saying that the average Japanese output per worker was just 70 percent of U.S. levels (2–10–86, 25).

In other words, in 1978, Japan paid on average 71 percent of U.S. wages to produce 60 percent of U.S. output. That made Japanese labor, according to these statistics, 19 percent *more expensive*.

If you recall the previous chapter, West Germany's Dresdner Bank concluded in 1984 that higher U.S. productivity paid completely for higher U.S. wages. That was before the yen rose in value and made Japanese labor costs higher than in the U.S. once more.

The next time you hear of low foreign wages or "cheap" foreign labor, don't be fooled to think U.S. workers are necessarily overpaid. Just the reverse may be true.

Currency Exchange Rates. According to many sources, including Steve Lohr in the *New York Times* (4–11–83), Japan's currency, the yen, was long considered undervalued in international currency exchange markets, and the dollar was considered overvalued. Here's why.

Usually, when a country has a large trade surplus with another, as Japan has had with the U.S., its currency rises in value, and the deficit country's currency is devalued. But that didn't happen with the yen and the dollar. The dollar was strong compared to the yen for many years.

Both the strong dollar and weak yen stem in part from interest rates, which have been high in America and low in Japan. For example, in early April 1983, the bank prime rate was 10.50 percent in the U.S. and only 5.75 percent in Japan (*Business Week*, 4–18–83, 107).

There are many ways to keep currency and interest rates low. Some critics claim for example that Japan protected its capital markets by preventing foreigners from borrowing money in Japan. By lowering demand for debt in Japan, this kept interest rates lower. Then demand for the yen was less: investors wanted the higher interest rates available in the U.S., and they had to buy dollars, not yen, to lend in the U.S. Consequently, prices of Japan's exports were lower as the yen stayed lower, and Japanese exports were strengthened, which is clearly the prime directive of Japanese foreign economic policy.

Finally in September 1985, with a hemorrhaging trade deficit, leaders of the U.S. got together with finance ministers of Japan, West Germany, Great Britain, and France—the famous Gang of Five meeting at the Plaza Hotel, New York City—and decided to lower the value of the dollar with respect to the yen. Prior to that, "everyone" had said currency exchange rates were set purely by market forces and couldn't be managed. But afterward the dollar fell exactly as the U.S. wanted it to. The lesson is simple. To repeat what was said in an earlier chapter because it is so vitally important, foreign exchange rates can be managed within large ranges over long periods of time. The dollar in fact was managed. The yen was managed to keep it and Japanese products and labor costs artificially "cheap." And Japan could not have done that without close U.S. cooperation.

The higher dollar undervalued the wages of Japanese workers, who are paid in yen but get compared to American workers paid in the higher-valued dollars. For example, if the yen were revalued upward by 50 percent compared to the dollar, Japanese workers' wages would suddenly rise by 50 percent too. Large fluctuations have been common. In just two months at the end of 1982, the yen was revalued upward by 20 percent, from just under 280 to the dollar to 230 (*New York Times*, 4–11–83). Several years earlier, the yen had been below 200 to the dollar, showing a total range of roughly 40 percent, with more fluctuations in between (*Business Week*, 1–3–79: Spot = 195; 1 year = 179. 12–22–80: Spot = 208; 1 year = 196).

From 1980 to 1985, the dollar increased in value by a full 70 percent against an average of the world's currencies. And U.S. workers' wages were similarly moved upward by 70 percent against foreign wages even though American working people received no such increase in actual wages. Then, following September 1985, the dollar fell to under 150 yen by the spring of

1987. That's almost a 50 percent drop in the dollar from 280 and a doubling of the yen in less than five years. And suddenly Japanese workers had become twice as expensive as previously in American terms.

What is the "real" value of the dollar? In 1980, reports said 200 yen, but the dollar exceeded it by as much as 40 percent and made American labor seem overpriced. Consequently, imports increased and the real value of the dollar fell further. In early 1987, the impression was given that the dollar was worth 150 yen or less.

Due to these fluctuations, "real" wage costs of Japanese auto workers—the part of the differential attributable strictly to workers' pay—can fluctuate just as much. *When* the wages are compared is important, and the comparisons can be strongly biased by management just by choosing the dates most favorable to prove the debater's point.

Undervalued foreign currencies are at the root of many complaints about high labor costs in the U.S. Despite the dollar's drop against the yen (and European currencies), such countries as South Korea, Taiwan, and Brazil, which kept running up huge trade surpluses with the U.S., did not have their currencies move upward correspondingly in value.

Taking together these undervalued currency exchange rates with productivity, hidden costs, and subsidies to foreign producers (who may be American companies in disguise), the end result can easily be in many cases that foreign labor is more, not less, expensive than American labor, even at high U.S. union wages.

Real Pay. By 1986, after the yen ran up and the hidden costs began to be added in, a number of reports showed that Japanese pay was close to or even higher in some cases than U.S. pay.

According to a study by Japan's Labor Ministry, a typical Japanese factory worker in 1986 earned $1,872 per month, 12 percent more than the $1,671 earned by his U.S. counterpart (*Business Week,* Economic Diary, 8–11–86). According to Dean Witter sources, Japanese factory wages surpassed U.S. wages in 1986 (WNYC radio, 1–16–87).

In late 1986, *Forbes* reported "Japan's factory wages are already 12 percent higher than America's at recent rates of exchange" (11–3–86, 235). It also reported, "With the yen at 175, some estimates put the annual disposable income of a typical Japanese factory worker near $25,000, more than either U.S. or West German workers earn" (5–5–86, 41).

As early as 1983, James C. Abegglen wrote an "Ideas and Trends" piece in *Business Week* stating that average manufacturing wages were almost equal in Japan and the U.S. (8–15–83, 14). Still earlier, average gross earnings for General Motors production workers in 1980 were $20,000, while Toyota and Nissan (then Datsun) averaged $18,000, according to statistics from the International Metalworkers Federation and the UAW in *We Are Not the Problem!* (Institute for Labor Education and Research). That $2,000 is a small gap at most, and still subject to questions about the yen, productivity, hidden costs, and taxes.

Interestingly, the *New York Times* reported that Japan's per capita income in 1983 was $7,908 compared to $10,559 in the U.S., and hourly wages averaged $6.05 versus $9.17 in the U.S. (10–30–85, D1). But once taking into account the upward revaluation of the yen, and adding in hidden, nonhourly costs, these figures too show equal pay in the U.S. and Japan.

In a final example, *Business Week* in 1985 compared the lives of two auto workers, a welder/team leader for Toyota in Japan and a UAW member for Ford in Michigan (9–30–85, 76). The Japanese worker earned $26,250 annually, 45 percent more than the average Japanese manufacturing worker. The American earned $29,200 annually, also 45 percent more than the average for U.S. manufacturing jobs. Once more, the yen was well above 200 then. The Japanese worker(s) would be earning more than their U.S. counterparts at the "real" 1980 yen rate of 200, and considerably more at the "real" 1987 rate of 150. Further, the Japanese worker paid $2,300 less annually in income taxes and $4,250 less on mortgage and property taxes.

A simple calculation from the above report would make the average Japanese manufacturing income about $18,000 a year. In fairness to a lot of workers, it must be emphasized that many Japanese factory workers earn less, less even than the $18,000 at 1985 currency exchange rates. For example, the leading Japanese electronics manufacturer, Matsushita, paid assembly workers an average of $12,000 per year at its VCR plant in Okayama (*High Technology*, 8–86, 31). That was at a rate of 167 yen. And other reports talk of horrible conditions in small industrial suppliers, paying as little as $12 a day in sweatshops and for homework (*New York Times,* 4–22–86, C18).

Accounts of the horrible conditions in Japanese sweatshops show they have miserable productivity (just like miserable productivity in many small American job shops). Do their low wages make them competitive? If they did, why did major Japanese companies raise pay and working conditions in their factories? Remember the 25 percent productivity rate in 1960. The small, brutal shops are the most likely to have stayed at that level—and to have stayed uncompetitive, unless they stayed brutal and low-paying too. But the high pay and good working conditions in major companies raised productivity and quality and proved both competitive and profitable.

Meanwhile, the U.S. has its low wages and hard work too. For example, at a new plant organized around teamwork and problem solving in College Station, Texas, Westinghouse paid new workers $960 per month to make military electronics gear. If they scored well on skills tests, they could boost pay to $1,550 a month after three years (*Business Week,* 7–28–86, 76). That's $11,520 annually to start and $18,600 for nontraditionally skilled labor.

Sidney Harman of Harman International Industries (large audio equipment) said that direct wages at his Northridge, California, plant were $13,000 annually. They were the same as Japanese competitors and he got slightly higher productivity (*Inc.,* June 1986, 28).

After a tough strike, Teamsters won $5.85 an hour at a Watsonville, California, canning and frozen-food plant, while food packers in Texas earned $3.75 an hour—the U.S. minimum wage (*Business Week,* 3–30–87, 90B). And American food packers got Mexican workers for only $4 to $5 per day.

The U.S. also has a large array of sweatshops and employers who are quick to use captive, illegal aliens as labor. And U.S. auto makers use lower-wage, nonunion subcontractors and Mexican labor too.

But such cheap labor won't help U.S. managements after all. As noted earlier, Japanese companies increasingly are using Mexican labor and threaten to take away, by virtue of better management, any and all advantages American companies thought they would get when they began to send jobs to Mexico in the first place.

One hears also of crowded and cold housing in Japan to imply the Japanese are poor. But once more, that's because Japan is overcrowded and lacks natural resources. Its situation is poor and its people suffer because of circumstance—regardless of what they get paid in world currency terms.

Despite its problems, many reports say Japan has both more equitable income distribution and larger accumulated wealth than in the U.S.

The *Economist* published statistics from the Organization for Economic Cooperation and Development (OECD), a leading international economic agency, showing that in both 1972 and 1982, variations in wages among industries were virtually identical in the U.S. and Japan (the variations were greater, by the way, than in Britain, West Germany, and France) (8–30–86, 57).

Forbes reported that income was distributed more evenly in Japan than in the U.S., with more going to the lower end (8–18–80, 58). Steve Lohr reported a similarly equitable distribution in the *New York Times* (12–21–81, D1), as did Robert Lekachman in a review in the *New York Times Book Review* (5–4–86).

The wage comparisons of auto workers, as well as of many other workers, show that factory wages generally in Japan are, and have rightfully been, close to or even higher than those in the U.S. This occurred at precisely the same time that Japan achieved economic superiority in those industries.

Japanese savings reflect their high pay. According to the *New York Times,* average household savings rose to $28,660 in 1985 (3–29–86, 29). Adjusting for a higher yen, that could easily be $40,000 in 1987—far higher than in the U.S. Of course Japan's tax and social-service structure is different—Japan has no social security and the people must retire early—so they need to save, but no one can save that kind of money on low wages.

The evidence is overwhelming that Japan never was the "cheap-labor" country American management claims it was—or still claims it is.

Better Workers

The neat finishes and well-fitting parts of many Japanese autos give the impression that Japanese workers are more highly skilled and work harder and more carefully than American auto workers. Consumers conclude that the lower quality of American cars and other products is caused by sloppy, lazy, uncaring American workers. The truth is very different.

Hard Workers. Paul Aron, a top analyst for Daiwa Securities-America who has been to many Japanese factories, said that Japanese workers didn't work harder than Americans; rather, their machines worked harder (*Wall Street Week,* 9–7–84).

A survey of foreign-owned companies reported, "Foreign managers say American workers compare favorably with workers of other lands" ("Foreign Managers Make a Hit with U.S. Workers," *U.S. News & World Report,* 1–8–79). A senior Japanese manager of a Toyota truck-bed manufacturing plant in Long Beach, California, said, "People here are working harder than people in Japan."

After visiting many factories, Andrew Weiss, an associate professor of economics at Columbia University, said he felt that the work pace was faster at several Western Electric plants in the U.S. than at five of Japan's largest and most successful electronics companies (*Harvard Business Review,* July-August 1984). Weiss reported that a Japanese manager who had visited several Western Electric plants also found the American work pace to be faster. And other observers were cited in the article saying that American factory workers worked faster.

As a computer programmer, I occasionally walked through the production floors of Western Electric's manufacturing plant in lower Manhattan. I can only describe the pace as breakneck. Workers there were truly "Driven!" To a considerable extent, I was driven too. Management from the manufacturing plant was in charge of the computer room and filled it with the same pressure as the rest of the plant. At another Western Electric plant, a huge factory (since closed) in Kearny, New Jersey, computer programmers called the high-pressure regimentation they found there "Communist Poland." Both factories were unionized, as were most of Western Electric's production workers.

Testifying before the International Trade Commission (5–9–84), USWA President Lynn Williams cited data from Paine Webber's *World Steel Dynamics* showing that U.S. steel companies produced on average 11 percent more tons of steel per man-hour worked than Japanese companies for the period 1976 through 1984. In 1984, the U.S. productivity advantage was projected to be the most of the entire period: 25 percent. Jerry Flint of *Forbes* concurred, calling U.S. steelworkers' skills and productivity "the untold miracle of American industry" (3–10–86).

Ordinarily, greater U.S. productivity is explained by better equipment, but the U.S. steel industry has notoriously obsolete mills. For example, James Cook of *Forbes* reported in 1983 that because 79 percent of Japanese steel was continuously cast versus 29 percent in the U.S., Japanese steel makers "have been able to realize enormous economies in capital, labor, and time" (5–23–83, 32). Yet U.S. steelworkers, mostly unionized, produced dramatically more tons per hour. That's superior workmanship, with a vengeance.

Why are Americans so quick to believe that Japanese workers work harder and that U.S. unions impede productivity? Most Americans just don't see how fast the pace is and how hard the working conditions are in many American factories. And unionized workers in the U.S. don't see the pace in Japan. Certainly American managements and the news media keep saying that foreign and nonunion workers work harder. The propaganda is so strong that even Professor Weiss admitted that he was surprised by how wrong he was.

With auto and mortgage payments to meet, higher educations to buy, dreams of "making it big" as a professional or in business, or just to pay food and rent bills, many Americans at almost all income levels "work their butts off."

Skilled Workers. It takes special, superior kinds of human beings to get work done in the hard conditions of many American factory and office workplaces. It's not workers' or unions' fault if American employers make shoddy products.

Quality is a management responsibility. If low quality gets through, it is because management lets it. After American auto managements began trying to upgrade to Japanese quality, reports began saying that auto workers were finally being allowed to stop the assembly line—previously unheard of—if they spotted a defect. In other words, management previously ordered that defects be passed on to the consumer! Workers had been ordered to lower their quality in order to speed up their output. Yet workers were blamed.

To get top quality, an intelligent blend of automation and skilled workers is necessary. Brute human labor alone can't possibly work as fast, accurately, or with as much power or technology as many machines. Yet trying to eliminate skilled human labor entirely produces such complex machines that they are too costly or unreliable to be used in most cases. And many human skills of sight, dexterity, adaptability, and judgment are still far beyond the most advanced machines.

Many Japanese companies produce greater quality because they automated earlier, more extensively, and yet more modestly than American companies. For example, Japan uses more robots than the U.S., but most of Japan's robots are simple devices that are less complicated than those that American companies try to install. It seems the Japanese did it in large part because they had shortages—not excesses—of skilled labor.

At least until recently, the U.S. long had the finest mass public education system in the world. Many American working people have college educations or at least went to junior college or community colleges. In Europe, general public education usually stops around age 15 or so. In West Germany, the weeding out for college reportedly starts as early as the first grade, and three-fourths of students went to vocational school after the ninth grade in 1986 (*U.S. News & World Report,* 1–19–87, 62).

In Japan, standardized tests begin weeding out students after the ninth grade and deliver the coup de grace after the twelfth grade (*New York Times,* 7–12–83, A1). Consequently, the U.S. Census Bureau believed in 1985 that although the quality of U.S. schools did decline in the 1970s, superior test scores by some foreign students resulted at least partly because lower-scoring students had already been filtered out (*New York Times,* 10–20–85, 39).

Paradoxically, while Japanese colleges are exclusive, they do not necessarily have high educational standards. The pressure on students to perform well in high school begins in the sixth grade and is so great—it's called "examination hell"—that students reportedly are burned out by the time they get into college. Many spend the four college years recovering rather than working.

After they enter companies, the younger graduates with the most impressive test credentials "seem worn out by the brutal competition of schooling and examination" (*Inc.,* 4–86, 60). The result: "They show little enthusiasm for their work." The *New York Times* published a similar report headlined "Japan's Youth Seem Old Before Their Time" (3–11–84).

Worries abound in Japan about the stifling nature of its educational system and its conformist social structure. Lack of a creative, freewheeling approach is thought to be behind Japan's inability— to date—to develop world-class computer software. The planning manager of Japan's premier software project, Sigma, went so far as to say it was necessary to "impose creativity" (*New York Times*, 12–3–86, D9). If attitudes like that prevail, Japan could have a very long way to go.

Factories and offices also need creativity and initiative. They too are highly complex working systems, and their overall productivity depends greatly on how they are organized. *Business Week* reported in 1980 that because of poor coordination among departments and poor cooperation between management and labor, most industrial plants ran only an estimated 50 percent of maximum potential, and steel plants, which depend even more on a smooth flow of production, ran at just 30 percent utilization (8–18–80, 98).

In major Japanese companies, management organizes work and enlists workers for suggestions. In America, management ostensibly runs everything, but often it implicitly leaves production to workers: It hires skilled employees (including professional staffs) and expects them to get work done, preferably without supervision. They do it too, and they do it best by organizing their own jobs and how they work with each other. Unfortunately, management doesn't like the power that workers get in running production, and it often interferes to assert its own power, messing up production royally.

Given the superiority of Japanese management, nothing explains higher U.S. productivity so much, especially in the steel industry, as American workers' gifts at self-organization and creative problem solving. Their very outspokenness and relative fearlessness, which American management hates so much, also result in free thought and expression and creative energy. They are America's most vital productive asset.

Besides a less-skilled work force, Japan also had shortages of labor after World War II. Birth rates dropped so much that its leaders feared that "a critical worker shortage would commence around the late 1960s" (*Science News,* 11–6–82, 299).

The shortages appear to have continued into the 1980s. "Foreign competitors appear to have more to gain by flexible automation, and less to lose. The Japanese have suffered from a labor shortage, while the U.S. has chronic high unemployment" (*High Technology,* July 1983, 42). In other words, Japan and other nations lacked America's large skilled labor force—the very workers American managements bad-mouth—and felt they had to automate to compete. "The explanation of high [Japanese] quality lies in the investment in design, and in the investment made to take labor out of the product" by automation (James C. Abegglen and Akio Etori, advertising supplement to *Scientific American,* October 1980, J14).

"Labor" could hardly be an advantage when less human labor actually goes into Japanese products. It's hard to imagine why Japanese companies would take labor out of manufacturing if Japanese workers were the competitive advantage American managements say they were.

According to John T. Eby, head of Ford's operations in Japan and a director of Toyo Kogyo (Mazda), the Japanese auto companies automated many jobs because they "just wanted to get men out of dirty, uncomfortable jobs because they know if they keep a man in a job like that, the quality will be erratic" (*New York Times,* 3–28–83, D1).

Why were Japanese managers worried about "erratic" quality? In the 1950s, "Made in Japan" meant "shoddy." It appears that when Japanese manufacturers depended on human labor as American auto makers did, Japanese labor could not compete with American labor. So Japanese managements had to automate and design labor out of the most difficult jobs. And they automated in such a way as to augment what skills their workers did have.

Japanese managements upgraded workers' output by designing every human job so that it could be done most easily. For example in the U.S., cars have traditionally been moved along an assembly line at roughly ground level. Auto workers had to work from a trench underneath the car or reach and stretch from the side to add parts to the chassis. In Japan, however, such large parts as doors are assembled separately, making the work on the doors much easier and better. Major body parts such as doors and the chassis are hung from an elevated line and tilted so workers can work much more comfortably—and under finer control ("Making Cars in Japan: A Lesson in Efficiency," John Holusha, *New York Times,* 3–23–83, A1). By carefully organizing the process of assembly, Japanese management eliminated the most awkward and back-breaking tasks, such as bending, stooping, crawling, and reaching—things American auto workers had to do all the time because management never made the effort to improve the system.

It's notable that when American unions demand better working conditions, management complains about "restrictive work rules." But Japanese management clearly shows that trying to get better working conditions can stimulate superior engineering. U.S. managements would do better to listen to unions and employees rather than fight them in knee-jerk fashion.

Japan also created a far-sighted form of labor relations to augment what skills its workers had. The much talked-about "lifetime employment" in Japan was not the result of a kindly or brotherly attitude of management toward workers or unions. Rather, it "is a relatively modern invention that results from the concern of Japanese employers with attracting and retaining skilled laborers" after World War II. "Only about a third of all Japanese workers are sheltered by lifetime employment promises" ("Japan's Enviable Jobless Rate," Steve Lohr, *New York Times,* 12–21–81). Those promises were given mostly to skilled workers and were concentrated in heavy industries that needed skilled workers to be competitive. American companies, however, which had an abundance of skilled labor, laid off workers periodically and did precious little to train, retain, or upgrade worker skills.

Was lifetime employment something only Japanese companies could think of? Hardly. Japanese companies also waged war on unions in the 1950s, and the companies were more successful in crushing, or at least beating, unions than their American counterparts. But "Made in Japan" still meant "shoddy." So Japanese companies turned to U.S. productivity experts, whom American managements scorned. The result: lifetime employment and other ways to cultivate skilled labor.

When American unions fight for social programs such as unemployment insurance, job training, and comparable worth, American management complains of "costly social programs." But Japanese managements' actions show that efforts to reward and build a skilled work force create superior productivity.

All this shows that because of a less-skilled work force, Japanese managements designed work better to make up for lower work skills. Workers got better results, and that appears—deceptively—to be superior workmanship.

What's more, Japan also had to build products that didn't need service because it had little or no initial dealers to provide service in America—another kind of shortage of skilled labor! As a result, they got lower costs, more sales, more profits, and great customer loyalty.

The quality in Japanese products today comes from management's efforts to eliminate the problem of a *less* skilled human work force. To compete against American and European industries, Japanese managements took workers from high school, trained them, and continued to train them to build up skills in their work force. They invented "lifetime" employment to keep the skilled workers they had, because they couldn't rely—as American management did—on a large pool of skilled labor that could be hired or laid off at every turn in the economy. And they automated to increase the quality and output of their skilled workers. The dominant position of many Japanese industries in the 1980s results from its superior production in the 1970s, and that superiority was built by decisions in the 1950s and 1960s when Japanese labor was less educated and less skilled than it is today.

In contrast, many American managements have been counting on a highly skilled and hard-working work force to get the job done despite inferior design and management's indifference to quality. They have pushed for harder rather than smarter work, wasting the skills employees possess, especially adaptability, ingenuity, and initiative.

This analysis reveals that America has an immense undeveloped asset in its highly skilled work force. American working people are simply not the high-cost, low-quality burden they are accused of being. Carrying American management's reliance on skilled workers to its logical conclusion, how much of American management is an unnecessary expense and a costly obstacle to progress? The following chapter sheds light on this question.

6

How American Management Made Itself Uncompetitive with Japan

The problem with American competitiveness lies not in labor but elsewhere: in management, government, and the financial markets. It's there we have to look to achieve greater efficiency, quality, and lower costs in many American businesses.

With a work force that was in many cases inferior to American labor, Japanese manufacturing managements set about finding ways to cut nonlabor costs and improve every nonlabor aspect of their businesses. They succeeded far beyond the dreams of their counterparts in American management. And they started by cutting the size, cost, and inflexibility of management itself.

Management Overhead and Profit Margins

Size of Managerial Bureaucracy. Many reports show that Japanese management allowed fewer layers of bureaucracy above production workers. *Business Week* wrote in 1981, "Salaried staff costs for Ford's North American automotive operations are a staggering $4 billion a year—a figure that Ford executives readily admit is probably twice that of rival Japanese auto makers. Indeed, Ford is laboring under 12 layers of management, compared to Japanese competitor Toyota's seven" (12–21–81, 69).

Smaller Japanese management means less pay for management, less "overhead," and less total "labor" costs. It also means greater managerial communication and flexibility in decision-making, and more reliance and trust in workers to get things done.

Percentage Taken by Bosses and Creditors. Reports show that the entire management and capital structure of Japan took less money out of production and put more capital back into modernizing production. For example, James Cook wrote in *Forbes* (4–13–81, 128) that Japanese auto makers paid only 20 percent of earnings as dividends, while U.S. auto makers paid 50 percent. Interest rates have long been higher in the U.S. than Japan. And the Japanese continued to modernize through the 1970s while Americans did not. Japan's continuing modernization, well into the 1980s, refutes the excuse that Japan had a unique advantage because it could modernize after World War II. What stopped the Americans from modernizing when they had more capital than Japan? Greed: Managements, bosses, stockholders, and creditors just kept bleeding American industry dry.

According to *We Are Not the Problem!*, the top 34 Toyota executives each got paid approximately $44 per hour, but the top 55 GM executives each got $264 per hour (data from Harley Shaiken in *Dollars and Sense*, Jan. 1982, converted to hourly rates). Now that is a real pay gap! Confirmation of this statistic comes from comparisons of wages within Japan. According to Steve Lohr of the *New York Times*, in 1981 "the wage gap between management and workers is much smaller in Japanese companies than in other nations" (12–21–81, D1).

In "Is American Management Too Selfish?", Thomas Friedman and Paul Solman, two editors of broadcast business news reports, answered yes: "All the professors agree that we've got a problem: American managers are too selfish and unaccountable" (*Forbes*, 1–17–83, 77).

How selfish? A 1986 survey of 906 of America's largest companies by Gilbert Dwyer & Co. found that 54 percent offered "golden parachutes" to protect their executives (*Forbes*, 12–29–86, 8). These are contracts that pay executives benefits when they are forced out—even if their companies fail. The potential costs of these contracts for large industrial companies in 1986 averaged $5.2 million per company, while Merrill Lynch's deals could cost $60 million alone.

Yet workers can get little or nothing when profit-sharing schemes are offered, which is not often. From 1983 to 1986, GM made billions of dollars in profits and paid its executives hundreds of millions of dollars annually in bonuses but paid workers no more than $515 per person in its profit-sharing plan. In 1986, GM made $3 billion in profits but shared nothing with workers. In 1984, one independent financial analyst defended executive bonuses by saying that "the bonuses paid to [management] don't amount to a dime a car" (*Newsweek,* 5–14–84, 51). Actually, they were close to $42 per car. It's a peculiarly inverted perspective that understates management's rewards by a factor of 420, or 42,000 percent. Perhaps that's why weekly steelworkers' pay of $407 was called "high-paying" and "hefty" (*Business Week,* 10–28–85, 95) while top managers can make millions of dollars in golden parachutes and the like for failing!

How unaccountable are executives? In 1984, the 500 companies in the *Fortune* 500 replaced only 11 chief executive officers (excluding retirement). At that rate, one of those companies would replace its chief for reasons other than retirement only once every 50 years (*U.S. News & World Report,* 2–18–85, 75).

In "America's Imperial Chief Executive," Steven Prokesch of the *New York Times* reported at the end of 1986 that despite a lot of talk about holding chief executives accountable for the performance of their companies, management experts concluded that little progress had been made and there was no visible prospect of any major change (10–12–86, F1).

Beginning with the recession of 1982, middle management in large manufacturing companies came under great pressure and many middle managers lost their jobs due to less business, some management streamlining, mergers, and computerization of the information analysis that middle managers were hired to do (not to mention having fewer employees to manage).

But before 1983, management had grown enormously. Headlines to a report by Karen W. Arenson in the *New York Times* announced "Management's Ranks Grow" and "A 9 Percent Gain in Two Recessions" (4–14–83, D1). According to Ms. Arenson and statistics from the federal government's Bureau of Labor Statistics, management growth stretched "across all segments of the economy."

In other words, after four severe recessions beginning with the one in 1969, management, far from becoming leaner, had grown fatter and more unaccountable than ever, except perhaps for middle managers in large industrial corporations. We should expect to find that management grew especially in the ranks of service companies, which continued to expand without productivity gains and which had little foreign competition, and among military producers, which had little market competition and few regulatory watchdogs at all.

Management survives and grows huge because it exists in America for far more than doing specialized work. Some managers do work, and those who depend on their work to earn their pay may be in trouble as *their* bosses look to eliminate *their* labor. But management exists also to serve itself with personal gain and easy lives. Top managers are indeed the "Boss." The rich, well-connected, and comfortable parts of management will survive or find other positions.

Most of all, management exists to push employees. A large management overhead provides a willing, knowledgeable work force to use to break strikes. That part of management that is bloated as "strike-breaking insurance" would have a self-interest in keeping labor relations hostile, for that justifies its existence, even if that hostility lowers productivity and the bloated management raises costs. Ironically, with the weakening of unions, large corporations have less need for a bloated management and have indeed been savaging the ranks of middle managers.

Despite the cutting, management may have grown still more unproductive if the working managers have been cut and replaced with self-servers. It seems likely. Almost four years after Ms. Arenson's report, Senior Editor Jerry Flint of *Forbes* wrote, in "Who Gets the Parachutes?", that "too often, the executives who made mistakes escape the sacrifice." And he asked at the end, "Is it back to the good old days, meaning back to corporate bloat?" (1–12–87, 38).

Worse, if the growth in middle management occurred in the first place because higher management failed to do its own job in using and evaluating workers and middle managers, a premise many working people and *Business Week* (12–21–81, 69) support, then cuts will have created only chaos, resentment, closed communications, and havoc.

Mis-Management at the Networks. This certainly happened most visibly at CBS in March 1987. Citing a news budget that rose from $89 million to $300 million between 1978 and 1987, its new financial managers decided to cut production people.

Experienced and respected reporters and writers were fired for no cause other than that they got too little airtime. Management sought to replace experienced writers with temporary workers, precipitating a strike by the Writers Guild of America. As a result of cuts in the mailroom staff, letters and important documents were reportedly piling up or getting lost—but definitely not getting delivered (*New York*, 4–6–87, 11). And in response to employee complaints, management instituted a dress code "to give the mailroom staff some identity in the company." As if CBS, of all companies, had previously lacked pride and identity! It is ironic that a company that sells its ability to tell us about the world would cut itself off so completely from the world.

Were these cuts and the attacks on the Writers Guild necessary and appropriate? According to many reports and comments, most of the increased costs had gone to million-dollar stars, expensive technology, overemphasis on scoops and spectacles, the raging inflation of the early 1980s, bloated management bureaucracy, and simple mismanagement throughout the company.

For example, CBS headquarters "Black Rock" was built with many expensive features, such as Canadian granite that "had to be buffed just so lest it reflect sunlight" (*Fortune*, 10–13–86, 64). Industry experts estimated CBS spent $50 million too much to buy several magazines from Ziff-Davis in 1985. A reporter for a local radio station cited the opinion of many knowledgeable observers that CBS was a "management mess." According to them, top executives who had never covered news indulged in perks and high salaries, spent money on the wrong things, and ignored experienced reporters who knew how to report effectively and cheaply.

Astonishingly, CBS spent $8 million and four years to build a new studio-and-newsroom complex. Yet insiders said that twenty high-tech editing rooms had to be redone. According to one staffer, "Editors have trouble monitoring a tape's brightness and color shading. There isn't enough room for an editor, correspondent, and producer to work in the same room" (*New York*, 6–1–87, 13). Staffers dubbed the editing rooms Lubyanka, after the infamous Russian KGB prison, because the rooms were "inhumanly small."

In addition, CBS gave 57-year-old Thomas Wyman, whom it

had just ousted as CEO, a golden parachute of $4.3 million plus $400,000 a year for life (*New York Times*, 4–7–87, D1). *Business Week* estimated the total payment to Wyman would cost $11.4 million (5–4–87, 51). CBS also paid $1 million, plus unspecified yearly bonuses through 1990, to Van Gordon Sauter, the former president of CBS News, who left along with Wyman.

A commentary in *Business Week* contradicted the idea that excessive news costs were due to working journalists (3–30–87, 33). While doubling the hours of news programs, CBS "added only seven correspondents and 50 producers during the period when its budget exploded." *Newsweek* agreed, saying "the star system that allows huge salaries for on-air talent...is one of the principal reasons that news budgets at the networks have more than tripled in 10 years" (3–16–87, 80).

An apparent case can be made that, since CBS News declined in ratings precisely during the period that work loads increased dramatically, CBS News suffered from too few, not too many, producing personnel. If so, any cost problem CBS had was with spending in the wrong ways, on the wrong goals. And any revenue problem it may have had was due to inferior products brought on by the shortcuts in production. Nevertheless, the new management decided to continue the failing policy of stars, spectacle, and entertainment. It cut instead the kind of people who had made CBS News preeminent in the first place.

It's all painfully similar to the plot of the last episode of *The Mary Tyler Moore Show*. A new, inexperienced boss came in, kept bumbling anchorman Ted Baxter, and fired the professional news staff headed by Lou Grant.

But what brought in inexperienced bosses? Underlying the turmoil at CBS News appears to be a cause that has nothing to do with operational costs, reporters' effectiveness, and simple mismanagement.

In 1985, "smart money" viewed television stations as licenses to print money. And the networks owned highly profitable television stations. So Lawrence Tisch bought into CBS, General Electric bought NBC, and the smallish Capital Cities bought ABC. All three buyers were supposed to include some of the smartest men in business: the epitome of professional management. They saw the money clearly and went for it. Rupert Murdoch, another "smart" businessman, did the same thing in trying to create a fourth television network. Unfortunately, advertising revenues soon flattened out and then declined, and prices for network affiliate stations, measured as multiples of the subsequent year's projected cash flow, fell from 18 in June 1985 to under 12 in November 1986, a decline of more than one-third (*Business Week,* 12–1–86, 38).

Assuming that the new owners didn't cause these revenue drops by somehow damaging the TV product, they still made the colossal mistake of buying at the top of the market, with less-than-expected revenues to cover their costs. That's an enormous cost problem, but it may not have been the only one.

Typically, raiders on Wall Street borrow to the hilt to make their purchases and expect to sell quickly at higher prices to pay off their debt. And financial managers demand high rates of return as matters of principle. The more the new network owners had counted on rising station prices or rising ad revenues to pay for the costs of their purchases, the more they would have been in serious trouble as prices and revenues fell below expectations.

Significantly, they attacked the networks and programming as if they were in serious trouble. They sought to raise profits the only way they seemingly knew how: not by producing a better product to win back viewers and advertisers, but rather by cutting wages and workers. Although CBS made the most headlines, ABC cut its work force substantially and suffered a strike too. Murdoch's Fox Broadcasting Co. cut Joan Rivers soon after signing her and had losses well in excess of $50 million (*Business Week,* 6–1–87, 50). Even ratings leader NBC brought in consultants McKinsey & Company to "rationalize" news operations (*New York,* 5–25–87, 20). And like CBS and ABC, NBC sought to increase the percentage of temporary workers, setting off a strike by the National Association of Broadcast Employees and Technicians (*New York Times,* 6–30–87, C18).

When four of the "smartest" financial managers do the same "right" thing at the same time but fail nevertheless, and when at least three of them create turmoil in their efforts to save themselves, the process is not simple mismanagement. It's professional mismanagement.

The only thing that might save the major networks is that they all have the same kind of financial managers at the top; ignorant of production and quick to ax people. But then who will save the public from them? Certainly not the Reagan Administration, which has long felt that broadcasters have no responsibilities to the public, even though they have governmentally sanctioned monopolies over their bands in the airwaves.

Arrogance and Greed. At Time Inc. as at CBS, employees were cut "to cut costs." But the worst costs were fiascos like the $47 million loss for *TV-Cable Week* in 1983, where, according to insider Christopher M. Byron, management made grandiose plans but totally failed to coordinate, oversee, or execute operations, producing situations that were too improbable even for a Marx Brothers farce (*Vanity Fair,* January 1986, 66). In 1987, producing employees were terminated as scapegoats (*New York Times,* 3–31–87, D1), but many of the top managers who caused the losses at *TV-Cable Week* had long ago been promoted.

The arrogance is awesome, and the greed is even greater. American "bosses"—owners, stockholders, bureaucrats, and creditors—in business and government pay themselves more and produce less for their pay than their Japanese counterparts. Taking more profits, they cost more. Being more greedy, arrogant, and ignorant, they do a lesser job. Both ways, they raise costs, reduce quality, and produce a cost/profit gap that has nothing to do with labor costs. And the larger the gap, the more they try to make someone else— workers, taxpayers, consumers—pay to make up the difference.

What do Japanese businessmen think of American management's behavior? James Fallows reported from Tokyo that his friends among Japanese businessmen, "no fans of Karl Marx," talk of a central "contradiction" of American capitalism that rewards the brightest people for such "unproductive" work as corporate law, stock market speculation, and mergers and acquisitions instead of for teaching, industrial engineering, and the like (*U.S. News & World Report,* 1–12–87, 37). One of Fallows' Japanese friends, speaking for many of his associates, called *seppuku,* or "suicide," the preoccupation of America's political leaders with "Contragate" instead of with America's rapidly worsening economic competitiveness.

"One of Japan's greatest businessmen, Sony's Akio Morita, said, 'When things get bad too many of your American compa-

nies lay off their workers; it's the bosses who should be fired.'"
So wrote the editor of *Forbes*, James W. Michaels, in his "Side
Lines" column (4–12–82). Three years later, *Forbes* repeated that
charge in a paraphrase (11–18–85, 178).

Workers naturally become angry and unwilling to "share"
when all they do is give back and all management does is take.
And then of course, workers get blamed by management for being "uncooperative" and "fat cats," and the news media—employers themselves—broadcast management's claims to discredit
the idea of involving workers in management.

Unit Costs

When management talks about labor costs, it often expresses them
not as wages per worker, but as the labor cost per unit produced:
All the money collectively spent on "labor" is divided by the number of units produced. More generally, "unit costs" are derived by
dividing total costs by total units. Either computation can hide a
multitude of marketing and production sins, as well as true management costs.

One reason that mass production is desirable is that large machines can be very efficient producers. However, they cost a great
deal to buy and can be paid for only by making large numbers of
products; their cost per unit goes down as the number of units goes
up. This is called an economy of large-scale production. It applies
as well to the buildings and office staff, which are fixed costs, like
machines, and whose cost per unit also goes down as the number
of units goes up.

The statistics concerning the mythical $2,000 labor-cost gap
in autos were expressed in unit costs—costs of manufacture per
car. Those costs depend very much on how many cars are made
and how many are sold. As Japan's auto sales go up, its unit
labor costs automatically go down. And as American auto sales
go down, its unit labor costs go up—regardless of what workers
are actually paid!

Management can cut unit costs in many ways. Reducing them
is a crucial reason Japanese companies get lower unit labor costs
while paying relatively high wages.

Larger Markets and Better Marketing. Major Japanese companies and government agencies go after larger international markets and do it more effectively than Americans.

One great Japanese strength is the trading company, which specializes in selling in foreign lands. Small manufacturers who could never invest large sums of capital or labor to learn how to export, and then to export and sell, can do so through trading companies. The trading companies can penetrate multiple foreign markets for many manufacturers, achieving larger markets, larger production efficiencies, less investment by manufacturers, and faster returns for trying to sell in foreign markets. They can sell more products and spread fixed costs over more units, thereby arithmetically reducing the cost per unit and the unit labor cost.

Cheaper Capital. Capital—money to invest for the long term in production—has long been much cheaper and more consistently available ("patient") in Japan for major companies. Some say it is Japan's most decisive advantage, not only for heavy industry but for high technology, which increasingly requires highly expensive plants and research budgets.

Japanese interest rates have been much lower than U.S. interest rates. Reasons include tax laws that encourage saving, workers' need to save for retirement, and conscious government policies to restrict foreign borrowing in Japan. Large Japanese companies also have special arrangements with banks, which are often major stockholders (*Forbes,* 4–13–81, 128), so the cost of capital to preferred borrowers is often cheaper still. And according to John Shoven of Stanford University as reported by *Forbes,* new capital in Japan was taxed at an overall rate of 7 percent in 1980 versus 37 percent in the U.S. (10–21–85, 186).

In America, capital is expensive or unavailable at any price. It's the high cost of consumption. For example, tax laws favor borrowing over saving. The super-liquidity trap, huge budget deficits, escalating military and medical costs, junk borrowing on Wall Street, and illegal drugs consume over $600 billion annually and make capital scarce and expensive for productive civilian purposes.

Because large Japanese companies get preferentially low interest rates (even if that reportedly denies capital to small, innovative companies), they have lower costs for machinery, research and development, and every other business expense and investment. That means higher productivity, higher quality, lower unit costs, lower prices, higher sales, and higher exports.

Lower interest rates also reduce the value of the yen. That reduces export prices, increases exports, and protects the home market effectively by raising the prices of all imports, including the most advanced computer chips (*Business Week,* 4–18–83, 114C). This produces larger total sales, larger markets, and larger production runs, which increase economies of scale, lower costs, lower prices, increase sales further, etc., etc., etc.

In all these ways Japan's cheaper capital produces cheaper unit costs, which can then be transformed by sleight of hand into "cheaper labor costs," even though they have nothing whatsoever to do with wages or how hard or how well workers do their jobs.

Automation and More Efficient Production Methods. Superior organization and design of automation and production processes in major Japanese companies lowered initial costs and operating expenses and produced more profits from high-quality products. These lowered unit costs greatly while employing higher-paid skilled labor.

As Japan achieves productive dominance and builds factories in the U.S., and as the yen appreciates and other Asian competitors arise, Japanese companies too may seek to eliminate labor. They certainly avoid unions in the U.S. if they can. Yet that doesn't detract one bit from the strategy that brought them so much success: working closely with labor.

Higher productivity offers management at least two options:

1. Cut labor, or

2. Upgrade the value of the unit and keep the labor
   to do it.

Upgrading value can include adding service, technology, features, options, designs, new models, and finding out what customers want. All this takes labor, and it often pays off: A superior product can be both competitive and profitable.

American companies usually cut labor, and their often-shoddy products and business failures show the lack. But many reports have shown how at least some Japanese companies and, in the U.S., IBM sought to retrain and redeploy displaced workers. They felt they got increased loyalty, experience, and skills.

Of course this doesn't always work, but neither does any other single business strategy always work. Yet it's always worth the effort to at least consider redeploying employees. And many people, businesses, and communities would benefit from it.

Easy Access to American Markets. Japan has easier and cheaper access to American markets than American companies have to markets in Japan. Japanese leaders such as Hisashi Shinto, president of Nippon Telegraph and Telephone Public Corp., dispute this by saying that they had to work hard and long to sell successfully in America (*Business Week*, 12–14–81, 44). But they are talking about consumer acceptance, not government and industrial resistance.

Many reports tell how informal or subtle restrictions such as unusual product standards, inspections, closed-distribution networks, and "buy-Japanese" attitudes among large companies and government powerfully limit what Americans may do or sell in Japan. (See, for example, "The High-Technology Gateway," *Business Week*, 8–9–82.)

Yet Japanese companies have free access to all levels of American government. Astonishingly, more than 100 former senior U.S. officials and 85 law and public relations firms were working for Japan in the U.S. by the end of 1986 (*Newsweek*, 12–22–86, 48). The Reagan Administration's former chief critic of Japanese trade practices, Lionel Olmer, even went to work for Nippon Telephone and Telegraph, which has a history of shutting out American telecommunications suppliers.

Protection makes perfect sense—as long as other countries allow it—for a country that must export or die, especially a country as culturally close-knit as Japan is. And protection makes sense for a country trying to maintain its capacity to be independent.

However, not everyone is equally protectionist. Many reports tell how Japanese consumers often snap up foreign products as status symbols or when their quality is high. Companies such as McDonald's have reportedly succeeded in Japan by selling top-quality American products, tailoring them to Japanese tastes and needs, and employing Japanese personnel to stay as close as possible to the Japanese market. According to one story, a young Japanese tourist in the U.S. was overheard to exclaim, "Look, Mom, they have McDonald's here too!"

Unfortunately, many American companies have not adapted to consumers in Japan as Japanese companies adapted to consumers in America. For example, the Japanese, like the British, drive on the left side of the road and need steering wheels on the right side of the car. But American makers long tried to sell the usual American car without modifications. A general version of this "left-hand drive" syndrome is reportedly a common cause of American failures in Japan (*Business Week,* 2–15–82, 60).

Sometimes, adaptation takes more than simply supplying a "left-hand" car. Japanese auto salesmen visit prospective buyers at home in Japan, reportedly because customers don't like showrooms (*New York Times,* 1–18–81). And for cultural and regulatory reasons, some times of the day and year are better than others to make a sale, so salesmen carry information about prospective buyers and show up when they are most likely to buy. A traditional, high-pressure American car salesman would never stand a chance. One would hope an aggressive American company would hire Japanese workers and learn from them.

American tastes must have first seemed just as "inscrutable" to the Japanese, yet they learned to adapt. Why can't many American managements learn to sell in Japan? And why do many not even try?

Part of the answer is that many American companies fail to market effectively even in the U.S. Many Japanese companies beat them in their own home American market where there are no "inscrutable oriental" customs to deal with. Japanese managers just did what American companies should have been doing all along. There's nothing mysterious or sinister or unfair in that.

Japan has gotten a lot of public pressure to be less protectionist, but perhaps it didn't get as much pressure in private. It is no secret that business interests and the American government are pleased that Japanese auto and steel imports are killing American unions.

There are dangers in saying one thing privately and another thing publicly. One report in *Newsweek* suggested that the conflict between Argentina and Britain was fanned because British negotiators before the war misled Argentina by privately suggesting that Britain would not fight over the Falklands. If Japan keeps taking American jobs, American nationalist resentments must inevitably mount. And if resentments are fanned by duplicitous private American negotiators who encourage Japanese imports to break unions, then trouble between America and Japan could become serious. One theory has it that when America denied Japan materials it needed, Japanese leaders responded by attacking Pearl Harbor. And now the American government is pushing Japan to rearm!

Competitive Protectionism. Japan is not the only country to practice protectionism. In fact, many countries protect their home markets. Usually, they just protect inefficient companies. But some do it to build industry and jobs. Why is it, and how is it, that countries such as Japan and Brazil can protect their home markets, increase industrial production and employment, and close or shrink the industrial gap they have with the U.S., just as the U.S. used protectionism to catch up to Britain in the 1800s?

The industrial successes of the U.S., Japan, Brazil, and Taiwan, among many other nations, show that protectionism is not necessarily the uncompetitive crutch that antilabor world traders say it is. Their success proves that protection can actually increase competition if it gives small producers the chance to grow before foreign companies eat them up. That is how protectionism helps backward countries advance.

Rather than being caused by protection, economic obsolescence and uncompetitiveness seem to result from restrictions on trade and competition in the home market.

Whether import protection helps or hurts depends heavily on whether a country has small markets and suffers nearly monopolistic stagnation of them. In many industries, Japan competes in world markets and has fierce competition among domestic companies in its large home market. It has at least eight auto companies to America's three. Protectionism in that context has fostered growth and competitiveness. But countries of Western Europe have small markets and cartel-like restrictions of trade, and they have lost competitiveness.

America appears to be in between. It has a large home market, but not as large as the total world market that Japan targets. Often, U.S. markets have been dominated by one or a few producers, as the auto market has been dominated by General Motors. And most U.S. companies just do not try or care to export, so they restrict their market enormously.

The charge by world traders that protection of American industrial jobs would necessarily hurt American productivity and competitiveness is overly simplistic, misleading, and highly self-serving. It implies, and the statement is often made, that America should allow its industrial jobs to be exported. But backward industries—and American auto and steel are indeed now backward, while high tech is falling behind—need protection from predatory foreign competition to grow competitive. With protection from foreign competition, they could grow competitive if they made the effort.

There's the rub: if they made the effort. The U.S. auto industry long showed very little interest in competing on quality. And it has pretty much given up on small U.S.-built cars, switching to foreign producers or suppliers of parts instead. Even GM's highly touted effort to make the small Saturn turned out to be much more hype than substance ("On a Clear Day, You Still Can't Quite See Saturn," *Business Week*, 8–12–85). As it kept getting delayed and redesigned into a lower-volume, higher-priced car, the only victories Saturn appears to have won were to hide GM's plans to import Korean and Japanese cars and to force concessions from local governments and the United Auto Workers Union.

It's not as if subcompact cars were actually money losers. According to *Forbes*'s Jerry Flint in "The Winner—by Default," Detroit executives do concede they made money on subcompacts (9–10–84, 44). But apparently subcompacts just weren't profitable *enough* for them. In this case, the cost for abandoning a low-profit item was to give Japan huge parts of the U.S. market. This loss in turn gave Japan huge economies of scale and experience to capture more and more of the rest of the U.S. car market.

Other industries similarly have been abandoned without a fight or transferred to foreign producers. All this because money chasers in management and Wall Street wanted more profits quicker—and didn't want to share any of their profits with U.S. workers.

Steel went like autos. USX abandoned both steel production and its own name. As early as 1982, steel was just 28 percent of its total revenues, down from 74 percent in 1978 (*New York Times,* 2–21–83, D1).

America needs a strong steel industry so that it is not dependent on foreign sources or easily broken sea lanes in times of military or economic war. As in steel, America needs new management in old-line industrial companies if they are to survive and support vital national interests.

U.S. steelworkers have long been complaining about the abandonment of U.S. steel capacity. But their warnings went unheeded and demeaned. They were and still are way ahead of economists, politicians, and other "leaders" because they are at the heart of production. They see and feel first what is happening, and they are best suited and motivated to do something about it. Perhaps steelworkers, who have a commitment to steel production, can introduce competition into America's steel industry and make it competitive again.

Rather than forcing steelworkers to give back all their wages to a fat and uncompetitive management that will abandon steel in any case, maybe America should sack the management and allow steelworkers to manage steel production themselves. They might need protection at first to make up for what past managements failed to do. But in the long run they would bring vast energies and new commitments to make American industry competitive.

The people who advocate a knee-jerk, simple-minded pursuit of unrestricted world trade have other things in mind than American competitiveness. They want to defend the business and profits they make outside America, even if it hurts American jobs—all the more because it does hurt American jobs. America protects its home market less than other nations because American business and government are squeezing American workers to work for less. It is just astonishing, however, how much dominant policymakers have been willing to erode their own markets to gain control over labor.

Other Nonlabor Factors

Easy Use of American Technology. It is widely acknowledged that at least until the mid-1980s, "Japanese technology" was usually just American technology applied better, or American discoveries that were ignored or underdeveloped by American managers.

For example, American management gave away America's vast treasure trove of technology virtually free to Japan. According to Steve Lohr in the *New York Times Magazine* (7–8–84, 21), "From 1950 to 1980, Japanese companies entered into more than 30,000 licensing and other technology-importing agreements for which the Japanese paid an estimated \$10 billion." The agreements involved "virtually all the known commercial technology of the West." And "the total price tag amounted to less than 20 percent" of what the U.S. spent *in 1984 alone* on R&D. Consultant James C. Abegglen called it "the biggest fire sale in history."

Often, American companies invited Japanese managers into their plants to take notes on how to produce more efficiently. As recently as March 1987, United Parcel Service ran television ads boasting how Japanese executives took lessons on how UPS ran "the tightest ship in the shipping business."

Many reports show that Japanese companies have wide and deep information-gathering organizations in America to pick up every bit of American technology available, as they have strong marketing efforts to tailor their products to American demand. These reports also show that most American companies collect little of the vast technical and marketing information available in Japan.

In the August 1986 issue of *High Technology,* Bruce F. Rubinger, a Boston consultant, wrote that in a survey he conducted, "only three of 24 high-tech firms interviewed actively follow Japanese technology." In April 1986, *Business Week* reported, "By some estimates, about eight times more information about U.S. companies goes to Japan than leaves that country for U.S. shores" (4–28–86, 66A). And in its September 22, 1986, issue, in "High-tech America's Myopic Mind-set," *U.S. News & World Report* said the U.S. ignored "the vast outpouring of high-quality research from foreign laboratories."

Even if it were true in the distant past that Japan had neither the market size nor the technology to justify large investments by American companies in information gathering, it doesn't explain why, as late as 1986, Japan was still being ignored. It doesn't explain why Japan does a better job of gathering America's own technology and meeting America's own market tastes than many U.S. managements do. And it doesn't explain why even though the criticism of American management has been going on so long that *Business Week* called the criticism "conventional wisdom" yet complained "the message has gone largely unheeded" (9–1–86, 31).

The answer is that American management has dangerously squandered America's demonstrated superiority in innovation and basic research. By early 1987, even the Pentagon began to worry, based on highly visible and growing evidence, that large parts of high tech, and eventually the American economy and national security itself, could fall under Japanese domination (*New York Times*, 2–13–87, A1). For example, the *New York Times* printed a table in which Japan already had the lead in 9 out of 13 key areas of semiconductor technology (1–6–87, D1).

As with computer chips, so with quality control. While American management ignored American experts on quality control following World War II, Japan made them heroes and named Japan's most coveted industrial award after Dr. W. Edwards Deming, an American quality-control pioneer (*Forbes*, 1–3–83). That was in 1950 or soon thereafter!

Mr. Deming's opinion? He "lays the blame for America's failure to keep up with Japan in quality on the desk of management—especially managers with no factory-floor experience—not on workers" (*Business Week*, 11–1–82, 67). According to Deming, "Management robs the hourly worker of his right to be proud of his work." That means American workers are denied the chance and rewards to contribute to quality or to any other efficiency. And a legion of other experts have agreed over the years.

The result is that Japanese products have a superior reputation for quality. "Public opinion" blames workers, but quality is a management commitment, and the Japanese example shows that American management failed en masse to get it.

And as with quality, so with industrial processes and production technologies. U.S. steel managements have been notorious for their "do-nothing" arrogance. In one example, Westinghouse tried for a decade to interest U.S. steel companies in a plasma-arc process for heating ore (*Business Week*, 7–27–81, 32G). Maurice G. Fay, manager of applied plasma systems for Westinghouse, explained that "whenever he talks to a U.S. steel executive, there comes a time in the conversation when the prospect's eyes glaze over and he asks, 'Tell me, Fay, how many tons of steel has Westinghouse ever produced?'" This closed-minded attitude is most revealing regardless of the merits of the process itself. But apparently the process did have merit. Westinghouse eventually tried Europe and found enthusiasm there, with two steel makers actively trying out the process.

Many reports have said that a large number of production experts like Mr. Deming tried exhaustively without success to get American managements to listen to them. They could have starved had not Japanese companies sought them out, welcomed them with open arms, and learned from them. Those lessons included not only quality control and industrial processes but organization and—most significantly—cooperative labor relations (or at least working closely with labor to get the most out of it).

In short, major Japanese managements are not superhuman. They just did the job American management could easily have done but failed to do—because it focused on crushing unions and dominating employees instead of serving the nation's interests and remaining internationally competitive.

Forbes, Business Week, and *Inc.* have reported innumerable examples of how small American companies have beaten back foreign "cheap-labor" competition by modernizing, reorganizing people, innovating, and using advanced technology. Unfortunately, those small companies have little power to change policies of big business or government. They do, however, show the way and expose many large corporate and government managements as being fat, slow, dumb, disorganized, and very costly.

While Japan has had easy access to American technology, many reports have shown that Japan forced American companies that wanted to sell in Japan to reveal their expertise, through joint ventures or the like, as the price to enter the Japanese market. Then, after Japanese companies had mastered the product, the original American company became expendable and got frozen out of new business with other Japanese companies. Something like that reportedly happened to IBM, which enabled Fujitsu Ltd. to take over leadership in the Japanese market for mainframe computers (*Forbes*, 11–23–81, 123; *Business Week*, 4–6–81, 42).

Despite promises by the Japanese government in the early 1980s, the Japanese telephone company, Nippon Telephone and Telegraph, strongly resisted purchasing the most advanced technology products from American sources (*Business Week*, 8–9–82, 40), and it dragged its feet too on medium- and low-technology American products (Trends, *Forbes*, 7–18–83). Four years later, *Business Week* reported that U.S. companies were still only "starting to crack" Japan's $32 billion telecommunications market (11–24–86, 102). How far along were they? They had only $186 million in business in 1985—0.6 percent of the market.

In its foot-dragging, NTT long claimed that American companies were inflexible and wouldn't adapt to Japanese specifications. Very likely, given American unwillingness to export, this claim was partly true, but as a blanket for all American companies in high technology, the claim is unbelievable.

Despite large sales in Japan, even IBM was viewed in 1987 as an outsider, a *gaishi* (foreign) company that had to buck a "buy-Japanese" mentality (*Business Week*, 2–2–87, 71). This was in a country where to be foreign was often to be a freak (*Forbes*, 7–14–86, 88); where foreigners were not considered human beings (*Manchester Guardian Weekly*, 12–29–85); where all foreign residents, even Americans married to Japanese natives, were forced to be fingerprinted (*New York Times*, 3–29–84, A2).

Motorola, which has a successful record making and selling in Japan, fared worse than IBM. To get into the cellular car-phone business, it first agreed to provide a competitor with cellular phones and transmission equipment. Then it proved that its product worked well with NTT's system. But for all of Motorola's efforts, the Japanese government gave 70 percent of the business to that famous electronics company, Toyota—yes, the car maker (*Business Week*, 2–23–87, 122J). Oh, What a Feeling!

Saying all this of course doesn't excuse American managements from evading their responsibilities to market properly in Japan—or in the U.S.

Despite subsidies and Japan's past natural advantages as a

follower (it's always easier and cheaper to copy than create technology when it's given away), Japan has had a most powerful, unwitting, and witless ally. A large part of American management has failed to use America's own inventions and discoveries and the people who make them. And it has ignored developments in Japan and failed to adapt to Japanese (and other) market demands.

The result is that a growing list of consumer products and high-technology products cannot be made at all in the U.S. That too has absolutely nothing to do with "labor costs" and is a colossal management failure.

Military Spending. For years American governments have been trying to force Japan to spend more on arms, and Japan has been resisting. Aside from the considerable potential dangers to world peace from an arms race with an insecure and newly militaristic Japan, military spending has become so destructive to the economy that America should be emulating Japan by seeking ways to reduce expenditures on excessive, unreliable, and expensive weapons.

A strong defense is unquestionably needed, but the present means of achieving it are open to severe criticism. And they must always be open to criticism for reasons of national security. Open criticism is the only way to introduce "free-market" efficiencies into military policy and production. Books have been written, but here are a few ways that Japan has major industrial advantages for not having a military economy:

Military spending costs a lot. That means higher government spending, higher taxes or borrowing, higher interest rates, and perhaps a higher-priced dollar in foreign currency markets due to higher interest rates.

Military spending is inflationary. It puts money into the economy through payrolls and profits, but military products cannot be bought by that money, and military production takes productive resources out of the civilian economy. The effect on the economy is to increase purchasing power but decrease products that can be purchased. It is like purely printing money, which is pure inflation. All these things raise costs, prices, and lower international competitiveness.

Simultaneously, military spending lowers employment in several ways compared to equal amounts of money spent on civilian projects. First, tax money spent on a tank creates no jobs but the jobs of building, housing, running and repairing that tank. Otherwise the tank just sits there and does no one any economic good. But tax dollars spent on roads, for example, create construction and many other jobs. Roads mean that people can travel, build, and trade. That means jobs for car making, home building, banks, real estate, trucking, insurance, leisure, retail services and trades, and every other business activity flowing from them. And, for the benefit of those who hate government spending of any kind, most of these jobs are in the private sector.

Second, money spent on weapons goes to relatively few people. Profits are high, but employees don't get them. And the employees themselves tend to be engineers, administrators, lobbyists, and other highly paid professionals. The higher the pay, the fewer the people who can be paid out of a given budget. So fewer people are employed, and they are less likely to spend their money on goods and services that will employ less-skilled working people. There is less stimulation per military buck too.

Third, military spending diverts efforts toward products that cannot sell in the civilian economy. Even the computer chips that missiles must have are different from personal computer chips. No home computer user needs a chip that is "hardened" to survive a nuclear explosion! This diversion inhibits development of products that people can use and buy and opens the door to foreign—especially Japanese—competitors who will offer attractive consumer products. Consequently, more jobs are lost.

Fourth, military spending encourages production inefficiencies. The entire process is full of bureaucracy and lacks a market to keep it honest. Frequently, contracts are not awarded on a competitive basis, and often all costs are paid for, plus a percentage profit. A manufacturer can hide an awful lot of waste and unmerited costs (including fraud and graft) in that "cost-plus" system, all the while claiming a low official "profit." And of course the Pentagon has subsidized costly, deficient, job-destroying forms of automation. Inefficient industries mean uncompetitive industries and eventually jobs are lost to foreign competitors.

All the while that the American government calls for "free trade" to increase competitive pressure on American working people, it is increasing spending on military projects that drag down the economy and give Japan an advantage but make huge profits for America's rich and powerful.

Finally, by enriching a few, destroying jobs, raising taxes, and cutting social programs, military spending impoverishes the middle class, makes the poor destitute, and increases divisions in American society. "A house divided against itself cannot stand." Rampant military spending weakens America socially as well as economically.

"Labor Relations." The term "labor relations" often seems to be used by management as if management were a given constant and the only variable were what kind of labor management had to work with. But management is not a given. As we have seen, the quality—or lack of quality—of management is far more important than labor in many industries in determining economic competitiveness. And management invariably sets the tone of "labor relations" because management is the boss and has all the freedoms to act as it wishes toward workers. Workers—and unions—respond initially to management's treatment, not vice versa. Only later do workers' interactions feed back to affect management. And the terms "labor-management" relations and "management-labor" relations are hardly better because they imply an equality between workers and bosses that simply does not exist.

If management wants cooperative labor, all it has to do is treat employees well. Where management gives a little cooperation and fair rewards for good work, it gets a lot of cooperation in return from employees. Anyone with some work experience knows this, but it runs so much against the grain of "management prerogatives" that it is virtually buried by the reporting media. Publications that attempt to provide useful information for business and have strong, pro-business credentials occasionally and quietly remind management that workers are not their enemy.

"For high wages, a company might expect to get high productivity. But it doesn't. It gets *exceptionally* high productivity. One of the biggest mysteries in today's uncertain economy is that so few management people realize this." This quote was selected by *Forbes* Editor-in-Chief Malcolm S. Forbes from an article in the *Wall Street Journal* by John A. Patton, a management consultant (2–28–83, 20).

Once more from Malcolm S. Forbes: "On the sound premise that better quality results when workers are happy on the job, Ford CEO Phil Caldwell started asking what would make them so.... The amazing and most productive by-product, President Don Peterson told us, was the range of highly usable suggestions for ways of doing their jobs better and more quickly" (*Forbes*, 2–28–83, 18).

If there are "so many" uncooperative unions, then it is the surest sign that managements are failing to treat their employees well. When many bosses say "cooperation," they don't mean the respectful give-and-take among equals. Except in some small businesses and high-tech fields where employees have valuable knowledge, and true cooperation is cultivated as a necessity, many bosses mean by "cooperation" that they want virtually slave-like compliance. And slave-like labor is just what they get in many of the less-developed countries they export jobs to.

"Management gets the kind of union it deserves" is a well-known saying in some business circles. It eloquently admits that uncooperative workers and unions result from heavy-handed, insensitive, arrogant, incompetent, or brutal bosses. But failing businesses also result from such bosses. Unions claim that managements in autos and steel, especially at the plant and floor level, are often arrogant and uncooperative. Not by coincidence, those industries are on the ropes and individual companies are failing or are on the verge of bankruptcy. *Business Week* has often mentioned within reports that management, especially in steel, creates labor trouble with arrogance or bad faith.

United Steelworkers members felt betrayed and became fighting mad when U.S. Steel announced it would close its large Fairless Works near Trenton, New Jersey, after previously demanding and then getting pay cuts in return for preserving jobs. What happened? U.S. Steel decided to import steel from Britain—despite being one of the loudest complainers against "subsidized" foreign competition (*Business Week*, 4–11–83, 34). Why should any worker agree to "give-backs" when jobs will be exported anyway, and the remaining American workers will just have to work for less? Why should any worker cooperate when management is so quick to go back on its word and betray workers? And why should Americans feel sympathy for company managements that abandon America and betray American jobs?

In another case, Teamster machinists and ground workers for Western Airlines were "so upset [by a bonus for nine Western executives] that they have canceled a six-month, 10 percent wage cut agreed to earlier" (*Business Week*, 4–18–83, 44). That was while Western expected to report a first-quarter operating loss substantially greater than the $6 million of a year ago. Here, management caused "labor" trouble, directly raised business costs, and endangered a weak company with its own outrageously high salaries.

Worrying about American industry's growing notoriety for shoddy merchandise, one *Business Week* editorial stated, "Achieving [quality] is not a matter of simply flogging the work force. It is a management responsibility, primarily that of top management" (11–1–82).

When industry consultants say things like "the real secret of Japan's success in automobile manufacturing is its freedom from restrictive union work rules" (John Holusha, *New York Times*, 3–23–83, A1), they are just scapegoating and finger-pointing, for they have only management to blame for uncooperative workers. But even if the charge were valid, the implied solution of giving management more power over workers is not valid.

Given the demonstrated inferior performance of many American managements, we have no reason to believe they could get better results even if unions caved in completely. All they could succeed in doing is to push workers to death. And in fact, they have always been very good at killing workers. That is why there are unions in the first place in so many dangerous industries.

If American companies have a "labor" problem, the problem is mostly with management—again!

Financial Dominance of Short-Term Accountants. Companies in America are increasingly dominated by financial gamesmanship on Wall Street. In 1984 for example, financial institutions accounted for 90 percent of the volume of shares traded on the New York Stock Exchange (*New York Times*, 11–25–84, F1). Raiders have repeatedly bought up and then sold off companies whose only "crime" was to invest and cultivate assets for long-term use. These long-term investments lower current profits, lower a company's stock price, and make a company vulnerable to being bought and broken up. To ward off raiders, many more corporate managements have done the same buying and selling themselves.

This short-term churning of the markets, fashioned by the super-liquidity trap, represents a major market failure for American capitalism. Few American companies can afford to work for years laying the groundwork in foreign countries to export successfully. Most successful Japanese exporters, however, worked many years to discover how to sell in America, which probably explains why Japanese claim America is not any more "open" than Japan, and why they say Americans can't sell in Japan because they don't put in the long-term effort to conform to Japanese standards.

At the same time that some companies were being broken up, many others were being bought up in a huge wave of what was called "merger mania" or "deal mania." Yet *Business Week* has estimated that between one-half and two-thirds of mergers in America "simply don't work" (6–3–85, 88). Is it any wonder?

Because the financial markets are so powerful, many companies are run by financial accountants rather than by marketing or production management. In addition, they hire and reward into high management positions large numbers of managers, including graduates fresh out of business school, who know the latest financial fads but who lack experience in production, sales, or engineering. Obsessed with the "bottom line," they see only arithmetic things like labor, material, and transportation costs, and they make decisions based on how their arithmetic comes out. And the trend is accelerating as "MBAs Are Hotter Than Ever" (*Business Week,* 3–9–87, 46). This can lead to some pretty clever but disastrous decisions.

It is like the TV sausage commercial in which a clever accountant tells the owner to use lower-quality meat because it will cut costs and raise profits. That is certainly an arithmetic truth, but an unreal conclusion. For as the small owner is quick to point out, if quality declines, so will sales, and then profits will fall more. Sound familiar? Just replace "sausage" with "auto."

You would think that with all the talk of cutting costs, the cost-cutters were accurately measuring costs. But astonishingly, they aren't. They aren't even identifying many of them.

President James A. Henderson of Cummins Engine, which prevented Japanese engine producers from getting a foothold in the U.S. market in the mid-80s for heavy-duty trucks, discovered in the process that "one of the things that nobody's cost system tracks very well in this country is overhead" (*Forbes*, 7–14–86, 83).

In "Cost Accounting's Blind Spot," John Holusha, the *New York Times'* excellent reporter on the auto industry, wrote that "what standard accounting procedures failed to see were some of the intangibles in [advanced production technology]—improved quality, greater flexibility and lower inventories" (10–14–86, D1). In "Accounting in Factories Is Criticized as Outdated," he reported conclusions from the National Association of Accountants that there was "an excessive emphasis on labor costs" that led to "the use of direct labor as the critical variable in measuring costs" and "an inability to measure the benefits of improved product quality and service" (*New York Times*, 3–23–87, D1). In the companies studied, "direct labor only averaged 15 percent of total manufacturing cost, compared with 53 percent for materials and 32 percent for overhead." The obsession with labor "has resulted in less attention to material costs and the problems involved with excess inventory and has obscured the fact that overhead offers twice the opportunity for cutting costs than do workers on the factory floor."

Fortune (10–13–86, 70) and *Business Week* (4–20–87, 60) reported similar findings, as did *High Technology* in a report on military production (March 1987, 33).

Many reports and financial analysts seem unaware of how the accounting systems they have helped create imbalance the decisions management makes. In a typical report, U.S. tiremakers were said to have "substantially cut the cost of tiremaking in the U.S." by closing plants and spending heavily on automation (*Business Week*, 4–13–87, 92D). As in so many reports linking automation with cost cuts, no cuts in actual dollar costs were cited; only cuts in labor were cited, even though heavy automation can be so expensive it can actually raise costs. For example, Robert E. Mercer, chairman of Goodyear Tire and Rubber Co., claimed that Goodyear needed less than 10 man-minutes to make a 13-inch tire, while many foreign competitors needed 25 to 50 minutes. By equating labor cuts with cost cuts, the accounting system can make very expensive actions look cheap and force managers to cut labor rather than truly cut costs or raise efficiency.

Consequently, when financial managers talk of "cutting costs," they often merely mean firing people, cutting wages, and getting inexperienced personnel. Meanwhile, they fail to cut larger costs that are staring them in the face, and they raise costs and lose business due to breakdowns in quality, service, employee skills, and operational effectiveness. Even by their own professed standards of "controlling costs," the financial managers are way out of touch with reality and failing miserably.

Where do financial and money managers come from? One whom I spoke to graduated with an MBA from a prestigious Ivy League business school. She said the program was an easy way to get an advanced degree in a well-paying career; it wasn't hard like a real academic course. This is what she meant: When she entered the two-year program, she didn't know how to read the stock market listings in the newspaper. But two years later, she was investing millions of dollars for a city agency.

It is easy for financial people to embrace the antiunion, four-dragon squeeze. They have few human connections to production and working people. Employees are inevitably rivals for control (as well as rivals for the business's money). So financial managers are biased by the logic of the situation to see little good in human employees and lots of bad. It's only natural for them to resent and want to eliminate people.

Bankers add additional biases. They make money either by charging interest for loans or charging fees for mergers and acquisitions. They love to see managers buying expensive machinery and generally substituting capital for labor. And they love to see financial managers take control and then buy and sell companies, because it means more fees and profits.

Consequently, financial managers have little means or desire to measure the intangibles that profoundly affect business success, such as attention to detail, responsiveness to the market, organizational effectiveness, and a relentless drive for improvement (which are in fact the chief characteristics of winning Japanese companies).

And their efforts to cut costs by terminating people are more likely to terminate the business in the long run than save it.

Astonishingly, dominance by financial wheeler-dealers has not changed significantly in over 30 years, giving it roughly the same age as the antiunion squeeze, except to the extent that financial managers are more dominant than ever.

In 1986, *Business Week* reported that manufacturing was "a ticket to oblivion" in all but a few companies (5–19–86, 118j). The article quoted C. Wickham Skinner from 1969 to show that little had changed in 17 years. Managers who went into a factory or into product development could still expect mostly low pay, low respect, and lots of frustration and shoddy working conditions.

Nor was manufacturing alone in being neglected. According to *Forbes,* the same applied to managers in purchasing, data processing, real estate, and anyone with special skills or overseas experience (4–6–87, 162). Although these jobs vitally affect a company's costs, quality of production, and export sales, job placement experts described them as "murder," "deadly," "nowhere," "black hole," and "the worst career traps in business." In its special report "Can America Compete?" (4–20–87, 57), *Business Week* stated that as far back as the 1950s, "manufacturing had ceased to be a factor in strategic planning."

In 1987, the CBS Evening News (5–11–87) showed Tom Peters excoriating GM, saying that every time he got into his GM truck, nine defects in his car reminded him why he hated GM and would never buy a GM truck again. William Holden played an executive who said virtually the same thing in the 1954 movie *Executive Suite*. In that movie, accountants had gradually taken control of a furniture company and reduced its products from high quality to junk. In the fictional furniture company in the Hollywood movie, producers led by Holden's character won out in the end over the bean counters. But then that's what made Hollywood "Hollywood."

Sony Chairman Akio Morita says it would be easy for America to regain competitiveness. All American management would have to do is decide to "produce real things well" (*U.S. News & World Report,* 11–17–86, 57).

But of course, that can never happen on a large scale with financial managers in charge.

7

Failure and Irresponsibility of American Management

BUSINESS PEOPLE SAY AMERICAN MANAGEMENT HAS FAILED

American management's failures are well known but not widely known. Intense criticisms of management are voiced in business, the business press, and occasionally in the general press, but the reports are mostly sporadic, scattered, after the fact, and slanted to show improvement. The impression is given that even if management has its problems, the system is working to fix them. But just as with Japan, a closer analysis of these reports shows a very different story: a deep and worsening crisis that runs through all of American business and government.

Here is evidence that a large part of American management is falling down on the job:

Nuclear Power. In a cover story considered so important that the text was begun on the front cover, *Forbes* blamed the failure of the nuclear power industry in America on management, pure and simple ("Nuclear Follies," James Cook, 2–11–85). Calling it the "largest managerial disaster in business history," with $125 billion already spent and $140 billion to be spent before the end of the decade, the article says, "The truth is that nuclear power was killed, not by its enemies, but by its friends." That is, not by environmentalists but by the people who built and administered nuclear power.

Two years later the National Academy of Sciences reported that the Nuclear Regulatory Commission (NRC) was so riddled with egregious management problems that "nothing short of candor would have an impact" on changing it (*Science News,* 1–17–87, 38).

Candor: the last resort of management!

Nobody Asked. An interview with Tom Peters, the best-selling author and management consultant, echoes what many people who have worked with American managements already know. "The major failure of American business is seeing the employee as part of the problem instead of part of the solution" ("'Something Is Out of Whack' in U.S. Business Management," *U.S. News & World Report,* 7–15–85).

When Peters walked around a plant and talked to long-time production workers, they kept telling him of numerous improvements that could be made cheaply but never get done because "nobody asked."

Management sometimes does not want to know. I have in mind a computer center where I saw impending trouble very much like what I had gone through at Western Electric. I mentioned my concern to the data processing manager, but he sloughed it off with a wave of his hand and a shake of his head. Soon thereafter, that computer center began to have serious trouble. Twelve years later it was calling in computer consultants who, I was told, kept having to fix the same problems time after time.

It's bad enough when "nobody asks." But it's much worse when management wants to hear nothing from employees and shuts out what they say.

No Teamwork. A study by the U.S. Chamber of Commerce Productivity Center "pins the major blame for slowing efficiency on *stubborn management.* New techniques for sparking a team spirit among work forces have been largely ignored" (*U.S. News & World Report,* 8–24–81, 54). Neither this study nor a study from the Brookings Institution "gave much weight to the often heard contention that workers simply are not as smart or dedicated as they used to be."

Little Employee Involvement. According to a broadcasting council study on productivity, the main conclusion of many productivity experts was that the bulk of productivity problems rest on management's shoulders and that 90 percent of workers would do much better if management involved them in decision-making (National Public Radio, "Morning Edition," 2–15–83). Time after time, Japanese companies have bought out failing U.S. companies and the same "shiftless workers" have then equaled or outproduced their Japanese counterparts.

Office Work. Workers spend a lot of idle time "just waiting for material" from other departments. Because of this, "white-collar workers are unproductive at least four out of the normal eight hours" each day, and blue-collar workers work 55 percent of the time. Major blame is put on managers for not having adequate backlogs of projects to fill gaps (*U.S. News & World Report*, 6–29–81, 58; quoting Theodore Barry & Associates, management consultants).

Construction. As the construction industry appears to be similar to office work in the need to coordinate the hiring of temporary workers, so construction appears to be similar in how that work is managed. According to John Borcherding, associate professor of engineering at the University of Texas, construction workers at nuclear power plants spent 29 percent of their time waiting for tools, scaffolding, materials, or another crew. Another one-third of the time was spent traveling to get tools, going to the bathroom, taking breaks, getting instruction, and on other incidentals. When management made the effort, idle time was reduced considerably ("The Difference Management Can Make," *Forbes*, 7–6–81).

A similar conclusion comes from *Cockshaw's Construction Labor News & Opinion* as reported in *Forbes* (5–18–87, 17). Studies of productivity figures from the late 1960s to 1986 show that in the $377-billion-a-year construction industry, "construction crews do effective work for only two hours out of every eight. [They spent] a third of the day moving around a job site and another third waiting." And the problem was not union rules; 70 percent of work in 1986 was nonunion. Peter Cockshaw, who wrote the report, blamed general contractors for paying attention to legal and liability problems instead of carefully coordinating schedules.

These reports make clear why union construction labor can be cheap despite high wages. As Boston contractor Jim Ansara found out when he invited union labor in, a better coordinated work force can get much more work done. And the union workers did the co-ordinating themselves without expensive management overhead.

Productive Workers. Here are more productivity reports that debunk the talk of "lazy" American workers: The gross domestic production per employed person—roughly the average output per worker—in Japan in 1980 was only 70 percent of the U.S., and West Germany's was 90 percent (Jerry Flint, "The Myth of the Lazy American," *Forbes,* 7–6–81). And Marshal Loeb (WCBS radio, 11:40 A.M., 4–9–81) reported that the U.S. output per hour was 49 percent ahead of the Japanese and 17 percent ahead of West Germany.

Both Flint and Loeb give evidence that despite Japan's and Germany's obvious success in a few dramatic industries, many economic activities in those countries were less productive than in America. So on average, the U.S. was more productive. If workers get blamed when productivity is low, isn't it right to give them credit when productivity is high? If management is not com-petitive, shouldn't workers get even more credit for overcoming management's mistakes?

Flint's article similarly debunked the myth of cheap foreign labor. It showed U.S. unit labor costs in manufacturing were be-low West Germany's and comparable to Japan. Making the point repeatedly that Americans work hard and well—union and non-union alike—Flint concluded, "The American worker is taking the rap for a lot of things that his politicians and executives are doing wrong."

Steel. Calling the management of U.S. Steel Co. (now USX) "one of corporate America's most hierarchical and bureaucrat-ic," *Business Week* reported that transforming it into "a lean, aggressive, market-driven team" is such a "daunting task" that it is the toughest job in business ("The Toughest Job In Busi-ness," 2–25–85). Tougher, we presume, than competing against the Japanese. Steelworkers and their union, the United Steel-workers of America, have been saying this for decades.

Perhaps no one is more qualified to speak about the failings of major U.S. steel companies than the "father of the minimill," F. Kenneth Iverson, chairman and chief executive officer of Nucor

Corp., a highly successful "minimill" company that turns out finished steel from scrap metal. In an interview with *Inc.* (4–86, 41), Iverson made the following points:

- Major U.S. steel companies were so loath to modernize that "in 1980, [they] still had rolling mills that rolled steel back in the Civil War."
- The idea "that unions per se have a negative impact on worker productivity [is] nonsense!"
- "The real impediment to producing a higher-quality product more efficiently isn't the workers, union or non-union; it's management."
- He thinks U.S. steelworkers are not overpaid. They "earn every bit" of their relatively high wages. "What people forget is that in every industrialized country in the world, the steelworker earns more than the average industrial worker.... And there's a reason for it. It's hard, hot, dirty, dangerous, skilled work."

Iverson has only two layers of management between himself and foremen and consequently, even with workers earning $30,000 per year, he says he feels that "we can make bolts as cheaply as foreign producers and make a profit at it."

Autos. On the *MacNeil/Lehrer Report* (9–1–82), auto industry consultant James Harbour said that the problem in the auto industry was neither the hourly work force nor costly labor rates. Most of the problem was management systems. "We're talking about quality of work life.... We're talking about eliminating these enormous staffs of people who overcontrol.... We're talking about getting rid of inventories...two years ago you had the old Secretary of Transportation [Neil Goldschmidt] on your program...and he told you that was a major problem then."

Just in the Warehouse. The U.S. auto industry is a leading proponent in America of the Japanese concept of "just in time" (JIT), wherein supplies are delivered just in time to be used. This is supposed to cut warehouse costs. But the warehouse industry in Detroit is doing just fine, thank you (*Inc.*, 1–86, 18). Why? Auto makers "announced plans to switch to JIT without laying the groundwork, such as producing accurate schedules so suppliers could coordinate shipments. Rather than eliminating inventory, they have pushed it onto their suppliers." In *Inc.*'s opinion, "The Japanese must be laughing now."

Robots. On the *MacNeil/Lehrer Report* (11–26–82), Joseph Engelberger, an American inventor of robots, said the problem of American industry was with American management, not labor. Far more Japanese managers showed interest in his robots than did American managers. A Japanese film on using robots in auto making, shown in the same report, said that robots were needed in Japan because of a shortage of skilled workers—more proof that cheap labor was not Japan's main advantage in auto making, since that labor did not even exist.

Executive Polls. "Poor management is the greatest obstacle to productivity growth, [according to the] vast majority of 220 company executives surveyed by *Productivity,* a monthly newsletter.... The respondents gave little credence to the notion that a declining work ethic has slowed economic growth" (*Business Week,* 2–16–81, 34H). According to one executive, "U.S. management has got to stop looking for someone else to blame."

Of 101 service and manufacturing companies surveyed by Organizational Dynamics, a Burlington, Massachusetts, consulting and training firm, "fifty-nine percent put the blame [for low quality] on management shortcomings—inertia, resistance to change, lack of commitment, communication, strategy, etc.—and only 11 percent fault the rank and file" (*Forbes,* 4–27–87, 16).

Lagging Indicators. Speaking about the economy's future, Seymour Zucker, senior editor, economics, for *Business Week,* remarked that business executives' opinions are lagging economic indicators: They remain bullish well into a recession and stay bearish well into a recovery (WOR Radio, *Sherrye Henry Show,* 10:35 A.M., 1–27–83).

Looking backward is no way to run a business.

Uncontrolled Purchases. "Do corporations know what they spend?" No, according to a report in *Forbes* summarizing a survey by *Purchasing Magazine* of the 100 top industrial spenders. "In many cases, particularly among conglomerates, no one at the top level really knows what the company's buying total actually is" (12–15–86, 8).

Orders Without Follow-up. "When a captain of industry snaps out a command or fires off a memo, what happens? Half the time, nothing"—according to a six-month study of many firms by university professors J. Bonner Ritchie and Ray Miles. Sometimes the executive would "overcommit" his resources, so his people could not fulfill his commitments. Sometimes subordinates "didn't think much of the order and ignored it." And sometimes subordinates resisted out of spite. "Many of the executives [said] they never thought much about how their decisions would be carried out. 'These people,' said one of the authors, 'get caught in an activity trap, and the activity trap for managers is making decisions.'" (Trends, *Forbes*, 4–12–82).

Action Without Preparation. Describing the types of people who buy personal computers, *Personal Computing* magazine (December 1982) created this profile of "The Boss" from interviews with computer-store owners from New York to California: "He selects and buys the computer, takes the training, asks all the questions, then carries the system back to the office, dumps it on his office manager's desk and tells him to use it.... About four hours [after the boss leaves with the computer], the store telephone is ringing. It's the [boss's] secretary or office manager, hysterical because the machine has been left on his desk and now he's expected to run it."

Form Over Substance. In "Why So Many Bosses Fail in Their Jobs" (*U.S. News & World Report*, 9–17–79), Roland S. Parker, a consulting psychologist, says, "Almost always it's a mistake by management, either in the hiring process or in the way the company is run.... A good many executives in responsible jobs get by on style rather than on substantive ability." He also blames promoting competent people into jobs they are unsuited for.

In other words, management not only cannot manage employ-

ees and capital and technology and marketing and production ad
infinitum, it can't even manage itself.

Professional Ignorance. A recurring theme in many analyses is
management's inexperience in manufacturing, marketing, and engineering. In "Major Cause of Business Problems: Poor Managers,"
Professor Robert H. Hayes of the Harvard Business School said
that at least 50 percent of business problems can be traced to bad
management (*U.S. News & World Report,* 12–8–80, 69). One problem: Financial and legal specialists have been replacing production
and marketing experts in top management. Another: Top executives change frequently, and with every change the new boss brings
in old friends and associates rather than trust the people already
there. So organizational structures then change, experienced people then have to change jobs, there is less "hands-on knowledge,"
and corporate strategies change frequently.

Arch Patton, retired director of McKinsey & Co. (a consulting firm), blames "industry's misguided shift to staff jobs" (Ideas
& Trends, *Business Week,* 4–5–82). "Staff positions have far out-
stripped line jobs in number and influence.... Bright people have
gotten the message. They avoid line jobs. Japan, on the other
hand, wants its brightest men in line jobs. After all, that is what
manufacturing is all about."

A report entitled "Business Refocuses on the Factory Floor"
(*Business Week,* 2–2–81) tells a similar story of a decade of management neglect for the fundamentals of production that caused
"products [which] are too costly to produce or too shoddy to
sell."

In "A New Target: Reducing Staff and Levels" (*Business
Week,* 12–21–81), "Management experts say...corporate streamlining is long overdue. 'Ever since the 1960s, when we started
believing that a professional manager can manage anything, we've
been on the wrong track,' claims John M. Stewart, a director at
McKinsey & Co. Stewart notes that companies rotated managers randomly among divisions. The new managers, unfamiliar
with the businesses they were expected to run, hired staffs to
advise them. When they moved on, a new manager repeated the
cycle. 'The problem was compounded when companies started
going international.'"

A Japanese View. Discussing economic growth, Saburo Okita, whom *Forbes* called one of Japan's leading economic planners, repeatedly stressed that technology and management are the decisive factors ("Innovate or Die," 11–1–81). We can add that applying technology is the responsibility of management.

Corpocracy. President Reagan's Secretary of Commerce, Malcolm Baldrige, charged that American business management is too fat, too dumb, too happy. Declining productivity is the fault of American management, not labor. Management should become sharp, lean, and hungry (Ken Prewitt, WOR-TV, New York, *News 9 at Noon,* 10–1–81).

A year and a half later, Baldrige repeated: Management is responsible for America's sorry record on productivity, and workers are not responsible. Management rested on its laurels in the 1960s and 1970s, and U.S. management pursued short-term, quarterly profits instead of the long-term goals of U.S. foreign competitors (WPAT Radio, Patterson, New Jersey, approximately 5 P.M., 4–1–83).

Distrust. According to a report in *Business Week* in 1981 (12–21–81, 69), Donald E. Petersen, then president of Ford, commented, "In the U.S...top executives assume they cannot trust their subordinates, so they added layers of staff to check on line operators. The result is confrontation, delay in decision-making, exploding costs, and a deterioration of the business. In their struggle for power, the staff people too often ignore the problems of the business, seeking what is best for themselves instead of what is best for the company."

Chaos. "Listening to the Voice of the Marketplace" (*Business Week,* 2–21–83) tells how companies failed to match their products to market demand. That is pure management failure. It also tells how engineering, manufacturing, and marketing must be coordinated so that each is working for the same goal, and each tailors its work to the others' needs. Disorganization is also a pure management failure.

Business Week's special report, "A New Era for Management" (4–25–83), tells one of the most detailed and extensive horror stories of chaos in management that this reader has yet seen in the business press. The purpose of the report appears to be not to discredit management, but to defend it by saying that management is at last changing, and to give positive examples for others to learn from. However, it fails to answer how the top managers who allowed staff managers to acquire power in the first place can now get rid of them and manage without them. In other words, if management was incompetent, then how can it suddenly change if the same people remain in charge?

Can You Bank on It? Financial corruption spreads far beyond Wall Street. Insider abuse involves one-half of all bank failures (*Business Week,* 10–7–85, 78; CBS Evening News, 6–25–86). Bank employees reportedly steal eight times what robbers steal (*MacNeil/Lehrer News Hour,* 10–2–84). One estimate put 1986 bank losses from fraud and embezzlement at $1 billion (NBC Weekend News, 7–19–87).

Executive Pay. Management is growing increasingly unaccountable because the people who are supposed to evaluate management's performance cannot do the job, and no one can currently replace them. This story is told in "Executive Compensation: Looking to the Long Term Again" (*Business Week,* 5–9–83).

It tells how for almost 20 years, performance was measured and compensated based on earnings per share. But earnings could be easily manipulated by liquidating inventories, selling assets, or cutting needed research and development, for example. Indeed, executive pay, tied to earnings growth, "climbed at a virtually unbroken pace during the 1970s," demonstrating a "severed connection between work input and reward."

Consequently, *Business Week* said, boards of directors began to recognize that "another performance measure ought to be considered....[They talk about the] need to reforge the link between pay and performance." And management consultants began to discuss "nonfinancial milestones by which managers can be measured...combining management-by-objective with salary, bonus, and long-term incentive programs."

Unfortunately for the competitiveness of many U.S. companies, the article goes on to say that the "biggest obstacle" to changes in compensation is people at the chief executive level. Pointing out once more that CEOs have become accustomed to seeing their salaries rise almost automatically regardless of their performance, the report predicts they will be loath to tie their compensation to long-term results, which take longer to bear fruit and are inherently riskier. And CEOs' ability to command boards of directors makes changes even harder.

Finally, the article quotes a consultant who speculates that golden parachute contracts, 70 percent of which paid over $1 million in 1983, are so comfortable that they are bound to affect CEO behavior. Under such contracts, CEOs could "live better if they bail out" as their companies fall in takeovers.

Many things wrong with management and its overseers become apparent from this story: Broad measures and broad incentives that focus on average performance substitute for detailed evaluations of each manager's performance. Why? Presumably because no one presently knows enough to evaluate what each manager does, or those who do know, such as working people, are not trusted to do so. Or those who may know, such as chief executive officers—the top bosses—cannot be trusted to do so.

Current business analysts and overseers can't find a workable standard to hold management accountable because they are outside the company's internal operations. Market analysts, boards of directors, investors, management consultants, even CEOs—all the people who ostensibly are management's boss—can't look at each individual manager and say how well he or she is doing. Because they can't do management's job, and don't work with management, they can't use internal, discriminate, detailed, and realistically flexible measures to evaluate and reward each individual manager on his or her performance. So they must resort to all these fancy external measurements—mere average indicators—to judge management, and they must use the same *average* measures to reward *individual* managers.

Finally, we see that despite all the brave talk in the subtitle that "Managers' Salaries Are Now Tied More Closely to Their Successes—or Failures," even the new measures are still average measures and don't get at the root of the problem of evaluating each individual manager's performance inside the company. And the top executives, who are the real bosses, will not allow detailed evaluations to take hold, since they themselves will be hurt most.

Two examples in the story reveal that management's attitude toward its own people is still in the Dark Ages, as if even middle managers were dumb and untrustworthy animals to be mastered and used up.

Having gotten rid of about half of Mead Corp. Containers Division's 20 general managers, division President A. Clark Peters III declares, "We've arrived at a stable of thoroughbreds."

Despite high prices for thoroughbred horses these days, most thoroughbreds are run like businesses to recoup investments. They are broken down by overuse and then shot. Many managers in American business also break down or burn out from overwork. They are not shot, but they are often abandoned.

Also quoted is Robert S. Kaplan, outgoing dean of Carnegie-Mellon University's Graduate School of Industrial Administration: "'We know if we put rats into a maze and feed them for going one way, that's the way they'll go. If we want managers to do something different, we should pay them for doing something different.'" This gives new depth to the expression "rat race."

These quotes from *Business Week*'s report of May 9, 1983, suggest an attitude that top management, and the people who nominally oversee management, view individual middle managers as animals to be trained and beasts of burden to be worked. Is it any wonder that "attitude surveys conducted by Hay Management Consultants suggest that communications between executives at the top and the middle have never been worse" ("As the Rules of the Game Change, the Faithful Feel Betrayed," *Business Week*, 4–25–83). Or that "middle-management anxiety can wreak havoc." And that "top managers themselves are not sure what their next steps will be."

If privileged managers have been treated so impersonally, just imagine how hourly workers are and have been treated, and imagine how that kind of brute treatment can cause problems with "labor relations."

Business Week's two major reports (4–25–83 and 5–9–83) on American management make several things strikingly clear:

- For a long time, managers were not being paid according to their performance. That is why the link between pay and performance must be reforged. And that is why many

corporate managements, and many American businesses, have failed or suffered such hard times.

- There is considerable confusion and disagreement about
  how to best measure and reward management. That
  means the management "experts" have no convincing solution to the problem of management's unaccountability.

- All these measurements are done by people outside the
  work environment, and the measures themselves consist of average financial figures totally unrelated to each
  individual manager's work contribution. That is why
  their solutions are not convincing.

- Any change must begin at the top, for that is where
  orders originate, but that is also where unaccountability is greatest, and where resistance is greatest to holding management accountable for its actions. That is why
  whatever solutions are attempted will not go to the root
  of the problem and will not solve the problem.

- Working people, even middle managers, are not valued
  for what they can contribute. Rather, they are treated as
  dumb brutes to be used up and discarded. That means
  that the proper and most promising solution—of raising
  quality by rewarding internal feedback within organizations—will not be attempted.

These reports give a damning portrait of the "boss" in business or government. He gives the orders, doesn't think how they
will be carried out, and has little practical experience due to rapid
job changes or inappropriate promotions. Therefore he doesn't
know how orders will or should be carried out, doesn't give instructions, presumably doesn't know what instructions to give
(due to inexperience), doesn't follow up, paralyzes everyone in
distrust, ignorance, and mutual conflict—and then blames subordinates when things don't turn out right. Top executives command high pay, and the higher the pay, the less accountable they
become.

Not every manager has all these faults, and many working
managers don't deserve to be associated with the faulty managers, but many more faults can be added to the list, including fa-

voritism, nepotism, laziness, corruption, and outright crime. The miracle is that any of these people stay in business. The bigger miracle is that working people continually bail them out. And the greatest injustice is that working people continually get nothing but criticism, abuse, and blame for their heroics.

Even if employees had nothing to contribute on their own—though in fact they have enormous amounts of energy, information, and organization to contribute—there must be a place for employees in management just to keep higher management honest and accountable. No one else seems able to do it. And we really can't afford to have foreign competition destroy a substantial part of American industry as the price to pay for forcing American management to improve—perhaps by only a little.

MANAGEMENT'S ABDICATION OF RESPONSIBILITY FOR PRODUCTION

In the huge wave of stock market and junk-bond deals that began in 1983, corporate raiders and "sharks" seized on growing concerns about corporate accountability to legitimize their takeover attempts. They made the claim that they would clean out bad managements and keep good ones from going bad. Unfortunately, the raiders and sharks were themselves so unaccountable that they wreaked havoc. And top corporate executives eventually developed many strong defenses against hostile raids. These defenses ranged from changing corporate bylaws and installing expensive "poison pills" to beating raiders to the punch: Managements initiated mergers, acquisitions, buyouts, selloffs, and "recapitalizations" themselves.

In its May 18, 1987, cover story, "Corporate Control: Shareholders vs. Managers," *Business Week* reported a new effort by shareholders, led by pension funds, to get control of professional managers. It concluded with the brave words "From now on, executives will have to be much more accountable for their performance." But the article had to admit that the balance in power between management and shareholders was only "beginning to shift." Such caution is well founded. Corporate management's power is deeply rooted in the basic top-down, bureaucratic way business and government are managed, and American markets accommodate themselves to it rather than attempt to change it.

The question of management's accountability is actually several questions, and each has multiple answers: To whom is management accountable? To whom should it be accountable? And for what?

Corporate managements have an explicit accountability to their owners and creditors, who usually demand some mixture of profit, growth, and market share. But corporate managements also have an implicit *responsibility* to serve the interests of customers and employees, for economic as well as moral reasons. And management generally has an implicit responsibility to the public to produce things that create prosperity and national security. Indeed, the public is led to believe that management makes profits precisely by being productive.

However, management has many ways to escape accountability. And the forces that hold management most accountable are often at variance with production. They undermine management's desire and degrade its ability to provide prosperity and security for customers, employees, and the general public.

Concentration of Power

Corporate and government managements have significant freedoms and powers to avoid or disregard serious accountability to anyone.

Monopoly Power to Act. Top management has a monopoly of power over the organization and command of large enterprises in business and government. Stockholders and the voting public may have a theoretical veto over management, but they cannot substitute for or replace management in its entirety, except to play musical chairs with other managers. It is like the hirings and firings of managers in professional baseball when one team fires a manager and another team then hires him. Many more managers get shifted from team to team than actually leave or enter the ranks each year. Similarly, individual managers may be sacrificed occasionally, but the managerial bureaucracy as a whole survives.

Survival of the Biggest. Some companies are so large that they dominate by sheer size, or are able to coast for a long time on enormous momentum before management's faults catch up with them. And in any period of high interest rates and credit crunches, survival often goes not to the best, but to the biggest, which have enough resources to ride out the storm.

Corporate managements do of course have to serve the marketplace somewhat, but competition is often limited to a few companies in many goods and services, and the presence and resources of giant corporations effectively shut out smaller competitors. As long as managements don't break down entirely, or at least if they perform in an average way, they can get by on sheer momentum and have considerable freedom to serve themselves and escape responsibility.

Monopolies, cartels, and other competitive restraints do have a way of degenerating of course, as the U.S. auto and steel industries have learned. Someone always comes along eventually with a cheaper or better product and consumers buy these alternatives. Indeed, beginning in the mid-1970s, a new, worldwide bout of competition opened up to keep managements hopping. But bureaucracies can take a long time to respond to competition, and then they may be too late.

Until they are forced to compete, bureaucrats will continue to serve themselves. And after the current bout of world competition is resolved, new global monopolies or cartels may arise that will stifle the world economy and leave bureaucrats more secure than ever—sort of a Pox Ameri-Japanacus.

Mutual Self-Support. Corporate management can escape accountability for production by getting government to supply tax breaks, contracts, loan guarantees, price supports, and bailouts. Corporate management controls huge amounts of money and effort that go into political campaigns, and huge numbers of administrators and executives in government come directly from business and go back to business when they leave government. Also American governments generally leave production to the private sector. Government bureaucrats and corporate managers are two identifiable, overlapping segments of the larger self-sustaining, self-serving class of managerial bureaucracy.

The American government too generates business for American companies and protects some marginal managements, especially among military suppliers. Foreign aid is often given so that recipient countries can—and must—buy American products. America's military and economic strength is used to bail out foreign blunders by private and corporate investors. Direct spending by federal, state, and local governments for public services and military contracts keeps many a fat and incompetent management rolling in dough.

If only one company or government agency had major faults in its management, it would quickly go bankrupt. But the faults are so commonplace among large corporations that the faulty managements confirm each other and support each other in their practices. In other words, when whole groups of companies have faulty managements, mediocrity survives and only the truly terrible—or daring—disappear.

The Insulated American Market. Special features of the American market still insulate many American managements from the most extreme pressures of global competition. The American market is the largest, most open market in the world. Being located in it gives many managers luxuries that foreign producers don't have. These luxuries include having lower transportation costs and larger economies of scale, being closer and more attuned to market tastes, and having easier access to American technology and skilled labor.

Divided Overseers. The people who oversee management have many divided interests and never speak with one voice. People such as consumers and citizens to whom management is implicitly accountable are similarly divided. The multiplicity of overseers and the divergence of their standards give management a great deal of freedom to play them off against each other.

A *Business Week* editorial acknowledged management's nimbleness (5–18–87). When management was criticized in the 1960s and 1970s by civil rights activists, environmentalists, and other social-issue pressure groups, it answered that it was obliged to promote the interests of the legal owners of its corporation and not get involved in social goals. Yet when those legal owners began to call management to task in 1987, it replied that it had employees, customers, suppliers, distributors, and communities to serve as well as shareholders. The chairman of Champion International Corp., Andrew C. Sigler, even asked, "What right does someone who owns the stock for an hour have to decide a company's fate? That's the law, and it's wrong" (*Business Week*, 5–18–87, 103).

Precisely because the public became alarmed over destructive raider tactics, many states passed laws to restrict what pressure shareholders can put on management. A law passed by Indiana and upheld by the U.S. Supreme Court in 1987 appears to have particularly disturbed supporters of corporate raiders ("Life Tenure for Managers?" *Wall Street Journal*, 4–23–87, 32; *Forbes*, 5–18–87, 33). At the time of this writing, many other states are expected to follow Indiana and add or strengthen barriers to hostile takeovers ("Ebb in Takeovers Foreseen," *New York Times*, 4–23–87, D1).

Control of Voters. In capitalism, the checks and controls on bureaucracy leave a lot to be desired. In many large companies, management effectively controls the stockholders' vote through proxies and controls boards of directors by appointing board members. In some cases a few stockholders holding a large, minority block of stock may exercise effective control, but then management serves that minority and not necessarily the interests of the corporation as a whole. And in reward for not fighting the private interests of dominant stockholders, management may be left in peace to escape responsibilities.

Most stockholders are perfectly willing to cede day-to-day freedom to management. Usually they buy stock precisely to share in profits without having to become bothered in operations. As a consequence, short of getting into serious difficulties, many managements are effectively their own bosses. In government, politicians and bureaucrats are so remote from the average citizen that they too escape effective public control, except in the most flagrant cases of abuse.

Perhaps most insidiously, bureaucratic managements in business and government, capitalism and communism, control voters by controlling the information voters get to make decisions. In America the control is rarely through outright legal censorship, but information is presented in the way most favorable to whatever management is in question. Whole batteries of experts, writers, public relations people, professional journals, and think tanks labor enormously to present information that defends corporate management in general, and sometimes government, against serious damage.

Pressed-on Teflon. Usually, the press gives the impression that workers are to blame for falling American competitiveness. That impression absolves management of blame, and the news media share in management's blame by not helping correct management's failures.

In a stunning example of how the press tries to put Teflon on management, *Fortune* (9–15–87) did a cover story on Ronald Reagan's management style just two months before the Iran-Contra scandal broke. In "What Managers Can Learn from Manager Reagan," President Reagan is pictured facing the reader with his arms folded, smiling confidently, in command, saying, "Surround yourself with the best people you can find, delegate authority, and don't interfere."

Markets and the Profit Motive

Markets and the profit motive are supposed to keep corporate managements accountable. But with the super-liquidity trap at work, that accountability degenerates all too often into serving greed at the expense of production and the public.

Profits, Profits, Profits. The profit motive is a mixture of blessings and curses. On the plus side, the profit motive can move people to work harder and better than they would if they didn't have a stake in the results. It requires that economic functions be profitable, or at least self-sustaining. In a general sense beyond economics, everything and everyone must pay their way somehow, by some process, in someone's or some group's estimation or feeling. Love, fear, and hate create labors and payoffs that money never does. Government "services" are paid by taxes because society judges that the services are valuable, although not strictly "economic."

The divisions of labor in modern economies, and widespread differences among people's circumstances, guarantee that goods and services will constantly be exchanged. People will always be looking and working to turn those differences and exchanges to their advantage. And markets will inevitably develop to accommodate such efforts. These profit motives and markets must be dealt with realistically. They can be neither eradicated nor worshiped.

Fickle Profit Motives in Controlled Markets. On the negative side, the profit motive too often operates blindly, causing frequent and dangerous disturbances as huge amounts of wealth flow rapidly around the world; or else, those who are extremely rich have no interest in profits at all except to preserve or increase their power, so they use their wealth against the public good.

Currently in America, enormous amounts of wealth are administered by financial, corporate, and government bureaucracies. They are so big, and they herd together so closely, that when they stampede, they wreck normal markets and destroy the theoretical efficiencies of market economies. Being big and bureaucratic, they are nearsighted or insensitive about what is really happening in the world. And they serve the interests of their own institutions before they serve the economy or society. When the profit motive works through them it works nearsightedly, insatiably, and with knee-jerk abruptness. Corporate and government managements feel compelled to flog workers or ignore the public interest to ring up immediate profits at the expense of long-term growth or social health.

Experts Can Be Wrong. Financial markets operate on the opinions of expert analysts and experienced executives. But when experts disagree, who can be believed?

When the chairman of First Chicago Corp. (the holding company for First National Bank of Chicago) left his job, *Business Week* (8–4–80, 64) found much to fault in him. Yet he was soon hired as president of Occidental Petroleum, and *Forbes* was quick to defend him ("A Question of Loyalty," 9–1–80).

Even in the absence of controversy, the "experts" can't be depended upon. When market analysts arrive at an overwhelming consensus, the stock market usually—but not always—does something very different. That at least can be explained if, by heeding the analysts' advice, investors change the situation and thus change the outcome. This is an application of the Uncertainty Principle of nuclear physics to the stock market: We change in unknown ways the very thing we are trying to measure, because the tools we use are large compared to the things we are trying to measure, and we disturb the objects of measurement when we measure them. But sometimes the experts are dead wrong.

When the oil boom went bust in Texas in late 1982, Penn Square Bank collapsed and caused a large loss for Continental Illinois National Bank & Trust Co. of Chicago. *Business Week* reported that the large losses "are only a symptom of a management malaise at the Chicago bank" (10–11–82, 82), but just four years earlier, "*Dun's Review* gave the bank its highest accolade by naming it one of the five best-managed U.S. companies." How bad had management been in reality? Continental Illinois's losses were so huge that they had to be bailed out by a "$7.5 billion rescue line" from the FDIC and money-center banks ("Who Was Watching the Store?" *Forbes*, 7–30–84). This, despite the fact that "the cream of Chicago business" sat on the bank's board.

It is scary that so much money and power is in the hands of so few people who know so little about what they are doing. They can ruin a company, as they almost ruined Texas Instruments Inc.

The Home-Computer Debacle at Texas Instruments. The institutions that dominate financial markets in America, such as mutual and pension funds, report the results of their investments quarterly. Every three months they are liable to stampede out of what has fallen out of favor and into what has become the latest fad. In mid-June 1983, following a report of losses in its home-computer business, the stock of Texas Instruments fell 40 points in one day, and 11 points the next, for a drop of 32 percent in two days. Clearly, the markets had overvalued the stock, and then had overreacted to bad news.

Most market analysts blamed TI for not warning them of the size of the losses ("Texas Instruments and the Analysts: Love Was Blind," *Business Week*, 6–27–83), but the problem was out in the open to anyone who understood computers. Basically, TI tried to use its home computer as bait to sell more expensive—and

profitable—add-on devices, so-called peripherals. Without the peripherals, the computer was little more than a fancy toy or game.
It's the razor-blade strategy of practically giving away razors to
sell razor blades. Apparently, TI also hoped to sell lots of computers, making up for low price with high volume ("How Texas
Instruments Shot Itself in the Foot," *Business Week*, 6–27–83).

TI priced its home computer low to attract a large customer base.
But those customers were too unsophisticated and inexperienced
to know they would have to buy a lot more equipment to use the
machine, they had spent too little to commit themselves to much
greater expenses, and many were not affluent enough to spend any
more. TI's customers must have been shocked, felt betrayed, and
refused to be suckered into a long series of expensive purchases.
When faced with the huge added costs, they gave up on the computer and TI.

That problem should have been foreseen by analysts. When I
went Christmas shopping in 1982, it was obvious that most of the
home-computer makers were charging too little for the computer's
system unit and too much for the peripherals. They were making
hyperbolic claims for the low-priced machines, and I certainly resented it. In the first half of 1983, led by TI's price-cutting, home-
computer prices dropped even further, from several hundred dollars
to one hundred dollars or less. In short, they used sales tactics like
the "low-ball" price of a stripped car. But to complete the analogy, a used-car salesperson would have to go further and say, "So,
now that you bought your car, you want seats and a transmission!
That costs more!"

TI got burned by misreading the consumer, and analysts should
have known better. They could have known if they had "gotten
their hands dirty"—which some management gurus forbid—by studying the product, playing with the keyboard, and asking how many
peripherals consumers would buy. But they didn't, and their failure sent TI stock on a roller-coaster ride.

The analysts failed in the same way that much of professional
American management fails, by being too far removed from the
details of their business and by concentrating too much on ques-
tionable financial data. They fail to perceive what is actually happening in the business and thus make faulty decisions based on
their faulty perceptions.

Notably, TI was highly respected for its technology. Yet it has a history of failures in marketing consumer-technology products. In the 1970s, it led, then failed, in markets for digital watches and hand-held calculators. And it added the costly blunder in low-end home computers.

TI had strong technology and military contracts that enabled it to weather its blunders, but many other companies are not as strong. A 32 percent drop in their stock could result in anything from higher capital costs to decapitation: being taken over and dismembered by a raider.

Mispricing in the Markets. Another part of the problem with the profit motive is the failure of markets to put true costs on all economic activities. For example, electric utilities are not liable for the full damage that a nuclear accident could cause. Private insurers so feared a nuclear disaster that they refused to insure nuclear plants for full third-party liability.

As a result, under the 1957 Price-Anderson Act, the federal government limited the liability per nuclear plant to $560 million. That limit had grown by 1985 to only $630 million—far less than the potential damage that a nuclear accident could cause to people and property in surrounding communities. In addition, utilities paid insurance fees on only $60 million of that initial $560 million; the federal government guaranteed the rest of the liability coverage (*Nucleus,* a publication of the Union of Concerned Scientists, Summer, 1985, 4). Since 1957, the act has been modified at 10-year intervals so that utilities in 1987 purchase $160 million in private liability insurance and cover the remaining $470 million liability through a retrospective payment pool: All utilities would pay fees into a pool only after an accident occurred.

Consequently, nuclear power plants have paid much less in fees for liability insurance than a market evaluation of its true cost would dictate. And quite possibly, few commercial nuclear power plants would have been built without the federal limit on liability.

Secondly, the federal liability insurance does not cover property damage to the plants themselves, and utilities' own property insurance could be far too low; but Wall Street analysts don't realize the risks involved ("Electric Utility Analysts Almost Never Discuss Financial Impact of Accidents at Nuclear Plants," *Wall*

Street Journal, 3–18–87, 63). Another accident like Three Mile Island could easily cause damage to a nuclear plant that could exceed existing property insurance by $800 million plus "the hefty cost of repairing or tearing down the damaged plant."

Meanwhile, little money has been set aside to retire and clean up nuclear power plants after they end their useful lives. Retirement costs per plant are estimated in the billions of dollars, and "the U.S. has still not chosen a radioactive waste disposal site" (*Wall Street Journal,* 3–18–87, 6). Finally, nuclear-generated electricity got $15.6 billion in subsidies in 1984 alone from federal tax breaks, loans, and agency outlays (data from the Center for Renewable Resources, *Nucleus,* Winter 1986, 3). These subsidies were 74 percent of the price of nuclear energy and were 7 to 16 times the subsidies given to electricity generated by fossil or hydroelectric means.

For all these reasons, nuclear power was long artificially cheap and the market price of nuclear-generated electricity was much lower than it should have been.

Similarly, the cost of illnesses caused by industrial pollution is not born by polluters. The benefits of mass transit in large cities are only partially accounted for when government subsidies for mass transit are discussed. Discrimination against minorities exacts a high cost in crime, injury, fear, decay of the cities, and social turmoil, yet the efforts to eliminate the causes of discrimination are viewed only as costs and not as small investments to eliminate the far larger costs resulting from discrimination. And the biggest misprice of all: subsidies that lower the cost of foreign production and send jobs out of the U.S.

When markets fail to put the proper costs and prices on products, they do not calculate true or honest profits. Instead, they rob some activities of honest profits, create dishonest profits for others, and drive profits to the wrong activities and people.

In such markets, the profit motive fails to serve consumers' and the public's needs. Eventually it hurts the economy and costs business plenty. But "eventually" can take a long time. In the short run it can grossly enrich a greedy few, grind up countless working people, and leave the public impoverished and unserved. Now, however, "eventually" may finally be here. National productivity has suffered and American companies have lost their ability to compete in world markets. The near-sighted, knee-jerk, insatiable profit motive in a defective market has revealed itself to be self-defeating, destructive, and dangerous.

Bonuses for Failure. With all the supposed checks and balances, with all the analysts and their analyses, with all the talk of free-market competition and the profit motive to keep management "lean and mean," many people in top management in big businesses (and government bureaucracies too) have escaped accountability so much that many are actually paid for failing! The cost of golden parachutes and other outrageous severance bonuses greatly exceeds their dollar amounts. How many top executives would do their jobs differently and better if they really were to suffer badly for doing a bad job? This is where the American economy suffers its greatest market failure: in top management.

Government Replaces Failing Markets. As a consequence of the failures of profit motives and market forces, government bureaucracies have sprung up and taken power to perform services that markets fail to provide and that corporate managements are unwilling or unable to do.

When the market fails to price the effects of pollution, the government is forced to write environmental protection laws. When the market fails to price the costs to society and business vitality of unemployment, underemployment, and disabilities, the government is forced to write unemployment, disability, and antidiscrimination laws.

When companies sell products with dangerous or costly hidden defects, the government must regulate and prosecute them. In any market where consumers haven't enough information to make intelligent choices, or where they fear purchasing what the market offers (Tylenol, for instance), the government must create and enforce standards to give consumers enough confidence to buy.

When banks failed in the 1930s, the government had to step in to insure depositors and regulate financial institutions. That "big-government interference" preserved liquidity and saved the financial system. It ensured that banks and other financial institutions could have access to ready capital to fuel the economy. As bad as the Great Depression was, it might otherwise have kept sinking into a Great Black Hole. In all these cases, far from inhibiting business, government builds the confidence to support and underwrite huge businesses that could not exist without consumer confidence.

Paradoxically the bigger the government, the better for business in many cases. When the Reagan Administration got out of the business of regulation, state regulators stepped in and threatened to "balkanize the marketplace." Companies in such disparate industries as electrical appliances, industrial chemicals, and pharmaceuticals begged for federal regulation to recreate one large national market out of the 50 small state markets ("An Industry Asks for Regulation," *New York Times*, 2–17–87, A18). In addition, federal reregulation has been introduced increasingly to remedy the excesses or failures of deregulation (*Wall Street Journal*, 4–21–87, 1).

Unfortunately, while the government can work well, it usually works best when it facilitates or structures market actions, such as building roads or reassuring consumers about product safety. When markets themselves fail and the government steps in to *replace* rather than fix or redirect market actions, however, then government increasingly serves itself or the people and institutions it is supposed to regulate. It becomes increasingly susceptible to corruption and prone to break down.

When corporate or governmental bureaucracies fail, other bureaucracies are then created to check up on them. For example, the Food and Drug Administration checks on ethical drug companies. Financial analysts check on corporate and government accounts. And the Center for Disease Control at times checks up on the Environmental Protection Agency. But then they fight on such limited battlefields that they seem only to employ more bureaucrats but rarely reach clear resolutions and get effective results. And they serve narrow constituencies and themselves at public expense.

There is an astounding paradox in all this. The more that profit is relied on to hold corporate bureaucracies accountable and solve the nation's problems in an imperfect market, the more will be the need and demand for government bureaucracy to support or check up on dangerous market activities.

With thanks to James Thurber, bureaucracies rush in where

efficient markets fail to spread, and the ideal market is in heaven, but none of the bureaucracies are dead.

Under-Ruling Class. When top management is unaccountable, forging alliances and connections count more to executives than being productive. Top bureaucrats defend their ranks to defend themselves, much as the British upper classes do, or as bull musk oxen stand shoulder to shoulder and face outward in a circular formation, with cows and calves inside, to defend against predators. In America the process is not all that explicit, but defensive networks and informal human relationships exist nevertheless that are quite effective on average. In communist rule, the bureaucrats have no bosses—they are their own bosses and get away with murder. The only threats to their existence are foreign military threats or insurrections of workers, such as in Poland, when internal conditions become unbearably harsh.

People high in management bureaucracies hire and promote their own kind. It's not all corrupt: Management's role of policeman demands an implicit esprit of similar values and reactions. But it does lead to a self-contained and powerful—but small—class of people and groups running many big businesses and government agencies. The fact that these groups are mostly male, white, and exclusive adds barriers of race, sex, wealth, and culture to keep outsiders out. People in this class can raise their children in their own image and give their children the educations, values, expectations, connections, and "skills" they need to succeed—or at least imitate—them. Their children can learn what to do and who to see and have a huge advantage in becoming recognized and accepted as members of their parents' class.

Without new controls or superior alternatives to the bureaucratic system of management, managerial bureaucracies will continue to grow, acquire power, and eventually may come to rule in America as they rule in communism. And all the while they will drag Americans down into a second-class economic existence.

Super-Liquidity Stigmatizes Productive Managers

In many situations where a job has to get done, good managers must become involved in the work of people they supervise. But managers who do no such work criticize this involvement as an inability to delegate authority—a desire to be indispensable.

This stigma of production arises because the super-liquidity trap converts companies into liquid financial assets that can be bought or sold at any time. When a company "restructures" and converts from running buses to providing financial or computer services, or any time a raider or company takes over another company, the executives on top must become financial managers and must develop ways to "manage" companies about whose operations they know little or nothing. They reward and promote lower managers who develop financial skills and have the ability to step into and out of any job quickly and easily—to "manage" any job. They call this "professional management."

The financial markets and the money managers in them also fail to evaluate and reward productive managers. According to a survey of 1,400 institutional investors reported in *Business Week* (1–21–85, 99), less than 25 percent of the money managers cared about management competence, and only 4 percent cared about the quality of a company's products.

It may be true that a manager shouldn't get so wrapped up in tiny details that important executive tasks suffer, such as working with other managers and keeping track of budgets and projects. But managers must be in charge of production if work is to be done well. They must have a guiding knowledge of whatever work is at hand to evaluate and direct the work of employees. Such knowledge is also needed to make good budget estimates, make and keep job commitments, solve problems as they arise, motivate and reward employees, bring together resources and suitable employees, and help employees find better ways of getting work done, especially in many technical and skilled areas ranging from sales to office and service work.

Notably, criticizing managers for doing productive work values the form of authority over the substance of production. Bureaucracy does that by nature and rewards respect for authority—abject loyalty—over respect for production.

There is no crime in a bureaucracy worse than "blowing the whistle" or merely going over the boss's head. It is the surest way to lose one's job. No matter how right a subordinate may be about production, no matter how right a "whistle-blower" may be about waste, corruption, mistakes, or anything else, the person who appeals to higher authorities or involves outside allies is rarely rewarded. Even if the appeal succeeds, that person becomes suspect or tainted—a pariah—to all the rest, who see loyalty as the "prime directive."

Bureaucracies cannot allow gifted people to develop their talents fully. Exceptional talents would make them indispensable and give them a rival authority: the innate authority of superior production. Exceptions are likely only during emergencies. When production becomes essential for survival, the old chain of command may be temporarily suspended and the best people thrown into frenzies of activity to get the job done. But then they are burned up. And after the emergency passes, the old power structure of intertwined loyalties reasserts itself. At best, the most able performers who remain are thanked and retired, as General Kutuzov was replaced after he saved Imperial Russia from Napoleon in Tolstoy's *War and Peace*. Or else, able people may be promoted out of their areas of competence and put into areas where they are not competent, where they must lick boots to survive.

By basing the command of production on loyalty rather than merit, and by enforcing that loyalty through personal ties, management-by-bureaucracy creates a profound corruption that spreads everywhere and attacks every aspect of production. Productive and indispensable people, regardless of whether they are hourly workers or high-level experts or executives, simply cannot be rewarded as they deserve. Rewards go instead to those who are the most dispensable—the most worthless. The gifted are suppressed, the average is enforced—and lowered—and shoddiness is encouraged.

Good managers work hard, long, and well at production. It is tragic that they cannot be appreciated more and rewarded better in American management. But as long as super-liquidity reigns, financial managers will require a "controlling" bureaucracy to exercise authority, and working managers will continue to suffer the stigma of production.

"Military" Command Undermines Production

The kind of command structure that management creates in bureaucracies is more suited to military command than to production, as befits management's role as policeman for authority. The crucial difference is the difference between blind, unquestioning obedience and intelligent cooperation.

In parade-ground military theory, and it is bad theory because it is often contradicted in combat (the military equivalent of business emergencies), the soldier is not supposed to think about anything but carrying out his own assignment. He must perform his orders, and he must perform nothing but his orders. He must believe that the authorities know what they are ordering, and he must be willing to risk his life for the authorities.

But modern production is so complex and extended that no job can be isolated easily to a narrow circle of attention. The attempt to do so may increase the theoretical efficiency of each worker, but it can and often will destroy the efficiency of the larger organization. No one in a large company or in a governmental agency knows everything that is going on, and few if any realize the full interactions of their jobs with the work of everyone else.

To increase productivity, intelligent employees and managers must broaden their scope of vision to what is happening around them. They must open their minds to how they fit into the larger organization of production. They must question orders to understand them and to figure how to fulfill them, and sometimes they may have to oppose orders when the orders can lead to costly mistakes. Every working person must bring some measure of independence, intelligence, creativity, and courage to the job. Otherwise, the job will not get done properly, or it will never be improved. In fact, without constant adjustment to inevitable changes, job performance and productivity deteriorate. And the company will not develop new products or services that it needs to remain competitive in the future. Many of the same observations apply, too, to military situations, but that is another story.

Most important, few working people are willing to risk seriously their lives, health, or bodies for a mere job, unless they are destitute and desperate. If they believe that management is putting them at risk and is unconcerned about the dangers, they will be defensive and much less productive. They will reduce their behavior to the level of a dumb (meaning silent) private in the army: They will obey but will not contribute any more than they have to. And they secretly may obstruct production if they feel that they have to defend themselves. After martial law broke up Solidarity in Poland, underground resistance became widespread and one widely reported tactic was to obey orders dumbly and contribute nothing in the factories, counting on management's incompetence to screw up everything.

Management creates "bad labor relations" by being too authoritarian, too insensitive, too punitive—too military. But bureaucratic management is a policeman and can't escape its role entirely. So it can never utilize its workers most effectively or employ their abilities to the fullest.

Arrogance toward employees can easily build into a general arrogance that can be self-destructive. It can lead to disastrous failures in the marketplace, such as offending and losing customers or not making what consumers want. Texas Instruments is the perfect example. A company "infamous for arrogant marketing practices" (*Business Week,* 4–28–86, 68), TI was also characterized by "arrogance and insularity" in top management (*Business Week,* 6–10–85, 50). Arrogant insensitivity can also undermine or bring down governments, such as providing costly and unacceptable government services, running roughshod over citizens' rights, or pursuing foreign policies that are as brutal toward foreign nations and peoples as management can be toward citizens and workers.

Leading Japanese managements have actively solicited employee ideas and have been able and willing to pay to win cooperation from their employees. And they have been highly successful in marketing as well as production. Yet even they cannot escape the consequences of the police role. They get greater employee obedience, but they are also saddled with a higher degree of employee conformity, and they wonder if they can get more creativity out of their work force without reducing its obedience and loyalty.

There is an inevitable conflict between the brute force productivity that is created by management's role as policeman and the intelligent productivity that is needed to cooperate, communicate, adapt, and innovate. Management can seek some spot between the two extremes, but it can't do both. Because bureaucratic management can't or won't share power, credit, and rewards with employees, except to the degree that labor shortages or unions or legislation force upon it, it can't or won't give up the role of policeman. So bureaucratic managements, even the more enlightened kind, must always tend toward emphasizing or implying the dominance of dumb brute force over partnership and cooperation. Production must always suffer as a result.

When Management Abdicates Its Responsibilities, Everyone Else Suffers

Since bureaucratic management's primary role is to exercise or be a conduit for authority, its optimal goal is to delegate authority. In practice, delegation leads to getting away from the act of production, for delegation means getting someone else to do the work. To prove they are not doing work, professional managers can make having "clean desks" a matter of pride and competition. The idea is that as soon as something plops on the manager's desk, a manager should send it to someone who can do something about it.

This approach of directing others' work, but doing no work oneself, allows upward-moving managers to change jobs frequently and not stay long at any one job. They can keep their desks clean because they do so little; they just rely on experienced employees to do the work. Some managers openly boast that they do nothing, that they would be nothing without good people working for them. The irony is that the truer these boasts are, the less they are taken seriously: People who believe managers should work take the boasts as false modesty, while people who believe managers should not work take the boasts as evidence of good "management."

The concept of professional management creates enormous career opportunities for nonproducing managers. It allows professional managers to look for jobs in any company or government position instead of being tied to one single specialty of production. It's also an excellent cover to justify giving jobs or contracts to friends, family, and members of a manager's extended network.

But managers who do little work also learn very little. They may know all about the form of a business—its budgets, finances, deadlines—without knowing anything about its substance—its products, work force, technology, internal workings, customer base, competition, etc. They are truly the most dispensable of all, yet they are considered and treated as the most indispensable. Thus it is possible for people with little working knowledge to reach the top in management, as if being a chief executive officer were a talent in itself and were independent of the actual business the company is in.

As a matter of course, when top management delegates authority, it delegates responsibility for organization squarely onto the backs of lower managers, and they can dump responsibility onto workers and staff. When problems arise, employees quickly learn not to consult their boss unless they absolutely have to, because the boss may not be able to help, might hinder production by interfering, and would fault the employee for not doing whatever is "expected." Thus "delegation of authority" often degenerates into abdication of responsibility for production.

Not coincidentally, that abdication insulates management from the potentially disastrous consequences of its productive incompetence. Individual bureaucrats are adept at taking credit, avoiding personal responsibility, and blaming others, an ability that they share with the best politicians. Life in a bureaucracy isn't called "politics" for nothing. Lines of authority and responsibility can get so tangled that even when it tries, management can't get to the heart of many problems. Yet somebody usually must be blamed when things go wrong, so often the wrong people get blamed, and they are usually the lowest in authority—working managers, office staff, and workers.

Managements' abdication of responsibility can be seen every time any company runs into trouble. While upper managements take credit and get huge bonuses when business does well, they are still likely to get raises when business turns down. When there is trouble, they rarely say "It's my fault." Or when they do, they take blame for nothing in particular. Instead they blame government regulation—environmental rules are big scapegoats—high interest rates, unfair foreign competition, and a myriad of other factors. (Just read the excuses of U.S. Steel to get a long list.) Above all, they blame high wages and "restrictive work rules" and imply lazy or sloppy workers. Even when management accepts partial blame, it says now it is on the right track, and employees must still make up for management's past mistakes.

Every time management blames employees for things that are wrong, it implies or admits its irresponsibility and irrelevance, and it acknowledges employees' importance. If doing better is within employees' capability, then shouldn't they be allowed to do it the best way they see fit? If management won't accept responsibility or pay the price when things go wrong, shouldn't someone else, or a better system, be found that will? And every time management is allowed to blame workers instead of taking responsibility itself, it grows increasingly fat, irresponsible, and unaccountable to anyone but itself.

When management abdicates responsibility, it betrays more than its own production workers. Through its incompetence, it betrays and jeopardizes its company or government organization, stockholders or taxpayers, all employees including working managers, and other companies and their employees with which it does business. It also betrays consumers who use its products or services, and it betrays the general public, which must cope with the consequences of an incompetent management's acts.

Management has so much power that when it abdicates its responsibilities for production, it can endanger the entire American economy. That in turn can endanger the peace and stability of the entire world.

PART

II

◇

HOW TO MAKE MANAGEMENT WORK AGAIN

8

Why Management Can't
Always Know Best

How can production be brought to maximum efficiency when top management is not responsible for production and doesn't take part in the acts of production? The standard answer is that the authorities, management and technical experts, know best: In the division of labor, they have the knowledge. But can anyone who is insulated from the realities of production by their lesser responsibilities know best? And should they have the authority to command production and receive the benefits of their command?

Complexity

Big business and government are immensely complex and far-ranging institutions. In most cases, no single human being can command them in all their details. Manufacturing and performing services can be difficult enough to master. But production in the larger sense of doing everything necessary to succeed is even more difficult to master. It includes obtaining supplies, managing inventory, distributing the product or service, research and development, maintaining computers and machines, hiring and keeping key personnel, researching and testing markets, developing new products, advertising, and selling. Further, flows of capital and money, changes in markets and technology, and disruptions in political, military, legal, social, or labor relations can upset literally overnight the foundations on which many businesses or governments operate.

175

Management's "No Control." How do top executives respond to such difficult complexities? Some say "no"—they try to restrict and "control" employee actions lest employees do something wrong, hostile, or self-serving. To such executives, "control" means inhibiting actions rather than directing and providing leadership for action.

American Cyanamid Co., a multibillion-dollar, worldwide corporation, provided me with many examples of this "no control." I worked for five years as a computer programmer and analyst for the data processing department of Cyanamid's Agricultural Division headquarters, which was in Princeton, New Jersey, and contained the division's administrative and research center. I worked with many managers in many areas of the business at levels ranging from corporate headquarters to local plants and offices.

Once my boss wanted me to take a college course in linear programming, which is a mathematical technique to optimize production schedules. It was to help me develop a system of computer programs for Cyanamid's phosphate strip mine in Florida. The course cost only $125, but one of the managers high in the division's hierarchy objected to paying for it because I would be getting a college course free. He wanted me to pay for 25 percent of the course as part of the company's tuition-reimbursement plan. That made no sense. My boss could have sent me out of town for a week to a business seminar in linear programming that would have cost perhaps $1,500, with no question of my having to pay a penny for it.

Although I worked on the mine project for over a year, and wrote a system of programs for the mine's credit union at the same time, I was allowed to visit the mine only once—in August—for just three days. One time when I was explaining a difficulty I was encountering, my boss's boss interrupted me to ask, "What are you trying to do, get another free trip to Florida?" As if a business trip to a strip mine in the middle of a pine barrens in central Florida were a vacation!

There were so many obstacles to action in Cyanamid that my boss periodically complained of "constipation" in the company. Perhaps the worst offender was a formal group in the data processing department of corporate headquarters that seemed to say "no" to everything. It subjected proposals for new computer systems to endless second-guessing and had powers to delay or veto what it disliked. Many new proposals were effectively squelched, regardless of their merits, by the tiresome process to get them approved.

Another example of this "no control" came up while I was making technical evaluations of Digital Equipment and Hewlett-Packard minicomputers for purchase and use by the division's research staff. The manager in charge of the purchase heatedly told me that he wanted a less powerful machine so that none of the division's scientists could run wild with a more powerful one. He ultimately got the weaker machine precisely because of its limitations.

A statistician who represented Cyanamid's products before the Environmental Protection Agency and the Food and Drug Administration in Washington explained to me that there was an entrenched corporate-wide inhibition of computer systems. In hushed tones and a secretive air, he told me that having had its share of nightmarish breakdowns of computer systems, top management had consciously decided to keep computer initiatives to a bare minimum. He told me that he was told this by someone in top corporate management.

When intelligent use of computers and information—and people—is suppressed in the name of "controlling" trouble or abuses, great opportunities can be lost and disasters can result.

A great tragedy occurred when the space shuttle Challenger exploded. Engineers were overruled. Temperature-sensing devices were removed from the rocket boosters. An inherently risky design of the boosters was pushed through. And a politically motivated rush to launch pushed equipment beyond its limits. In addition, there was undue reliance on a single launch system for the entire U.S. space program.

The engineers who had opposed the launch suffered abuse and punishment, but the decision-makers were not held criminally responsible for the death of the seven Challenger astronauts. Some got new jobs and others were allowed to retire. None of them appear to have been fired. In the end, the U.S. suffered a terrible setback in space, especially when one after another of the older launch systems—Atlas, Delta, and Titan rockets—also exploded.

NASA had long been considered a superb organization. And Cyanamid, like my previous employer Western Electric, was neither the best nor worst of companies. All were thoroughly in the mainstream of American management practices. Many things I saw reflected contemporary business ideas and practices as reported in business publications. And the offices I worked in were totally nonunion. Upper management was the chief impediment to getting things done. Many people in middle-management positions or in staff positions with management responsibilities have told me their own experiences confirm this conclusion.

The Explosion of Complexity in Production. Traditionally American management has designed machines and office procedures to make human labor as simple and repetitive as possible. So at first glance it would appear that many jobs in factories and offices are not complex at all. However, even a simple assembly or clerical task can get terribly complicated if it is pushed to a fast enough pace. What may appear to the outside observer to be minor distractions may become major problems to the speeded-up worker. And management commonly pushes workers to the limits of their ability, and sometimes beyond their limits, precisely to find the point at which they fail.

When things go wrong or just don't work exactly right in fast-paced production, even the appearance of simplicity breaks down. Then jobs must be redefined on the spur of the moment and employees must create new relationships among their tasks to keep getting work done. Even experienced managers sometimes seek the experience of their best workers to get work going again. As a result, many kinds of so-called unskilled industrial and office work are highly complicated and require many unappreciated skills to be done well.

On the other hand, when management can simplify human production tasks enough, it replaces skilled people entirely with computers, robots, and other machines. But that just moves the complexity of human tasks away from the previous points of labor in a factory or office and spreads complexity in a wide arc everywhere else. Tasks of maintenance, supply, distribution, and coordination may be scattered around a huge factory, and other tasks such as design, engineering, communication, finance, and marketing may be scattered in multiple offices around the world.

Many auto makers produce cars, sometimes called "world cars," that are assembled in plants around the world from parts that may be designed and produced anywhere in the world. The finished cars may then be sold anywhere in the world too. In such a case, the increasing complexity of production moves into the office with a vengeance, and performing all the tasks of a business or government service increases in complexity even faster than in the factory. So whether production is concentrated in huge office complexes and factories or is dispersed around the world, it is growing ever more complex.

Roughly speaking, the growth in complexity may be thought to be proportional to the existing degree of complexity. In other words, the more factors and interactions among them that must be considered, the greater is the number of new interactions that any new factor can enter into. In mathematics, that's called an exponential or "growth" function, and it increases explosively. Like the straw that breaks the camel's back, a new factor of complexity can add an overwhelming burden to any successful enterprise.

To see how rapidly complexity can increase, imagine that a middle manager must consider 10 financial variables, and the 10 variables interact in 20 major ways (plus hundreds of minor ones). If the value of just one variable such as interest rates or currency exchange rates is changed, it could change every one of those 20 relationships. What's more, in the case of a global company, those rates would have to be tracked for a large number of countries.

Before he can make the kind of decision he learned to do in business school, a middle manager with an MBA might have to compute those 20 relationships for 10 different values in interest rates, and then do the computations for multiple values of each of the other major factors. The result can be thousands of scenarios to evaluate arising out of just 10 factors.

Now add one new factor, such as a new production technology. Just comparing the new with the old may require substituting the new technology for the old and examining a whole new set of 20 relationships and thousands of possibilities. Then the complexity increased not 10 percent, from 10 to 11, but rather doubled.

It's no wonder that middle managers began to buy personal

computers in large numbers once electronic spreadsheets such as VisiCalc and Lotus 1–2–3 enabled them to perform calculations like this much more quickly. Unfortunately, the very existence of these fancy electronic calculators means that many managers attempt to control many more variables and increase their complexity beyond all rational control.

Faulty Knowledge, Faulty Designs, Faulty Equipment, Faulty Organizations

In the above examples, facts were assumed to be known and means to deal with them were assumed to be readily available. But in the real world, "it ain't necessarily so."

In theory, engineers and other experts are supposed to make systems and machinery work together. And managers are supposed to make people, capital, and resources work together. Unfortunately, that's only in theory. Sometimes the authorities do marvelous jobs, but often these are just the showcases or the refined products after a lot of initial problems have been eliminated. In the mundane, day-to-day world of production, many problems arise that run counter to the best-laid plans. Here are some of them:

Initial "Bugs." When first introduced, new products and systems usually don't work right, or they develop "bugs" and require extensive modifications to work. Such patches are awkward and inefficient. They may never live up to the original specifications. This is most true when the design is new, but newly bought replacement products, even if they come from an old design that has been refined and is free of the initial "bugs," can differ in small but subtly important ways from the ones they are supposed to replace.

Hidden Problems. More troublesome to employees are problems that develop after the designers and engineers have gone away. When they leave, they rarely return, and they always seem to leave too soon. Even if a system or machine initially appears to do what it is supposed to do, it may have hidden problems or develop new problems with time and wear, such as frequent or inconvenient breakdowns, safety hazards, unreliable output, or lower efficiency than expected. Even systems that work well can fall behind newer systems of competitors, or otherwise gradually fail to meet the needs of changing business conditions. These are ever more serious problems as technology and growing world competition rapidly change the nature and economics of products.

Misfits. Problems also arise in fitting new machinery or systems into existing business operations. Even if a new machine or system works perfectly, it may conflict with existing systems, which themselves may be patchworks of earlier systems and conflicts. Such problems can be physically dangerous for factory workers, and they can cause chaos in the office. Because the accustomed ways of doing business are invisible to the naked eye—office organizations, supplier and distributor relationships, for example—no one may know all the details and interactions of what really goes on. Ignorance is especially prevalent when management prides itself on moving its managers around a lot. Then only secretaries and other hourly employees, if anyone, would really know the ins and outs of many aspects of the business. The company's entire success or failure may depend on a few low-level people who are ignored in making major decisions, and who are paid much less than the prestigious managers. And this can happen in government services as well.

Uncoordinated Growth. A major problem with fitting in new systems is that when a company grows, it rarely grows rationally. It may start out as a simple idea of offering a product or service that is or will be in demand. But it grows in response to market demand, competition, available work force, changing technology, changing economic climate, and other external conditions that have no rational relationship among themselves, cannot be rationally predicted, and may conflict with each other.

Those unrelated external conflicts become internalized when a company creates in-house organizations to deal with them. For example, a product-driven company may find that the market dictates changes in its product. The result may be instant—and classic—conflict among engineering, manufacturing, and marketing organizations as each tries to dominate the others. And conflicts increase as financial limitations and legal restrictions intrude and are internalized. No matter how coherent a company starts out, it must grow less and less coherent and rational as its business increases. And then the need for new or higher forms of organization become paramount. But then the problem becomes how to reorganize without disturbing what is already working well, and without causing more turmoil among entrenched internal organizations.

Vestiges of the Past. When a company grows or changes, the past can never be discarded or ignored as if it never happened. Vestiges of past business always assert themselves, although they may not be understood for what they are, and they may not be treated appropriately in management plans. Unless the managers involved have a long and continuous experience and open communication among themselves—rarely the case—management often isn't aware that the vestiges even exist. Then it certainly won't see them for what they are.

Vestiges such as political empires, rivalries, and resentments can build up, especially in bureaucracies. Attitudes, knowledge, and capabilities become set among people and organizations. Nonproducing investments and expensive commitments impose restraints. Short-term shortcuts in construction, finance, or treatment of employees, for example, become increasingly costly and troublesome with time.

Government programs that encouraged growth may run out of money, and laws that fostered growth may be changed, perhaps because there was too much growth. Water supplies may become depleted or polluted, careless development may cause flooding and traffic congestion. And taxes can rise to pay for fixing the problems. An unwary company suddenly could be left with unsuitable capabilities, in a depressed local economy, with bad roads that hinder transportation and travel, and higher taxes.

These and other vestiges of the past, even of successful growth, can come seemingly from out of nowhere to affect a business. And problems associated with the vestiges are most likely to flare up all at once precisely when changes or additions are made to a business. Then all the old relationships among people and departments are disturbed, and the players all fight to restore the old balance or create more favorable new ones.

Internal Conflicts. Problems of growth and change are compounded in large companies, especially conglomerates, because they contain many unrelated or uncoordinated, and often partially conflicting, "divisions," as when multiple companies are merged into one parent. Accounting, R&D, inventory, sales, manufacturing, and legal departments all have their own different priorities, needs, expenses, and demands. None may know or care about the others. All may feel that their needs are most important, and they fight for a larger share of the resources in the company.

Conflicts may arise in manufacturing when skills, machinery, and product mixes are not suitably complementary. Conflicting systems of operation are frequently obvious in the office, for example when "accounting" keeps information about daily or weekly purchase orders only for itself—if it keeps such timely information at all—but "sales" or "manufacturing" can't get timely enough information to know how to respond to changing market demand.

Similarly, "data processing"—which historically has grown as an aid to accounting and has often been kept subservient to accounting—may be handcuffed by its close relation to accounting. At Cyanamid, the data processing manager reported to the controller. As a result, accounting got first priority of all data processing resources. At times it seemed as if the controller wasn't interested and wouldn't authorize work for other departments. And the company's financial data were organized according to accounting's classifications and time schedules. Its sales reports, for example, came out too late to be useful to the pesticide sales department. When I wrote a computer program to report sales on a more timely basis, I found that the data were scattered in so many coded classifications, with so many errors, that I was never sure I had gotten information about all sales.

At times departmental rivalries and management's traditional secrecy deny computer programmers the information they need to write any effective programs at all. Or else programs are written without complete or accurate information. Sometimes programmers don't even know their information is faulty. That's a sure way to create the kind of horror stories that make computer systems notorious.

Shakeups with Each New Boss. Frequent changes in management add problems of adapting to new or clashing personal styles. Every time a new boss enters an organization, especially in the office, he or she will likely do things differently, if only to be distinguished from the predecessor. New managers may be dissatisfied with employees they inherit with the job, questioning whether their loyalty and attitudes are tied to the previous manager and questioning their willingness and ability to do things the new way. Alternatively, new managers, especially in higher management, may want to bring their own people, and they have to get rid of the holdovers to do that.

Programmed Conflict. Some "professional" management concepts deliberately foster conflict. At Cyanamid, the CEO was said to like to reorganize occasionally just to shake things up. This theory of reorganization says that breaking up entrenched relationships keeps everyone competing and on their toes. This allows rising managers to get transferred among many jobs. But it also breaks up productive working relationships. And whole organizations are created just to check up on each other. So productive activities can neither take root nor improve.

Such programmed conflicts are predictable when top management trusts no one, not even its own middle managers. This distrust can easily arise when top management is inexperienced with operations. Someone from manufacturing might not know much about sales or R&D. Someone who hopped around in many jobs might never have stayed long enough in any one job to learn "the business." But more and more, top managers come from finance, the law, corporate headquarters, other corporations, or an MBA program. They know too little to trust their own judgment, their employees, and the organizations they command. So they program conflict to make "sure" that no employee takes advantage of them. That ties the company into knots and ensures that it won't adapt well to changing business conditions. And it wreaks havoc among employees, who spend most of their time fighting each other.

Organizing to Reduce Complexity

As production grows more complex and markets change and grow ever more rapidly, business and government have enormous and exploding needs for organization. That raises a simple question: If production is so difficult and complex, how does anything get done at all?

Intelligent human beings design and operate production to eliminate most possible combinations or make them self-adjusting. That way they keep production as simple as possible. The decisive factors in reducing complexity are not mathematical, technical, or mechanical. The decisive factors are human communication, cooperation, coordination, and overall organization, so that individuals can be motivated and rewarded for what they do well, and well-intentioned and effective individual efforts can work together to produce the maximum collective effect.

Timing and foresight also help. Some Japanese manufacturers try to deliver their raw materials and parts to the factory barely 20 minutes before they are needed and used. In that case, foresight, cooperation, and organization extend beyond the factory to many companies and industries and may make the whole world, in effect, one large "workplace."

The more complex that production and markets become, the more important is organizing ability to a business or government's final success. All things being equal, the people who can deliver superior organizing ability and increase the amount of goods and services we all can use are the people who ought to be in charge of managing complex economic or government activities. Who is responsible, who should have authority, and who should be encouraged and rewarded for improving production?

A quick look: We have already seen that most American managers in big business and government are rewarded the more they serve their own selfish, bureaucratic interests. Executives who survive and rise to the top are all too frequently the faultiest at creating and running large, effective, productive organizations of human beings. At best all they can do is create and run bureaucracies to grab and hold "control" for themselves.

The rest of this book will show that producing employees bear enormous responsibilities for production. They work together and build effective collective organizations to save themselves from management's excessive pressures and to bail out management's mistakes. They are the fittest at creating and running effective large organizations of people and serving the interests of a large majority of people in society.

No Control at All. In other words, when management tries to reduce jobs to simplistic tasks or eliminate human labor altogether, which is the overwhelmingly dominant management obsession in America, then organization of the many components of production becomes enormously important, greatly prone to failure, and fatal when it does fail.

It's no wonder that American management is so preoccupied with "control." Setting aside for the moment the enormous special interest it has in increasing its own power, it is compelled by the very complexity it has created to try to "control" it. But of course the job is so unmanageable that the "control" that management seeks all too easily degenerates into trying to constrain every conceivable action.

Blocked by such a dam, producing people within an organization seek to get around it by way of a myriad of uncoordinated, "underground" actions. They even have a saying for it: It is easier to beg forgiveness than to get permission. At the same time, some bureaucrats turn the dam into a wall that defends their own political empires so they can do whatever they wish. And of course the organization's performance suffers greatly from lack of coherent direction or drive. In such cases management's "no control" is no control at all.

On the other hand, when jobs are designed for and filled with skilled and responsible employees, and when employees have substantial authority and rewards for organizing and managing production themselves, then complexity diminishes and organizations can become much more simple and effective. At the same time, work becomes much more productive and rewarding for both employees and managers, and the business or government service gains huge competitive advantages in every aspect of its operation.

9

Working People: Survival of the Fittest

Hard work changes people.

People who work and produce in heavy industry or in low-paying offices and services (such as teaching, nursing, government, and clerical jobs) survive numerous life-or-death struggles to keep their jobs and keep working. These struggles refine and temper them in many ways. The productive power and social character of their work force them to acquire and develop the most difficult and valuable of human skills: communication, cooperation, and organization. This chapter begins the story of how that happens and the great gifts and awesome potential that result.

Life-or-Death Struggles

It is a life-or-death struggle to escape being killed or maimed in industrial accidents and avoid being sickened or worn out by high-pressure jobs.

My father worked as a welder for 15 years in an ironworking shop that my uncle called, with an upward roll of his eyes, "Dante's Inferno": the fires and fumes of welding; metal moving or being worked overhead and on the floor; the noise; metal and cables stacked in piles or lying underfoot. One of the men my father worked with lost his foot when it got pinned and crushed by shifting steel beams—and he was blamed for being careless. (That same ironworker told me in 1973 that the Japanese were building steel mills that would put Bethlehem Steel out of business.

It's another example of how industrial workers are far ahead of public perceptions.)

Here's how *U.S. News & World Report* described a Pontiac assembly line in 1984: "This is no place for the fainthearted. Walls vibrate like a drumhead with the din of sheet metal clanging against metal, the shuddering of massive two-story machines, the zapping and sizzling of high-voltage welding guns joining steel. Partial deafness is a veteran's mark" (7–16–84, 48).

The shop in which my father worked was essentially a big metal shed without heat in the winter or air conditioning in the summer. In the winter the steel he worked with held and radiated the bone-penetrating cold of subfreezing temperatures. In the summer the welding and its fumes added to the heat and humidity of 90-plus degree days, plus the heavy exertions of moving tons of metal and heavy clothing to protect the skin. It richly earned the name "inferno." My father told of at least one man who said that he wasn't afraid of going to hell when he died because he goes to work there every day already.

The Industrial Bloodbath. Most Americans have no idea how hard and dangerous industrial work is. In 1966, "2,200,000 persons suffered disabling injuries" in industrial accidents (Howard A. Rusk, M.D., *New York Times*, 9–1–68, 55). That was 300,000 more disabling injuries than were caused by motor vehicle accidents. And this industrial bloodbath was concentrated in a much smaller number of people than the total number of people who rode in motor vehicles.

Has work gotten safer since 1966? There were over 14,000 industrial deaths then, but *Inc.* reported in 1987 that there were "an estimated 100,000 work-related deaths annually" (March 1987, 48). Add to that an uncounted toll of people who are poisoned by industrial chemicals but may never be diagnosed as such.

Dangerous working conditions are a hidden factor in many work disputes. I say "hidden" because workers openly talk of them but the news media rarely report safety-related demands. A good example of this was the strike and boycott in 1985 and 1986 by meatpackers of Local P-9 of the United Food and Commercial Workers against George A. Hormel & Company's plant in Austin, Minnesota. The strikers reached out and got support from much of the upper Midwest community, raised hundreds of thousands of dollars in strike funds, and held out for a year before finally succumbing to pressures that included disputes with officials in the international union itself. The P-9 effort was a heroic feat of organization and determination that was occasionally televised by the national news networks. Throughout the strike we were told that the workers were haggling over a measly 69 cents in hourly pay. It made the workers seem stupid, petty, and every bit as unmanageable as management said they were. But we weren't told about the injuries inside that plant.

Hormel says the Austin plant had 30.3 injuries per 100 workers in 1984, 24.3 in 1985, and 3.2 in 1986, after the P-9 strikers were replaced. A spokesman attributed the huge drop to a different attitude of the new workers, saying P-9 had "milked the system" with lawyers to represent workers. The striking union put the injury rate much higher.

To put these figures in perspective, meatpacking is the nation's most dangerous occupation (*New York Times,* 6–14–87, F1). Yet plants can go years without federal inspections, and those inspections increasingly consist of checking just company logs of injuries, not injured workers or working conditions themselves. Consequently, cheating is believed to be widespread (Lisa Meyers, NBC News, 3–1–87; *New York Times,* 8–2–87, F1). The Occupational Health and Safety Administration (OSHA) estimates companies report only half the actual injuries (Lisa Meyers, NBC News, 11–15–86).

Even so, while all private industry reported an average of 7.9 injuries per 100 workers in 1985, the meatpacking industry reported a rate of 30.4. At OSHA's estimate of underreporting, meatpacking would average 60.8. Whatever the true figure, the official average is still awful and consistent with the sickening mutilations and other injuries described by *Times* reporter William Glaberson. In his view, the meatpacking industry is returning to conditions as brutal as those that prompted Upton Sinclair to write *The Jungle* 81 years ago.

Many meatpacking workers might not fully realize the dangers they run. Reliable information about injuries is scanty. Public data is generally understated. The alternative, unemployment, may seem worse. And many disabling conditions, such as carpal tunnel syndrome, arise from accumulated wear and tear and may not appear until after years of work.

It is to be hoped that Hormel's stated Austin injury rate of 3.2

in 1986 remains that low and can be verified by thorough independent inspections. Nevertheless, the P-9 strike was notable for its special intensity. Only threats of severe bodily harm on the job seem able to explain the enormous determination that the strikers demonstrated. The government and the press should have thoroughly investigated the Austin plant. But they didn't. Instead, the strikers lost their jobs and were made to seem they got what they deserved.

The harm done in the workplace is staggering. The 1966 *Times* story said accidents on the job caused "about 10 times as many working days away from work" as strikes. In 1984, job-related injuries and illnesses caused 8 out of every 100 full-time workers to lose an average of 63.4 workdays per case (*Business Week,* 11–25–85, 46). At five workdays per week and 100 million workers, that's eight million workers each losing three months of work each year! Yet many managements attack and vilify unions when they fight to protect employees. There is something unspeakable about that.

The Spiritual Drain. It is a life-or-death struggle in many jobs to leave work at the end of the day and feel like a human being. Teachers in many cities call their jobs "combat." When I was in high school, there were floors where students feared to enter and teachers were cowed by tough, white students. Nurses tell me they get abused by doctors who don't respect their professional training and experience; nurses also get abused by patients who— rightly—want more care than management allows nurses to give. And growing numbers of office workers are as regimented and hard-pushed as assembly-line workers.

Getting up and going to work every day, on time, without fail is also a struggle when the body is tired or sick and the spirit is unwilling, especially before 6 A.M. or on shift work. When pay is low, it is hard just to save a few pennies and find good food and housing to keep body, soul, and family well and together—especially for working single mothers.

In short, conservation of life's vital energy is a life-or-death struggle that many working people, especially industrialized workers, must fight and win.

The Daily Pressure to Produce. Most people who work have little luxury to "take off" when they want. They feel the daily pressure to produce, the drive for more and faster, with as little paid for the work as possible. Medical and unemployment insurance, holidays and vacations, and welfare can cushion their need to work every day, but only in the short run. A person who fails to produce every day as the boss wishes is "terminated," a word that strongly suggests what can happen to the life of a person out of work and without wealth to fall back on.

Adaptation. Office and service workers must often step carefully through a virtual minefield of politics and conflicts of interests and power. If they don't learn who to see and how to get things done, they find themselves isolated, without influence or respect, and unable to do their jobs well. If they step on the wrong people's toes or say the wrong thing to the wrong person, they could quickly lose all hope of promotion. And if they keep offending the wrong people, they will find themselves fired or harassed into leaving.

Few people can come in cold to a new job and pass all the hurdles of politics and production unless they get some kind of help from other people. Employees are impelled by their work conditions to seek mutual cooperation for mutual benefit. They may never become the best of friends, but they usually do feel substantial bonds of some kind based on sharing experiences and cooperating to get work done in difficult circumstances.

The need to adapt to the difficulties of employment (a social activity) develops in working people, and especially in employees in large organizations, many social skills that are sorely needed today and are largely unappreciated by outside academic or hostile management observers.

Decisive Actions. Many kinds of fast-paced work require snap judgments or decisive actions based on insufficient knowledge and complicated by the intrinsic variability of human relations and mechanical objects. And this often takes place in an environment that may be dangerous, disturbingly distracting, physically hard, or emotionally pressured. Then such judgments and movements require degrees of sensitivity, alertness, and intelligence that are rarely required anywhere else.

Sensitivity. Brutal conditions are antagonistic to sensitivity. Academicians, executives, army officers, artists, policymakers, and even politicians often justify their luxurious, sheltered lives on the grounds that they cannot do their best work amid turmoil and pressure. Yet sensitivity in a brutal environment is frequently demanded of working people, especially in industry and industrialized white-collar or service work. Remaining sensitive without getting burned out or worn out in a brutal environment is a struggle as fully exacting as the other life-or-death struggles. It adds and refines special qualities in the people who survive.

Self-Defenses. Organizing unions and conducting strikes are life-or-death struggles. A lost strike can easily mean less pay and worse job conditions, debts incurred during the strike, a broken union, lost jobs for many workers, and blackballing of union leaders. Many union organizers have lost their lives when attacked by company thugs, police, or the National Guard.

Employers in both capitalism and communism view union actions as life-or-death struggles too. Every strike contains within it the seeds to overthrow oppression, as the Polish workers so amply demonstrated. And each union action challenges the fundamental power of each boss to do as he or she wishes.

Industrialized Employees. Large employers in business and government have turned many kinds of white-collar and service work into "industries." They have made employees indistinguishable and easily replaceable so that work can be pushed harder and faster. This has begun to happen even to middle managers, computer programmers, and doctors and lawyers.

There is a rational process to industrialized work that develops powerfully productive abilities in people who survive it. Industrialized employees are put to difficult but well-defined tasks, and they quickly learn how good their work is. They develop rapidly in getting their jobs done or are forced to leave. The tasks may very well approach the limits of human ability, but they can't go too far because then mass employment would be impossible.

Simultaneously, industrialized work is an organized social activity using advanced means of production. Employees learn the power of organization and value working within organizations to get work done. As a result, large numbers of selected people develop valuable work-related abilities.

Self-employed people face different kinds of struggles, which are more likely to be overly harsh. They may do good and hard work, yet fail because they are not at the right time and place. Or if they are at the right time and place, whatever they do will likely succeed. The requirements for success are just less clear and the penalties can be terminal. As a result, there is less opportunity to improve work abilities through a process of surviving, adapting, and growing.

Many people also work alone or with no more than a few companions. They usually don't learn from their work how to work and cooperate within large organizations. And they have little experience with large-scale production and distribution. Isolated working people can easily be overwhelmed by the enormity of modern economies and cannot grasp how everything works together.

In summary, life-or-death struggles refine and temper industrialized employees but leave large numbers of them uncrushed. Those struggles condition the survivors to cooperate and share on a merit—but otherwise egalitarian—basis within the most powerfully productive social units the world has ever known: the businesses or government services of their employing organizations. The people who survive and prosper in industrialized work grow strong and fit. They carry within themselves enormous and unique social and moral powers that are still largely untapped by modern economies.

Personal Powers

Assembly lines and other machines, piecework, supervisors, speed-up, growing work loads, and now computer monitoring of office work drive industrialized employees relentlessly and develop within them a positive, constructive drive toward everything in their lives. They become with time disciplined, potent, reliable, punctual, determined, tough—and confident and secure through the exercise of all these abilities. It's worth looking at these personal powers more closely.

Discipline and Realism. To survive and prosper in a difficult environment, working people must above all else face, respect, and cope with reality. It takes iron discipline to look unpleasant realities in the face and cope with them without flinching. Discipline and realism cannot be turned on and off like a faucet. Industrialized working people bring their job-driven realism and discipline to everything they do in life. They can make hard, clear-headed decisions and commitments when they want to, and they can stick to those commitments and decisions because they are based in reality. They don't look for trouble, because trouble is a vanity they cannot afford; but they can fight very hard for what they believe in because they have the courage of realistic convictions. And they are not given to chasing impossible dreams; but they can act audaciously, unitedly, and decisively when even the most "impossible" dream appears realistically attainable to them.

Unbiased Respect for Good Work. Experienced working people are just too realistic to allow prejudice to cripple their judgment, for crippled judgment is often dangerous. And they are too respectful of the value and dangers inherent in production to denigrate people who do good work. Anyone who proves himself or herself on the job will find respect and a decent working relationship, regardless of race, sex, religion, or politics.

Many people demand respect from working people, however, without earning it first. "Leftists" and "radicals" who fault workers yet don't work themselves get little respect. By working little and by not being superior the few and brief times they do join the work force, these would-be leaders don't prove themselves capable of leadership. And when their performances are inferior, as workers, writers, thinkers, and organizers, they prove themselves incapable and unworthy of leading working people. Workers perceive such "leaders" to be losers, opportunists, or potential exploiters and refuse to follow them to defeat and suffering.

When organized workers really begin to act, most would-be "leaders" of workers' movements suddenly quail, call for caution or "self-limitation" (an organization's equivalent of asthma), and do everything in their power to restrain and defeat workers. Such "leaders" really haven't the strength and confidence in organized workers to see their fight through to the end.

One reason many working people resent employment quotas that bring in "disadvantaged" workers is the feeling that special allowances are being made for people who can't do the work. And perhaps some of the specially hired people can't do the work because they are indeed disadvantaged and they have been excluded from the education and training that would have qualified them. That is the fault of a system that throws inexperienced people into difficult work. It doesn't make working people prejudiced, narrow-minded, or "backward" if they insist on high standards of work. Indeed, it makes them just the opposite, for, to repeat, they accept anyone—regardless of race, sex, or politics—who proves worthy on the job. That can be said of very few other people. That's why industrial unions are among the most integrated and democratic institutions in America.

Rock-Solid Character. People who survive and prosper in industrialized work see that hard work gets results and that they themselves can work hard. They come to want to get things done and identify with the huge power of the investments in plant and systems that created most industrialized jobs. That conditions them to be instinctively confident and constructive in everything they do. They develop with time a long-term outlook on life—to work for the future—that is sadly lacking in management and most of American life today.

Although they can have problems like everyone else, underneath the problems is much more likely to be a rock, a foundation, an enduring strength in the stability that work gives their lives. It helps them deal with their problems, if not totally successfully, at least successfully enough to keep their jobs, support themselves, be responsible for their actions, and generally get along with society. They are just not as likely to "crack up" or become fanatic under problems that break others.

Elegance, Simplicity, and Greatness. Jobs often *appear* "simple-minded" or "easy" but are neither simple-minded nor easy to perform successfully. Nothing may seem so simple-minded and easy perhaps as working in a fast-food restaurant, but editors from both *Business Week* (10–13–86, 86) and *U.S. News & World Report* (11–21–83, 8) found to their chagrin that they couldn't keep up the pace. "Simple-minded" assembly-line jobs are equally difficult and a lot more strenuous and dangerous.

To conserve energy, keep a fast pace, avoid mistakes and accidents, and do a job properly, working people frequently have to develop extremely efficient economies of thought and motion. It is worth remembering that "simple" and "easy" are often hallmarks of greatness. The greatest creations of mankind often have an elegant simplicity that deceives the casual observer into thinking they are obvious and easy.

In mathematics, brevity and conciseness are called "elegant." In sports, the greatest athletes can make the greatest performances look routine. Babe Ruth's swing, for example, was so compact and quick that it barely catches one's notice in the old films. It certainly lacks the dramatic swish of many contemporary sluggers, but it was precisely its compact efficiency that gave it such power. Babe Ruth also achieved with that "simple" and "easy" swing a lifetime batting average of .342, the sixth highest in major league baseball, good enough in one of his "average" years to win a major league batting championship today.

In literature, Hemingway is prized for his elegant simplicity. Despite the length of their novels, Dickens and Tolstoy are unequivocally direct and say great things in simple ways. For all his greatness at character exposition, Shakespeare is remembered most for his exquisite "one-liners." In letters, one of the greatest all-around talents of the nineteenth century, Goethe, once apologized for writing a long letter because he hadn't the time to refine it into a short one.

"Simple" and "easy" are the hallmarks of greatness because conflicting forces, scattered efforts, and divided motions are invariably weaker than compact, coordinated, united ones. Greatness must be simple to concentrate all its power in a single thrust for maximum effect. In moving people deeply or getting profound results, greatness clears away all obstacles and makes the results appear direct, easy, and natural. (The effects can be complicated, but the source can't be.)

People achieve qualities of greatness when they focus all their faculties and reach their maximum potential in their personal lives. The full measure or extent of their greatness is revealed by how much they move people or what results they get. Every working person who survives in a difficult job has achieved at least some quality of personal greatness. Many working people are genuine heroes just to have supported themselves and their families with hard jobs in difficult times.

Sensitivity, Steel Nerves, and Iron Constitutions. When their working environment is uncertain, complicated, or dangerous, working people must be sensitive to nuance, adaptable to change, and alert to anything that could threaten them or their jobs. That could just as easily be office politics as a falling steel beam. Yet they cannot allow their sensitivity to make them skittish or prevent them from doing their jobs, for they will never have safety or certainty. They need strong stomachs and nerves of steel to endure their sensitivity, and the survivors develop them. They develop superior constitutional strengths and mental abilities to cope with a demanding and stressful world.

Little research has been done, or at least it hasn't become widespread public knowledge, about the effects of industrial stress. Not surprisingly, employers don't support research that might show that employees suffer cruel and unusual punishment.

Those who have studied stress, most notably Hans Selye, tend to say that the body can handle successfully only one major stress at a time, and only up to a limit. It is as if the body concentrates on that stress and can get "blind-sided"—hit and felled by a blow at an unguarded spot in its defenses—if a second major stress hits it. They define stress as anything that makes demands of the body. It is not just emotional. It could be an injury, an infection, severe cold or heat, physical exertion, mental exertion, poison, pollution, or noise. So when a person is under a major stress, an additional stress could seem to be small and yet be extremely harmful.

Many stresses have hidden components that affect the body through the mind. That doesn't mean their effects are unreal or shameful. No professional athlete or performing artist who ever came through in the clutch or got butterflies before going on stage can deny that they are responding physically and powerfully to a perceived challenge. Indeed, it is usually the ones who don't react strongly who fail. It isn't for nothing that Reggie Jackson is called "Mr. October"—meaning the man who rises to the challenge and wins the World Series.

Whenever our minds perceive a challenge, nerves from the brain stimulate our muscles and organs, and powerful chemicals are sent into our bloodstreams by glands such as the adrenals and pancreas. They raise blood pressure, set the heart beating faster, shut down—or accelerate—the digestive tract, maybe cause a sweat, and do countless other things. They are all part of the age-old, fight-or-flight reaction that the body needs to respond quickly and strongly to external challenges, like fleeing from a lion or chasing prey.

Those chemicals are meant to produce strong physical actions, and the actions are meant to use up the chemicals, since they corrode the body when they circulate too much. The body's action is also intended to be directed at or away from the challenge.

But in civilized life, many of the strongest challenges, such as pleasing a boss or meeting mortgage payments, don't call for strong or direct physical action. Frequently, the appropriate response to a problem on the job is to suppress action rather than increase action—like keeping your mouth shut and not talking back. And the response is directed internally to suppress thoughts and feelings that could cause trouble if expressed.

When people suppress actions under stress, they do not use up the chemicals and tension created by stress. They remain much longer than nature intended and do much more damage than nature intended too. Some people hold tension in muscles that fight each other and cause stiffness, pain, or damage to joints, bones, or teeth (grinding). Prolonged tension can contribute to high blood pressure. And internal organs will suffer from prolonged exposure to adrenal hormones and other chemicals. That is how stress weakens the body and can weaken any part of the body, usually weakening first and foremost the weakest organs.

Illnesses caused by excessive and prolonged stress can seem unrelated to each other and to whatever caused the stress. And they are rarely diagnosed as being stress-induced by modern medical "specialists." In part, that's because specialists concentrate on small parts of the body and ignore the big picture of the person as a whole. But perhaps most important, employers pay the largest part of doctor bills through health insurance plans, and doctors who cooperate with insurers and employers get a lot of institutional business. In addition, no doctor wants to spend hours or days in court without getting paid to testify in a complicated stress-related case.

Ironically, doctors in the past, who are thought to have known fewer medical facts than doctors today, were wise enough to put much more value on stress and on avoiding stress for people who were ill. They were also accountable to and paid directly by the patient.

Consequently, prolonged and unending stress on the job and in society is an often undiagnosed, underlying major cause of illness. According to Dr. Alex Cohen at the National Institute of Occupational Safety and Health, "Stress is one of the 10 leading work-related health problems...which can contribute to hypertension, heart disease, ulcers, and depression" (*New York Times,* 11–9–86, F1). According to Dr. Paul Rosch at the American Institute of Stress in Yonkers, stress costs American industry "as much as $150 billion annually" in absenteeism, reduced productivity, and medical fees.

Both doctors felt that lack of control over work is a major factor in creating stress. It's no accident that NIOSH found that "full-time VDT operators had the highest stress levels among workers," more even than air traffic controllers (*Newsweek,* 10–29–84, 122). Both jobs are computer monitored and make workers feel helplessly vulnerable to management control (*Forbes,* 7–2–84, 158).

Stress is also why "8 out of 10" employees used drugs in Silicon Valley, by the estimate of one engineer and former drug dealer (*MacNeil/Lehrer News Hour,* 4–19–84, p. 8 of transcript). Yet according to a former head of the organized crime unit at the Santa Clara County Sheriff's Department, "It just amazes me how little management does know" that there is even a problem (*New York Times,* 4–6–85).

Dr. Cohen felt that in reducing job stress-related illness, "Worker participation is a critical issue." If worker participation in job design could reduce a significant part of what Dr. Rosch estimated to be $150 billion lost by business to stress annually, it would be good for business and a major competitive advantage for the businesses that adopt it. It might also help reverse the sickening decline America is suffering in high technology and manufacturing. But will many managements voluntarily give up their "prerogatives" to terrorize and abuse workers? It hardly seems likely.

Stress is a major pollutant of our lives. Besides the cost to business and employees, the inner pain and loneliness it causes are reasons why many people join dictatorial groups or absolutist cults and religious sects. Their strict rules and grand promises remove uncertainties that cause stress and let stressed people trust in, and give up personal responsibility to, a "greater" power.

The many life-or-death struggles of working for a living mark it as a major stress. But infections, accidents, pregnancy, family troubles, financial troubles, and deaths of loved ones are also major stresses and visit working people like anyone else. So people who survive on the job must have such fit constitutions that they can survive, endure, and continue working under multiple stresses that would break many other people.

Productive Goodness. There is an undeniable identity between positive, constructive behavior and something we call "goodness." In daily life, people are called "good" when they work hard, keep their jobs, meet their family and social responsibilities, help others, give good cheer, and in other ways are cooperative and giving. These are all productive actions. And this is only natural, because survival depends on productive actions, especially working hard, meeting commitments, and cooperating with other people. Consequently, people feel *good* when they can be productive.

In most faiths, God *creates*. In the Bible, God *worked* to make earth and man. And Christ *labored* to save mankind. The productive instinct of working people and its fruitful results spring from the same source as the highest qualities of constructive goodness and decency that run like a common theme through many religions and moral codes. In their productive drives, working people are living embodiments of goodness.

"Evil," on the other hand, is widely associated with negative or harmful behavior and destruction. In Christian faiths, Satan tries to undo or destroy what God creates. In *Paradise Lost,* one of the most powerful and enduring Christian studies of good and evil, John Milton explained Satan's behavior by saying that Satan would rather rule in hell than serve in heaven. In worldly terms, Satan denies reality (God's dominance) and tries to destroy reality (everything God creates). Satan insisted on having "my way" "in all seasons" against superior and constructive forces. That sounds like many a criminal or "rugged individual" or business person who sees no virtues in productive activity (other than making a profit), belittles "do-gooders," feels no obligation to other people or society, imagines he or she can exist independently of society, resents the structures and responsibilities society imposes, and does his or her best to circumvent or escape them, thereby becoming a plague or parasite on us all.

Being inferior, being committed to destroying rather than building, opposing reality, Milton's Satan was doomed to failure. And any society is doomed that worships corporations' and a few individuals' "freedom" to get the biggest profit they can find anywhere in the world, even if they destroy productive people in the process, ignore people's and society's needs for productive activity, and suck the lifeblood from socially responsible working people.

There is a basic moral contradiction between family values and free-market economic forces. Super-liquid free markets pull people apart. As jobs change, relationships change between husband and wife, often breaking up a marriage. As jobs are moved around the world, they pull people with them and separate family from friends. That is especially bad for children; it's not good for adults either. When jobs are exported to the lowest-wage labor on earth, and can be moved every few years to wherever the lowest wages happen then to be, super-liquid markets destroy communities, regions, and nations. They also generate a free-market worship of individuality that destroys social feelings within people, especially the feelings and comforts of social interdependence, without which civilization is impossible. In short, super-liquid free markets *liquidate* morality and civilization just as they liquidate capital, people, and productive activities.

We face today terrible problems from failing to employ our people productively: rising underemployment and long-term unemployment; the increasing obsolescence of many skills, intellectual as well as manual; the "termination" and discarding like trash of the people who have old skills; discrimination that creates millions of second-class citizens and relegates them to inferior jobs or unemployment; abandonment of the disabled and forced retirement of many people who want or need to work; and a huge military economy that produces very little that is useful at all. Our nation and many people in it are growing sick as a result.

People's most basic mental and emotional strengths—their very human essence—are being destroyed on a vast, frightening scale. In what "is almost certainly the largest mental-health survey ever conducted...nearly 20 percent of American adults, a team of researchers from the [U.S. government's] National Institute of Mental Health reported last week, currently suffer psychiatric disorders ranging from disabling anxiety to schizophrenia." This news comes from "an ongoing survey of 20,000 Americans in five communities around the nation" (*Newsweek*, 10–15–84, 113). And "the criteria for mental disorder were strict and detailed" (*New York Times*, 10–3–84, 1). For example, "an antisocial personality was not just the neighborhood grouch, but a person who had serious troubles with family, school and community before the age of 15 and was often involved in crime and violence afterward." Twenty percent of Americans *disabled* mentally or emotionally!

Other reports confirm this study. Eleven percent of high school students in a New York State survey described themselves as "hooked" on alcohol (*New York Times*, 10–23–84, A1). And there are an estimated 10 million compulsive gamblers in the U.S. (WCBS radio, 10–24–84).

As long as the destruction of productive people and values continues, this country cannot prosper. We need to reverse the destructive, evil forces in our society. We need people whose goodness can guide them and us in doing so. Working people, especially industrialized workers, have the productive instinct highly refined and driven deeply into their souls. We need their productive goodness to prosper.

Large-Tool Skills. We don't ordinarily think of factories and offices as tools, but they are tools nonetheless. It is just that they are on such a large scale that people work *within* them, and the skills needed to make them work effectively go far beyond the manual and mental skills needed for small tools such as hammers, personal computers, or many kinds of expert technical knowledge.

Factories and integrated office or service operations are tools because they are created and used by people and extend their productivity. While they require mastery of specific tasks, their overall productivity requires even more mastery of high human skills, including discipline, honesty, communication, cooperation, initiative and creativity, and organization.

Measuring the output of individual employees tells nothing about the productivity of the larger organizations. Even slower and easier work can create higher value if people work together and more carefully. And often they must work slower, or for shorter time periods, to keep in touch with and participate in what's going on elsewhere.

It is outrageous that factory and office workers are called "low-skilled" and their individual tasks are called "simple-minded." Large-tool and large-scale skills are really skills of making a large organization work and are among the most difficult in the world. If you doubt that, just try to get a large number of people to work together.

Economically, employees in efficient factories, offices, and service operations deserve higher pay and bonuses for making their larger units work. Morally, they deserve higher pay for suffering the inhuman working conditions often found in industrialized jobs.

Increasingly, millions of Americans who are rushing to learn the newest fields of expertise will find themselves as "unskilled" (obsolete) and in debt as many industrial workers are today. They will all need the same solution: a system that provides lifelong opportunities for decent employment while maintaining the American standard of living.

In such a system the criteria for who is skilled or unskilled must range far beyond whether a person has command of small tools or personal knowledge, for these change and disappear too rapidly. The criteria must give great weight to who has the human skills to work well. Again, these include discipline, realism, cooperation, and organization. And they do not disappear with time but rather usually increase with experience and age.

Industrialized employees have these highly productive human skills in high degree and abundance already. And they have a strong long-term interest to create lifelong opportunities for employment. They and their skills must be saved or else every quality of social activity, and every social standard of quality—in production, behavior, and technology—will decline.

Wellsprings and Defenders of Civilization. If civilization is anything, it is the resort to negotiation rather than brute force to resolve grievances and bring about actions. People understand that by working together, they are better off. They accept many trade-offs on personal freedoms in order to gain other, better freedoms.

But there often comes a point when a small group of rulers threatens to dominate social organizations and create a dictatorship over society. Organized workers are a profoundly civilizing influence on such would-be dictators. By virtue of their collective and united strength, unions force some of the most powerful and arrogant people on earth—bosses and bureaucrats—to negotiate with and respect working people. That in turn influences people in government to understand that domestic and foreign policies must respect human rights and democracy.

Unions can be good negotiators and moderators because working people learn personally from their jobs that they have to talk things out to get work done. Sometimes it seems that organized workers do a lot of talking—perhaps too much talking. But considering the importance of issues and the large numbers of people involved, all wishing to learn and influence what their fellow workers are thinking and willing to do, a lot of talking usually has to be done. Then, after the issues have been aired and after feelings and thoughts have been expressed, effective decisions and actions are usually taken. That is why democracy is said to be slow to act, but mighty powerful when it does act.

Organized workers are people making decisions about some of the most important issues in their lives. Their talk is very much to the point. And it is effective. They develop enormous abilities to transmit and analyze information, negotiate, and build cooperation and respect for the truth.

In their organizations, working people are wellsprings of civilization. In a world full of just grievances and conflicting—seemingly irreconcilable—demands arising out of those grievances, we sorely need the best negotiators and talkers we can get to ameliorate grievances, build trust and cooperation among former enemies, and find or create solutions. We desperately need organized workers to become much more involved in the world's problems, for no one among the world's leaders seems both able and motivated to solve them.

10

How Employees Have Intelligence to Make Management Smarter

American Management Must Be Improved

If American managements are allowed to escape blame for their own failures, and if they don't radically improve their operations in big business and government, America is doomed to be a second-rate economic power, and American working people are doomed to suffer a lower, second-rate standard of living.

Who is going to increase U.S. competitiveness in all the non-employee related areas of American business and government? The rich investors, managers, bureaucrats, expert analysts, and consultants in business and government who got us into this mess? What is going to force them to change for the better?

Proponents of the present "free-market" system (as if all markets in America really were efficient free markets!) say that competition will force—is forcing—management to improve. They say that recession makes management "lean." Yet between 1969 and 1987, the U.S. had four severe recessions, and American economic competitiveness *declined* greatly during that period. Recent history shows that relying solely on "free-market competition" means that many companies will lose business permanently or go bankrupt because their managements will have failed to become competitive. It would be much better to clean up the act of faulty managements before they drag their companies and important parts of the American economy down with them.

The "free market" is particularly deficient as a source of vitality for the American economy when it comes to world trade. Many multinational corporations cry loudly for "free trade." But they receive a sinister form of protection in many foreign countries when the governments of those countries suppress workers and use the full power of the police and army to break strikes and imprison union organizers.

Authoritarian or right-wing military dictatorships suppress workers just as brutally as communist governments. Yet while loudly condemning communism, many leaders of America praise, do business with, and financially and militarily support many a right-wing dictatorship. Using American tax dollars, they support the very regimes whose brutality allows American multinational corporations to take jobs away from American working people. Let's see advocates of "free trade" prove that they are not hypocrites by fighting for workers' freedoms to assemble in foreign nations and collectively negotiate with their employers. While communist dictatorships fully earn our opposition, "anti-communism" does not justify supporting murderous rightist dictatorships in foreign lands.

Multinational corporations are free to export jobs by building plants in foreign countries, but American working people are not free in practice to leave. They are rooted and stuck in communities that have been abandoned or bled dry by the multinationals. A free market simply does not exist when foreign and multinational producers are free to sell their goods in America but are protected in foreign markets from American competition. Knee-jerk reliance on a "free market" will destroy countless American jobs and businesses and produce far fewer jobs and less business in return. It will leave America prey to giant multinational (probably Japanese or "American") corporations' monopolies or dependent on international cartels such as OPEC. And foreign competition will not make government more honest or efficient.

An effective defense against the international squeezes on working people will take a long and difficult global solution, but surviving in the meantime must start with improving the way the American economy operates. Its resources and people must be used more effectively and more humanely. The best place to start is to upgrade the quality of management in large corporations and government agencies that dominate the economy.

Top-Down Management Is Senseless

From a purely operational view, management's executive efficiency in large businesses and government services is unavoidably degraded because it is both autocratic and bureaucratic. Management is autocratic because it is modeled on the absolute power of a single owner. Management is bureaucratic because, while it is the theoretical representative of a theoretical owner, no individual really owns government or most big businesses. And no one person in large organizations directs all operations and exercises all powers, so no one has full powers to keep all of management honest even to itself, much less to anyone else.

Lacking the guiding, coherent hand of a single owner at the top, bureaucratic management often degenerates into a rat's nest of conflicting interests, divided loyalties, entrenched special interests, myopic vision arising out of divided or self-serving loyalties, and very little communication among managers. Bureaucratic management acts with the full power but without the intelligence and sensitivity and united purpose of a truly individual, private owner. It is debatable whether absolute power is good even for owners of small businesses, but blind and deaf power is senseless in large organizations.

Precisely because of this, many companies try to decentralize operations. But most stop short of ceding substantial autonomy to lower management, and they certainly do little to encourage or enable nonmanagement employees to exchange ideas and act on their own initiatives.

Improve Management with Better Information from Employees

As long as management has absolute authority, it is unaccountable to anyone. Most business and government operations lack internal pressures to keep management perpetually sharp. They lack internal incentives to encourage cooperation among employees and use untapped human resources. Without intelligent pressures and incentives, management will continue to treat working people—including, increasingly, their own middle and lower management—as fuel to be burned rather than as people to be consulted in improving operations. Many needed changes in the American economy will not be carried out by the managerial bureaucrats who got us into this mess in the first place.

The primary goal in improving management must be to internalize the discipline of competition so that corporations and government organizations are kept perpetually lean and regenerate, while at the same time nurturing a loyalty to the larger organization that avoids rapid turnovers or the vicious infighting of private empires within the organization.

Communication, cooperation, and mutual loyalty are necessary in any large organization. But instead of rewarding cooperation and group loyalty, autocratic and bureaucratic management uses fear and penalties, or selfish incentives, to motivate employees. So it cannot get, nor does it want to pay, tens of millions of working people to share their experience and unique knowledge about what is happening in production and in marketing, and it cannot get working people to volunteer initiatives, solve problems, and organize— or reorganize—superior system solutions.

Bureaucratic management cannot have both the dictatorial, top-down coordination of a strong boss at the top and the distribution of intelligence, communication, and decision-making at all points throughout the organization. It just cannot respond quickly and effectively to countless situations when and where they appear.

In bureaucratic management, top-down orders preclude diversity. Large-scale or widespread operations and decentralization make top-down coordination extremely difficult, if not impossible. Fear and distrust by subordinates of the boss, as well as fear and distrust by managers of other managers, interfere with all information and communication coming to the top from below. Distrust, ignorance, and paralysis, which arise out of fear of subordinates' distrust and ignorance, grip people at the top and make them extremely cautious. Personal ambitions corrode all orders from the top. The result often is that management is neither coordinated, aggressive, respectful of the company's best interests nor free to act in a decentralized way.

It is probably not coincidence that some of the most successful American corporations, notably IBM and Procter & Gamble, reputedly place dominant priority on marketing and attention to customers and customer service. Such externally oriented priorities exist in industries where technologies must be tailored to customers' needs or tastes. Companies in those industries must set up internal institutional structures that precondition it to listening to managers and service personnel on the ground level, where the company meets the market. Then the market would set the priorities, distributed management and staff would be charged with sensing and analyzing market priorities, and higher-up management would be charged with choosing and implementing policies to satisfy the market.

It also seems no coincidence that when IBM and Procter & Gamble ran into trouble, it was for being insensitive to their markets. By not giving corporate customers what they asked for, IBM lost them to Digital Equipment Corp. (*Business Week*, 3–30–87, 86). And Procter & Gamble lost "an estimated quarter of a billion dollars" in Japan because "they didn't listen to anybody" (*Forbes*, 12–15–86, 168). Fortunately for them, "Big Blue is relearning how to go the extra mile," and P&G "is learning, albeit slowly, from its mistakes."

Most governments and companies are not as market-oriented as IBM and P&G. And even IBM and P&G must still lose many opportunities for grass-roots feedback from "low-level" employees and employees in nonmarketing areas such as manufacturing and office work. Such areas have less contact with the market and may be less conditioned by the market to listen to "low-level" people.

Ironically, many companies that lack fine attention to marketing, notably companies in high tech, have tried to make up for their deficiency by hiring chief executives from successful marketing firms, such as Apple Computer's hiring of John Sculley from Pepsi-Cola. They seek the magic bullet but instead repeat the old mistake because they still take the top-down approach. Even a marketing man at the top cannot substitute for a whole management that is not market-oriented. Nor can a "marketing" executive succeed if the other top executives do not commit themselves to that approach. If top executives had been committed to marketing in the first place, the new executive probably would not have been needed. So getting a marketing chief executive may do no good and may create years of churning turmoil as managers fight among themselves for power or fight to avoid being replaced by more market-oriented managers, which also happened at Apple.

To operate efficiently and effectively, large organizations must get the full involvement of their employees. Full involvement means sharing in the decisions and rewards of management, as well as sharing the responsibilities, tasks, and risks. Workers already have more than their share of responsibilities, tasks, and risks. But involving employees in decisions and rewards is vigorously resisted because it runs directly against the strong grain of "private" ownership, which bureaucratic management claims to represent.

Many small businesses are truly private and deserve to stay that way, but what is private about publicly-owned GM? What is private about corporations in which the largest shareholder owns a tiny fraction of stock, and where up to millions of people hold shares, sometimes in multiple and competing companies? What is private about organizations that have tens or hundreds of thousands of employees? What is private at all about government? Nothing. When management claims the right of private property to enforce its own privacy, whom is it trying to be private from?

In most important ways, big business and government are not truly private, but they are kept private by management from employees, and also from stockholders, taxpayers, voters, and all persons in society. Involving employees in management will inevitably mean opening up management to the scrutiny of all the people who stand to benefit from its improvement or who stand to lose from its deterioration. The results will be better management in big business and government, which should benefit everyone in society, especially stockholders and taxpayers.

If the present chaos-producing system of professional mismanagement stays in place while management operations are opened up to scrutiny, many individual managers will feel betrayed and under attack. To defend themselves, they will make matters much worse, not better. To improve the present system, as well as to have a better system of management, many working managers themselves will need to participate much more than they currently participate in America in the process of management. That is, top financial management must be made to listen and respond more to its *own* management staff. And to get all that employees can contribute, increased participation needs to be extended to all nonmanagement employees.

Working people collectively know a great deal. Employees in the factory, office, lab, sales force, and field have many more eyes and ears than management. They are just as intelligent as management, and many are equally or better educated. They see first what is going on, they think first about it, and they have many ideas for improvements. They are ideally situated to gather information, judge the results of management's decisions, make their own decisions when appropriate, and act quickly when action is called for. Employees are currently an underused, formidable resource who must be employed much more effectively. Bringing them more fully into the management process offers an unparalleled chance to improve the quality of management with better information and feedback.

Employee participation in management will probably take many forms. It already does. Employees are involved in company paternalism, where management treats employees ostensibly like a family but allows them few powers to exercise intelligence and initiative, keeping employees more as children than as intelligent, responsible adults. Employees work closely with management by means of the almost-captive unions of Japan. Rapidly growing small companies involve employees in a sense of ownership as well as in management with stock ownership and profit-sharing plans. And West German unions in major industries have representatives on company boards of directors.

Union employees also tried to be involved in ownership and boards of directors at Chrysler and Eastern Airlines in the early 1980s, but that involvement broke down because management wanted money from workers and resisted sharing information or decision-making with employees. In other forms of employee participation that exist in the U.S., employees generally are highly restricted in what they can do and say by both law and management's practical powers.

Still, in the U.S., employees are usually ignored or penalized for even suggesting something to management. At worst, there is no feedback; at best, whatever employees actually do feed back to management is far inferior to the feedback that is needed for highly successful, complex living systems.

Feedback

In living systems, feedback entails some element of power by individual components to command the larger organism's behavior. For example, when the body needs food, hungry cells send out signals and take actions that we feel as hunger. Hunger forces us to eat or suffer for not eating, just as sated cells reward us with good tastes, smells, and feelings. When something cuts or burns the body, the affected areas make us feel pain, and pain forces us to do something or suffer the consequences. Similarly, we are driven to satisfy our emotional and social needs, or to defend ourselves, by feelings of love and friendship, fear, loneliness, anger, or hate.

If organs and individual cells within us lacked the power to issue commands and affect the body's overall behavior, any person or living organism would die from failing to attend to its own needs or failing to adjust to external circumstances. In other words, feedback is a highly sensitive and intelligent form of adjustment to reality, and feedback works only because individual components in the system have certain well-based powers to influence the system in their behalf.

In political democracies, citizens communicate their needs and desires to their political representatives, and the vote is the principal power of feedback citizens have to enforce their will. But where votes are suppressed by armed force, the rulers ignore and suppress the populace.

In market economies, consumers communicate their needs and desires to companies, and use of money is their principal power of feedback to get the kind of products they want. But where corporations or governments monopolize production and enforce their monopolies with legal and police powers, they ignore the market and impoverish their peoples.

In general, without compelling powers, the feedback provided by individual components can be—and will be—ignored by the central forces of the system. The result will be that the central forces will "take leave of their senses" and send the system or organism to destruction.

Similarly, in present forms of employees' participation in management, employees can speak—sometimes, and carefully—but management can ignore them and can punish them if it doesn't like what it hears.

Often the only feedback regulating management today is the final result of profit or loss, and the only thing that really shakes up management is the threat of bankruptcy or being bought out and merged into a larger company, both of which wipe out *management* jobs. Such feedback is as if the human body lacked all the finer senses of touch, taste, hunger, pain, pleasure, and muscular coordination. These senses tell us of subtle changes and move us to make subtle adjustments before the changes grow large and dangerous. Then managements' and the financial markets' one-dimensional attention to the bottom line is as if the body learned it must eat only after it had lost substantial weight, or as if it learned that it had lost an arm only after seeing the blood gushing and the arm lying on the floor.

Even the vaunted Wall Street analysts often know little that a company's management hasn't told them. So they too have to wait until the bones stick through the skin or the arm falls off. The only advantage they have is that they may add a new perspective and see the trouble a bit before management. But then they stampede like a herd of spooked cattle at the sound of thunder. And they usually trample not only the company that spooked them, but many others that even vaguely resemble it. That's no way to run a business or an economy.

Much more advanced forms of feedback are needed to make managements in big business and government alert to reality, responsive to change, and responsible to the stockholders and citizens they nominally report to. Yet advanced feedback cannot be implemented and maximum effectiveness cannot be achieved in large organizations unless working people have much more freedom to act within their places of employment. And working people will never get the freedom they need to make their full contribution unless they can organize and bargain in self-defense against management's own self-serving behavior, which includes trying to reduce employees' pay, taking dangerous shortcuts on the job, and punishing those who resist. In effect, feedback cannot be introduced into large business and government organizations unless employees have organizations that have authority, power, economic incentives, and responsibilities to control and command parts of their working environment for themselves.

This doesn't mean that individual employees should be free to do anything they wish. Feedback is meaningful only when it is an effective *counterbalance* to centralized authority. Centralized authority is necessary to produce effective and coordinated large-scale actions. But in many large organizations, central authority is absolute and local authority of working people—feedback—is nil. The point of this discussion is to raise a counterbalance to blind, deaf, and senseless centralized authority as embodied in bureaucratic managements. Until that is done, there is no danger of employees creating anarchy. Indeed, brutal or arrogant managements create great anarchy every day when they drive good employees to withhold initiatives, quit, or go on strike.

Like the senses that collect and transmit information to the brain, working people are at the working points in any large organization, where information first appears about internal operations and external conditions, where true feedback must originate. But since employees have brains and senses of their own, they are, or can be, far more intelligent and active participants in feedback to management than are the senses to the human brain.

In fact, the very analogy to a central brain is grossly misleading because many kinds of information are processed in human bodies outside of the brain. Many components of the central nervous system have large concentrations of nerve tissue that process information before it gets to the brain. They even take actions on their own—such as spinal reflexes—without consulting the brain. Several noncentral nervous systems link many organs directly, independently of the brain. Many organs have their own cells that analyze the blood and send chemicals of their own through the blood to affect every organ and every cell in the body—especially affecting moods and actions of the brain itself. And of course each cell has DNA that in turn carries enormous amounts of genetic information that affects behavior.

The Brain Proposes; Reality Disposes

Although we tend to think of the brain as the dominant organ of human evolution, there is much evidence to suggest that it serves rather than leads the feedback sensory organs. To put it another way, the senses tell the brain through the process of feedback what needs to be done, and the brain then figures out how to do it and issues orders to get it done. The fundamental priority of sense before thought comes about because information about the outside world must be sensed and collected, and preprocessed, before it can be effectively analyzed. There is no use or reason for a brain, or any analog to a brain, until it has problems to work on and information to work with. For example, primates, and our immediate evolutionary antecedents in particular, possessed an extraordinary confluence of information-gathering and information-using abilities: three-dimensional vision, color vision, dextrous hands, and diverse vocal abilities, for example. The more the brain used such information, the more survival abilities it would have.

In human activities, the real world predominates (although perhaps only belatedly), and the organs that interact with the real world predominate too. For example, mathematics is a "brain" or "computer" for science. Yet creative developments in theoretical mathematics frequently follow or are seeded by problems in physics, chemistry, biology, social sciences, and other "real-world" situations that add new dimensions and conditions to the old theorems.

The primacy of sense (the very word means intelligence) over thinking, and the priority of communication over thinking, crop up in the development of information technologies. Major generational advances in computers have come from the communications industry, especially Bell Laboratories, first with transistors and semiconductor technology, and then with optics. Many more researchers at AT&T won Nobel Prizes than at IBM. Scientists at AT&T pioneered or advanced whole new fields of study, including radio astronomy and communication and information theory. And of course AT&T grew large long before IBM.

Before computers or brains (or managements) can do any processing, they need to have problems and information about those problems collected, formulated, and presented for solution. Computers (like brains) need the communications industry (like the senses) to come before them and create the preconditions for their use. Communications and senses act in provinces outside the computer or brain. But dealing with the outside world is much more difficult than creating a self-consistent organ such as a computer or brain. The difficulties can be seen in the comparative evolutions of computer and robot systems.

Enormously powerful computers have already been built, but

they are not very smart. Like idiot savants (people of very low IQ who do miraculous things with dates or numbers, for example), they can so some technical tasks far better and faster than ordinary humans, but they need to be spoon-fed and nursemaided every step of the way and can't take intelligent or new actions for themselves. So-called expert or artificial intelligence systems are still extremely rudimentary and not very useful.

Similarly, robot systems are still very primitive. Creating a machine with consistent internal operations, an electronic automaton such as a computer, which is analogous to the brain, is easy, even trivial, compared to creating machines of sense and action that intelligently interact with reality. The "simplest" things, such as "grasping" a meaning in a tone of voice or grasping a particular object in a collection of objects, is still beyond the capacity of robots except in highly controlled and limited situations. Computer power has existed for many years to control robot behavior. Now computers-on-a-chip promise to make small and cheap computer brains available for robots. But the far greater challenge is in creating cheap and effective eyes, ears, hands, legs—or their equivalents—with sensitive feelings of touch, fine interpretations of nuance and small differences, and judgment for action.

In organizations of human beings, notably big businesses and government, management is an organ that acts like a "brain," but of course it is far less sophisticated and efficient. The best managements have only limited sensory connections to all their operations and have even more limited powers of feedback to adapt and adjust internally.

Given the right information, it is simple to make decisions. It is like saying that if 2 is added to 2, then 4 is the result. But are the figures really 2 plus 2? Should they really be added? Are they numerical at all? That's where judgment, interpretation, and reality all come in.

Few things in business are ever known exactly. Many are not known at all until a decision is made, actions are taken, and the results reveal what had previously gone unknown. The hardest part in any business decision is collecting and analyzing information about operations and external—especially market and political—conditions. Only after all that work has been done can someone say that 2 + 2 does equal 4, *if* the facts are accurate, *if* the rules are all known, and *if* the addition indeed corresponds to the facts and rules. Good management is of course involved in all of these steps, but so are employees involved, especially with good management. Working people, including industrialized workers, act like organs that sense, interpret, and interact with reality for management, especially where management keeps out of operations.

Management processes business information, but nonmanagement employees and lower management are the prime resources for making that information as complete, error-free, accurate, and high-quality as possible. Employees have huge resources of information because they are the prime contact with reality in operations and in the marketplace, and because they do a lot of information processing on the job every time they are called on to take an action or make a judgment. And those responsibilities are eagerly pushed on them by all stripes of managements.

So even if bureaucratic management were analogous to the brain, which its many faults prove it is not, the analogy would still be grossly inadequate all by itself to approximate the complex systems of analysis, command, and feedback that advanced living systems such as the human body have. The same crippling flaw afflicts political intellectuals who would attempt to substitute political bureaucracies for the managerial bureaucracies in business and government.

Managers, intellectuals, academics, consultants, and wealthy individuals who wield worldly power in big business and government often think they are "brains." The analogy to a brain is highly flattering, but it means little more than that they may be idiot savants. Worse, many do not "get their hands dirty" in operations. They leave dirty work to workers. That reveals they are out of touch with reality. And being out of touch with reality, they are irrelevant, useless, costly, potentially dangerous, and unfit for their high positions.

They like to imagine that they are superior to "average" working people. In truth, their money or position gives them power to buy, seduce, or intimidate others to praise and serve them. When they use that power wisely, they may be at least partly worthy of their own high regard. But when they misuse their power, which is almost inevitable, they cloak themselves in the fruits of the labor of their employees and appear far more worthy than they really are. They take credit and rewards from the people who really get work done. And they degrade operations immeasurably.

Information Overloads Short-Circuit
Authoritarian Managements

Information overloads cause breakdowns. No information system has an unlimited capacity for handling information. Bombarded with too much information, an information system will break down just as a car will break down under too heavy a load. Confronted with too many or contradictory things to do, even the most powerful computers can thrash about like fish out of water, moving more and more data around but getting less and less done. Perhaps the evolving brains of some human ancestors failed to cope with their increased burdens of information. Overwhelmed and befuddled, they could have lost effectiveness and died out.

Overloads can be handled minimally by shutting out part of the burden. When people are confronted by more than they can handle, those who survive shut out the least important things and things they can't handle in order to concentrate on the most important things they can handle. Those who shut out too many important things don't survive. In tennis, concentration on essentials is practically a decisive factor for victory. It explains Chris Evert's dominance over seemingly superior athletes. Computer systems suffer when they try to respond, or cannot avoid responding, equally to everything, without effective discrimination or priorities, and without effective filters to keep out, or postpone, less important information or demands. This leads to speculation that monkeys and apes, which survived without expanding their brains nearly as much as humans, did so by shutting out many kinds of information that their senses were giving them. So they stopped evolving.

Now the increasing need to work with large volumes and high qualities of information is placing a heavy burden of information on modern American managements. Some managements are evolving, but many are reacting by shutting out information from working people, thereby threatening extinction for themselves and all stockholders and employees dependent on them.

Employees' Distributed Intelligence

When things go right or wrong, employees not only see it and learn it, but they think about what happens and think about how things might be done better or differently. They also communicate among themselves, make associations, belong to informal groups, and occasionally create formal organizations that, taken together, are an elaborate network of decentralized information processing—a highly advanced form of distributed intelligence.

Distributed processing by many small computers is often and widely superior in data processing to a single, solitary central computer. And where there is a central computer, distributed data entry and verification by many remote terminals is far superior to performing all data entry and verification at the central computer. This is because the closer that information is kept to its sources of generation, including the people who know the most about it, the more accurate and sophisticated it is and the less it has to be massaged by the central computer. That raises quality and lowers costs of computation, communication, and error detection and correction. The distributed processors and the people distributed at many sites have their own intelligences: distributed intelligences.

Like distributed computing, decentralization of management is rapidly proving superior at keeping large businesses dynamic and flexible. That superiority is also the basis for the rapid growth and spread of personal computers into management, where it increases distributed data processing and aids decentralized decision-making. Similarly, the free market's most decisive advantage over centralized planning is the freedom of many individuals and organizations to take actions that suit themselves better than the remote government can. So why are the principles of decentralized management and distributed intelligence suddenly wrong when they are carried to their logical conclusion in giving managerial independence to groups of employees?

The Intelligence of Independent Employee Participation in Management

To keep management lean and "honest," people within business and government are needed who have the power and the knowledge to put pressure on management to change and improve.

Employees have immense knowledge and experience about how corporations and government work. Daily, they are involved and intimately associated with every aspect of operations. They see firsthand how policy affects operations and feel first—even before management—every operating result of policy decisions.

And they are such a large part of the public that they can informally represent the public's needs or wishes directly within the company or government agency.

Employees are best positioned to suggest the quickest changes as they are needed, from the production line to the sales line, and from the payroll line to the bottom line. Because they work harder, get paid less, and are laid off before management, they have the strongest reasons to keep their employers efficient and solvent.

Only employees collectively know enough about what really happens in business and government to provide adequate information for change. And only unions or other independent associations of employees have the potential power, if anyone has, to protect individuals who come forward—whistle-blowers—with needed information about faulty practices and suggestions for change. Groups of employees, unions, and professional associations must be substantially involved in all parts of management to restore vitality to large industries and government units.

Employees are a big business's or government's prime contact with reality, and reality must take precedence in the long run if an organization is to survive. The ideal system for managing big business and government must give employees the primacy and the respect that are due to reality. Independent employee participation has a vital, sometimes *primary* role to play in keeping a large organization close to reality. It can create, maintain, and safeguard high efficiency and effectiveness in *any* large organization. If practiced widely, it would also bring new vitality to many small businesses that do business with big business, government, and their employees.

If employees had full powers of feedback and participation in the management process to raise the quality of information and keep management alert and informed, then the new forms of management that may ultimately emerge promise to be as superior to present managements as the human brain is superior to the brains of gorillas and baboons.

——11——

Organization: Why It's Key and Who's Best at It

If management respected employees' intelligence, the American economy would be much stronger and more attuned to serving the needs of all working people. Unfortunately, the economy increasingly serves the needs of financial and bureaucratic managers at the expense of both working people and long-term economic strength. The intensifying super-liquidity trap virtually guarantees that no matter what doubts individual managers may have about prevailing management practices, the process of shutting out employees, abusing working people generally, and running down the economy will continue. In other words, abuse of employees in these circumstances translates into abuse of the economy and an inability to compete on world markets. And protecting employees translates into creating conditions to improve management, strengthen the economy, and raise the American standard of living.

The government has created some legal protections for employees, but it can't enforce them on the job. And under Ronald Reagan, it doesn't even want to. Before employees will be heard and heeded in improving management, they will have to organize so that they can defend themselves against management abuse. There is no other viable way.

Presently, trade unions and professional associations that bargain collectively are the only organizations of employees that protect employees significantly on the job. In America, these employee organizations have generally come to accept "management prerogatives" and kept a hands-off attitude toward telling management what to do. However, some of them are moving toward getting seriously involved in management.

The United Steelworkers of America, for instance, has negotiated contracts that exchange pay and benefits for stock ownership and nomination of directors on boards of many companies (*Business Week*, 5–18–87, 107). In 1987, the USW also began working with seven steel companies on creating better "labor-management participation teams," and other companies were informally participating as well (*Business Week*, 5–11–87, 84). A number of other unions, especially in heavy industry, are also involved in "worker participation," "employee involvement," or "quality of work life" and "quality circle" programs.

The National Education Association and the American Federation of Teachers are increasingly active on academic and government panels to improve education in America. They want teachers to have more say in what is taught, how it's taught, and who oversees the teaching. At the time of this writing, the Air Line Pilots Association is trying to buy United Airlines. And railroad unions had previously tried to buy Conrail, a railroad that serves the eastern United States.

So far, management has repulsed or taken advantage of many union efforts at cooperation. In one case hailed by some as a milestone in 1983, Local 100 of the International Association of Machinists negotiated pay cuts and work-rule changes in return for 25 percent of Eastern Airlines stock. But despite management's claims, it stayed hostile to labor and the IAM's 25 percent share in the company turned out to be powerless and costly.

In another celebrated case, General Motors allowed workers at its Hyatt Roller Bearing Plant in Clark, New Jersey, to buy the plant in an Employee Stock Ownership Plan, forming Hyatt Clark Industries in 1981 (*New York Times*, 10–26–81). Workers paid GM $53 million for a plant that the company was going to close. Additionally they promised to pay GM another $15 million over the next 20 years. And they borrowed the money to buy the plant from Chemical Bank, GM, and Prudential Insurance. Their capital costs were high and creditors and GM set the terms of ownership. In particular, workers' stockholder voting rights were deferred to an outside bank trustee until they paid off the $53 million principal (Warner Woodworth, *Dollars & Sense*, July/August 1985, 17). The creditors then gave management high pay and power to do as it wished, and they backed up management when the worker "owners" protested. The result: As of this writing, Hyatt Clark is in bankruptcy proceedings (*New York Times,* 5–3–87, F1).

Many nonunion companies tell their employees that they *are* involved in management. On an operational basis, some are. Perhaps no company involved employees more in "ownership" and managerial responsibilities for production than People Express Airlines. Employees owned stock in the company and were partly compensated in effect as business expanded and the stock rose in value. And Donald Burr, the chairman-founder of People Express, exhorted "worker participation" all the time. But he also engaged in a policy of rapid expansion that deferred profits from actually reaching employees' pockets (*Business Week,* 1–28–85, 90). Eventually, that growth became reckless and People Express wound up being taken over by Frank Lorenzo and Texas Air Corp.—a top-down union-busting combination that was the very antithesis of "participative management."

Although People Express's employees had managerial responsibilities and bits of ownership, they were powerless in financial and investment matters. And People Express itself, like most other companies, was powerless to fight the super-liquidity trap. The trap forces managements and companies to go for ultrarapid growth, and it allows other companies to buy up companies such as People Express that founder in that growth. People Express's employees consequently had no managerial powers at the highest level and paid a high price for their powerlessness.

On the basis of these events and their own experiences, many union workers are understandably suspicious of "participation" or "ownership" schemes which are actually *management's* plans. They view such schemes as ways of management to get more work for less pay in harder or more dangerous working conditions. But many employees also understand that better management can have its benefits, such as saving their jobs and creating more jobs and higher pay besides.

There are good economic reasons why union members—and all employees—can take advantage of bad management to fight for more control in the workplace and create a new kind of management: one that serves *their* interests better, by using their intelligence to work smarter and paying them more for it. These new kinds of management could then be role models to help nonunion employees argue for better managements of their own, to demonstrate the superiority of using and paying for employees' intelligence, and to fight the super-liquidity trap by demonstrating that hostile management attitudes toward employees are self-destructive.

Employee organizations of all kinds, from unions to nonunion professional associations and to individual employee groups, can also talk about these matters. In addition, they can share information, conduct public debates, start publications, encourage academic studies, underwrite think tanks, lobby in Congress, propose laws to protect whistle-blowers and restrain super-liquidity, support consultants who help employees work for smarter management, and generally give employees everywhere ideas, vision, and encouragement.

The key to all this—the beginning of the solution—is organization. Employees must organize themselves in groups and associations both to protect themselves and to improve management. And unions must get involved in improving management to protect themselves and their members as well. No change for the better can be accomplished without these actions. And no change can be for the best without having the best organizers as leaders. Who are the best organizers and potential leaders and how do they get that way?

Driven by Special Responsibilities for Production

As we have seen, even though companies have in theory the "best and the brightest" in engineering and management, problems for a business or government operation can arise from many quarters and appear within any part of an organization. But expensive capital equipment and deeply entrenched systems of operation can't be discarded casually or quickly just because they don't work perfectly or are growing old or outmoded.

When problems arise, the first symptoms appear in operations, on the factory or sales floor, or in the office. Employees are the first to experience them and the first to have to deal with them. They have to adjust or else risk their jobs. Raising a problem to the boss's attention is a risk itself. It can bring into question the employee's ability to get the job done. And some bosses, at least, don't like to be confronted with problems.

Some bosses act as if they don't believe a problem is real until employees prove it is real by suffering heavily for it, such as losing an arm to a machine or losing accounts in a faulty computer system. Working managers and professional employees can get this treatment just as much as hourly workers. It's as if employees were either congenitally lazy or were the enemy just waiting to screw management every chance they get. That could be a self-fulfilling prophecy: irrationally tough bosses turn employees into enemies.

Such "tough" bosses think that the more pressure they put on employees, the more they get from employees. Sometimes they are right, but more often they get high dissatisfaction, rapid turnover, declines in quality, and lost business from inferior production. To make sure that a problem goes beyond employees' abilities to adapt, management may even go through several generations of replacement employees before it accepts that it "has a problem."

Unfortunately, management's problem can easily become an employee's disaster. The original employee could have been dismissed, penalized, falsely blamed, injured, or even killed. Furthermore, management may let the problem continue so long that the whole operation shuts down and all employees lose their jobs.

The result is that management often passes the buck for production to working employees, who can't pass the moneyless buck to anyone else. This completes management's abdication of responsibility for production: Largely unaccountable to markets and overseers, except in ways that are mostly nonproductive, it gets working employees (including many a working manager and professional staffer) to carry out production.

Blaming the Victim

Managers who convince or force working people to shoulder more work are often promoted. But in a classic catch-22, employees and working managers who take on responsibilities for production may not be promoted because they are considered too valuable: the job couldn't get done without them. Their competence is reinforced by their responsibilities just as management's incompetence is reinforced by its abdication of responsibility. Consequently, when something does go wrong on the job, employees are usually blamed and upper management escapes relatively unscathed.

Three Mile Island. When the nuclear reactor at Three Mile Island nearly melted down and threatened millions of people in eastern Pennsylvania, "operator error" was blamed. Only later did investigators uncover a systemic pattern of management failure in General Public Utilities, the operator of the plant. It was so bad that a commissioner of the federal government's Nuclear Regulatory Commission, Victor Gilinsky, said that senior executives of the plant should be dismissed, protesting that in large part, "G.P.U. continues to be run by the same few individuals who ran the company before the accident" (*New York Times,* 6–24–83). If top management can stay in charge after an accident so bad that the entire nuclear power industry became suspect in America, just imagine how unaccountable and untouchable most bosses are in less extreme cases.

New York City Mass Transit. Lots of things go wrong with New York City's mass-transit system. Often, management blames problems on "inflexible" or "unproductive" union work rules. Yet working in NYC's subway system, for example, which was underfunded and allowed to run down for decades, is difficult and dangerous. The system has at times been plagued by broken cars, unsafe tracks, antiquated repair shops, rashes of fires and power outages, numerous accidents, and rampant vandalism and crime. And drivers carry heavy responsibilities for human life.

In such circumstances, employees' views would differ often and strongly from management's, even in the context of providing the best service to the public. Since top management does not work in the subways or the buses, many legitimate disputes would need to be negotiated or, at times, fought over. A union such as the Transport Workers Union cannot reasonably be blamed for fighting to defend employees from dangerous situations or opposing what it sees as bad operational decisions.

Unfortunately, the TWU at times took a somewhat truculent public stance that made it appear to be truly the problem management claims it is. But at the same time the union has long said it wants to cooperate with management to solve the transit system's problems. Outside auditors confirm that the union's actions really haven't impeded transit productivity.

After management won the right to change work rules in 1982, the state-appointed inspector general for the city's transit system, Sidney Schwartz, reported that management didn't change the work rules it complained of because of poor management (*New York Times,* 1–17–84, 1). Later, he said that blaming unionization was a "cop-out" by management (*New York Times,* 12–15–84, 26). At other times, Schwartz also said that mismanagement cost the transit authority hundreds of millions of dollars per year, and that the same old failings kept going uncorrected.

Among many more reports of mismanagement at the Transit Authority, the *New York Times* (5–27–85, A1) reported that four years after a team of business executives had made an exhaustive study of the TA, "most of the deficiencies the executives saw in 1981 were never corrected" due to "problems of management." And the TA lost $100 million because of billing errors alone (*New York Times,* 6–20–85, A1). But the most intriguing story is of a supervisor who kept a bull whip in his office (*New York,* 11–17–86, 48). According to broadcast reports, he was in the habit of brandishing it as he walked through his repair shop. How's that for a management style!

This mismanagement on a gigantic scale affects the entire greater New York City metropolitan area, comprising perhaps 12 million people "served" by public transit. Management spent many billions of dollars on equipment that often broke down while still new, forced the public to suffer with antiquated replacement equipment, and wasted immense amounts of labor patching up that old equipment. Yet management has been allowed to continue virtually untouched, except for occasional cosmetic changes. And it still blames workers and their unions for what goes wrong.

Air Traffic Control. When workers speak up or protest management's failures, they get punished as well as blamed. When air traffic controllers went on strike in August 1981, the controllers were condemned for "breaking the law." President Reagan used the full powers of the U.S. government to break their union, throw them all out of work, and brand them violators of sacred oaths. Yet subsequent reports widely acknowledged that the Federal Aviation Authority was an arrogant, excessively demanding boss and that the controllers had just grievances that they had been quietly attempting to fix for over ten years.

Transportation Secretary Drew Lewis admitted the validity of the controllers' grievances, and President Reagan was revealed to have admitted it in a letter he wrote to PATCO (the air traffic controllers' union) while still a Presidential candidate. Yet when the controllers went on strike in desperation and outrage, the same people who admitted their grievances treated the strikers like criminals; or worse, almost like traitors. Strikers claimed that government agencies used every means available to punish the strikers, including foreclosing on government-backed home loans of striking controllers. There were also accounts of vindictive harassment. One dismissed striker told how "a Federal marshal parked outside their home and warned children that the man who lived there was an outlaw" (*New York Times,* 9–28–86, F4).

Much was made that the strikers "broke the law" and "broke their oaths" not to strike, but their treatment wasn't really a question of enforcing oaths or the law at all. The FAA was the one that broke its oath: it pushed its employees mercilessly; the air controllers were just trying to defend themselves and make the FAA live up to its promises. That's precisely what unions are supposed to do.

As for breaking the law, the courts hold that some laws are not valid and may be broken, such as laws that enforce slavery, inequality, or brutality. And millions of Americans routinely break the law. When Americans drive over the speed limit or drive while intoxicated, they kill thousands of innocent people each year and are far more dangerous to public safety than any real or imagined crimes of PATCO. Yet speeders are practically heroes in many states and drunk drivers usually are allowed to keep on driving, sometimes even when they kill people. Similarly, tax cheats are heroes in business circles. Two Presidents of the United States, Reagan and Nixon, openly courted Mafia-tainted Teamsters officials in return for their political support. And President Reagan took no action against numerous friends and appointees who were forced out of his administration by scandals. The plain fact is that the strikers did nothing to deserve being treated so brutally. They instead did what any brave American would do: stand up and fight for their rights. That is the only way to keep freedom alive.

The air traffic controllers paid dearly for their protest against management's failures, but the FAA management was left in charge, unrepentant and unreformed ("What Could Ground FAA Reform," *Business Week*, 2–28–83).

The nation paid dearly for the turmoil the FAA created. General aviation traffic (small planes) was drastically reduced and commercial airline schedules were cut back for years, causing long delays for travelers, including many business people.

Worse, reports of near-crashes increased and two crashes occurred in the first year after the strike. The FAA's solution to break the strike was never officially blamed for the crashes. Yet published circumstances of the crashes raised questions about the air-traffic-control system manned by inexperienced, overworked, or rusty strike-breaking air traffic controllers.

When a jet skidded off an ice-covered runway while attempting to land at Boston's Logan Airport on January 23, 1982, winding up in frigid bay waters and killing two passengers, the National Transportation Safety Board reported that strikebreaking air traffic controllers had failed to request information or warn pilots about dangerous icy runways ("Board Blames Lack of Data for DC-10 Crash in Boston," *New York Times*, 12–16–82).

In the other, far more deadly crash that winter, at Washington, D.C.'s National Airport, a plane crashed after takeoff due to heavy ice buildup on its wings and fuselage. The ice had built up because the plane had been kept on the ground much longer than usual waiting for takeoff in snow and freezing rain. Would an experienced staff of air traffic controllers have known to alert the pilots to icing? More important, would an experienced staff have gotten the plane off the ground before the ice built up to a fatal load? And finally, how much of the delay was due to the FAA's undermanned, strikebreaking air-traffic-control system that required planes to wait on the ground during bad weather? No one in authority asked or answered these questions in any public way.

Both crashes involved relatively new, inexperienced airlines. To speed up their ability to offer service, and to lower costs of pilot training and screening, did they assume and depend on the same level of air-traffic-control support that preceded the strike?

It hardly seems likely that top-quality air traffic control could have been delivered in the most heavily used and cramped airports under the worst of winter conditions by understaffed, inexperienced, or rusty strikebreakers. The miracle is there were not more crashes.

Why was the FAA so willing to take a potentially dangerous strike of its controllers, and why was it allowed to go unreformed?

The FAA and the U.S. Justice Department began preparing to break a strike as early as January 1980 ("Carter Aides Drew Strategy for a Strike 20 Months Ago," *New York Times,* 8–6–81, A1). They succeeded in the short run because the FAA shifted the burden of flight control from the airport to the airlines by rescheduling flights to prevent the heaviest concentrations of traffic. Since it needed only enough controllers to handle peak loads, it got by with fewer controllers by reducing peak loads. And airline traffic itself plummeted as the deep recession of President Reagan's first administration began. Consequently, the FAA offered some service, albeit limited, and claimed—deceptively—to be serving the public.

Also, the FAA got the full use of military controllers to fill in for striking civilian controllers. And the FAA had the full backing of two Presidents and their administrations from the Democratic and Republican political parties. The national policy to squeeze and break unions had come a long way indeed.

For the long run, the FAA has been trying to increase computer control of air traffic (*Business Week,* 1–18–82, 100). If successful, it wouldn't need nearly as many traffic controllers as it needed in 1981. Given that labor-eliminating strategy, and given the long time of preparation for the strike, it appears that the FAA may very well have deliberately provoked the controllers into striking so that they could be fired for an "illegal" action. Getting rid of thousands of highly paid controllers and smashing their union saved the FAA a lot of money and freed it to do anything it wanted with the new controllers—unencumbered by "restrictive" union work rules. It also put the blame for the strike and the dismissals on the controllers rather than on the FAA.

All the antiunion warriors in America, including many in the Reagan Administration, applauded the FAA mightily. The firing of the traffic controllers intimidated the postal workers and their unions, who were nearing the end of their own contracts. And employers everywhere were emboldened to step up their own attacks on unions. The FAA had accomplished quite a lot, and it was rewarded by being left to do business in its usual way.

Ironically, the strike resulted in de facto reintroduction of air travel regulation because air flights were strictly rationed during peak periods. A President who fought in principle against government regulation found in practice a use for government regulation, and for the military too, to break a small, inexperienced government union—while claiming to support Polish workers to strike against *their* government.

Four years later, the air-traffic-control system was still in trouble. On September 24, 1985, an Eastern jet nearly crashed into the Potomac River at Washington's National Airport because an air traffic controller had put a helicopter in its path (*U.S. News & World Report*, 10–14–85, 153). Cockpit recorders of a Delta plane that crashed and killed 137 people on August 2, 1985, at Dallas-Fort Worth Airport showed that the pilots were highly critical of the controller (NBC Nightly News, 9–30–85; WINS radio, 9–30–85). Saying that air safety was diminishing, a congressional report released on September 10, 1985, urged the FAA to hire more controllers and improve working conditions, morale, and management practices (*New York Times*, 9–11–85, A18). In 1987, Malcolm S. Forbes wrote, "In the name of those who will die in air collisions that should never happen, Washington ought to tackle the killing problems plaguing our murderously overstretched air-traffic-control system" (*Forbes*, 3–9–87, 25). Not by coincidence, air traffic controllers began forming new unions all over again. *Forbes* said the FAA had no one but itself to blame (4–6–87, 35). And air controllers did indeed vote by an overwhelming 2-to-1 margin to form a new union, the National Air Traffic Controllers Association (*Wall Street Journal*, 6–12–87, 4).

Are these examples of management failure exceptional? Only in that management got caught enough to be embarrassed a little. Most of the time "human error" is loudly blamed to cover up for management decisions that make do with faulty equipment, cut corners on maintenance, create confusion and disorder, and push working people beyond their physical abilities. Management failures create many difficult or dangerous problems and force working people under the threat of heavy penalties to do both their own jobs and management's job as well.

Education. A very special case of abdication of responsibility by many different types of people and bureaucracies occurs when American teachers are blamed and expected to make up for all the different faults in American education. It should be obvious to anyone that no one can teach an unmotivated or hostile child. Ill, hungry, or lead-poisoned children can't be taught much. Good students can't be taught when disruptive children are allowed by parents, politicians, and school administrators to break up the class, when outsiders are allowed to terrorize the halls, or when drugs are sold and used by students in school. And potentially good students can't learn when they can't study at home, or when they don't believe their educations will bring them a good job, or when they see they can make more money selling drugs than they could ever make with a high school education. Teachers face all these problems but have neither authority, power, funds, personal time nor energy to correct them.

Many authorities above teachers profoundly affect the educational system. Yet when those authorities abdicate their responsibilities and failings in the educational system become matters of public concern, teachers bear the brunt of criticism.

Professional educators—not teachers—in universities allow courses like basket weaving to replace math, science, English, history, and languages. And publishing companies allow textbooks to be watered down to the least objectionable common denominator. On the other extreme, educators—not teachers—design math and science courses for future Ph.D.s instead of for use in daily life.

Colleges and universities accept subpar entrants into teaching programs, which then graduate and certify subpar teachers. State legislatures and boards of education certify subpar teachers, accept subpar teachers because they cost less to pay, and approve tenure for subpar teachers.

School-board staffs are favorite places for political appointees, who often have no loyalty to the educational system and little knowledge how to oversee or run it for the benefit of education. Some politicians and school officials turn school budgets into pork barrels for construction projects and equipment purchases. They may also get kickbacks. And then they cut into real educational expenditures to pay for their profiteering or sheer incompetence.

School administrators also accept watered-down curricula, watered-down courses, and subpar teachers from the professional educators and politicians.

There are principals who don't enforce educational standards or student discipline in the schools. Many teachers I have interviewed have said that the principal sets the standards in the school and teachers must obey those standards. That is how it should be. The principal is the boss and the teacher who blatantly disobeys established procedures will probably be fired. So why are teachers blamed for lack of discipline when neither parents nor principals nor the courts will support them in enforcing it?

And finally the public—including many parents, along with the President of the United States—fails to object for 20 years while the educational system deteriorates, but objects instead to paying for better teachers.

The strange—and revealing—thing is that America is not paying more for teachers. As a percentage of educational budgets, teachers' salaries actually dropped from 56 percent in 1956 to 42 percent in 1986 according to the U.S. Department of Education (*Forbes*, 12–29–86, 75). The low percentage of money going to teachers is a sure sign that the rest of the educational system is bloated at the expense of both teachers and education. And the large drop in teachers' percentage shows that most of the increased money spent in the last 30 years never went to teachers in the first place.

In light of all the actors and factors in the U.S. educational system, why are all the attention and blame dumped on teachers? Because they are at the bottom of the totem pole of authority and at the ground floor of doing the work. Like most managements, all the people above teachers can look the other way, pass the blame, and keep out of the classroom.

But teachers have to work in schools and can't escape that responsibility because upward of 30 potentially disrespectful and disruptive children won't let them. In the classroom, a teacher must be on stage every minute. That can be a hard act to keep up for a long time. When teachers can't keep up, or when parents or principals don't give them the support they need to enforce discipline, then education suffers.

Further, discipline—in the sense of being tough or strict—often is neither enough nor appropriate. When students are on drugs, or come to school hungry, or weep in class from abuse they suffered out of school, education calls for immeasurably greater skills than merely tough discipline and factual knowledge ("Teachers Tell of Daily Ordeal in City Schools," *New York Times*, Larry Rohter, 5–9–86, B2). Worse, when drug dealers assault teachers, they can destroy discipline and commitment altogether. It's not only a big city or slum problem, although that would be bad enough. Drugs are increasingly likely to be in every community, every school, every home. And child abuse can also happen anywhere.

Teachers have not gone unharmed by these kinds of abuse and lowered standards. Many are worn out and too many are either not prepared or not able to shoulder all the burdens this nation puts on them. Yet for at least 20 years teachers have been trying to tell the public just how bad things are going. But the American response has been to blame the messenger for the bad news. The miracle is that America has any good teachers left at all.

It will solve nothing to blame teachers for what is not their fault. The lax standards, low discipline, waste, and high costs that every other part of the educational system tolerates or encourages must be rooted out first. Any real solution must recognize that the entire educational system—including teachers—must be upgraded, for it and they cannot be replaced wholly.

Indeed, teachers are the first ones who want to improve the system, and they frequently go well beyond the call of duty. For example, Sandra Feldman, president of the United Federation of Teachers in New York City, said she knew of teachers "who had spent up to $600 of their own money for essentials like erasers, pencils, chalk, and rulers" (*New York Times*, 5–9–86, B2).

Perhaps not everyone knows that Christa McAuliffe, the teacher who died in the space shuttle Challenger explosion, was active in the National Education Association and had been president of her local chapter near Concord, New Hampshire. At its annual convention in July 1986, the NEA honored her posthumously and her husband spoke to the delegates not only about her but about them and their role in education ("A Reporter's Notebook: A Memory of McAuliffe," *New York Times*, 7–7–86). After urging them to get involved in the political arena to recruit and elect represen-

tatives who support education strongly, Steven McAuliffe concluded, "Most of all...stay in education at least until we in fact
have a system which honors teachers and rewards teachers as
they deserve." It was described as "a charge to action" and the
delegates responded with "sustained applause."

Teachers and their unions are ready. They know best what is
going on—and going wrong. They live and work with the system
and try to improve it every day. And they have strong organizations to propose and make effective change. We should listen
much more to them and support their efforts instead of ignoring
or fighting their every proposal.

Driven by Production to Organize

The penalties for not getting work done, or even for protesting
how it is not getting done right, can be severe. To keep working,
employees often have little choice but to solve problems quietly
on their own and make do with what they have. They may have
to keep up production as machines and systems slowly degrade,
or they may have to increase production in order to meet rising
competition or expectations. Sometimes they have surprisingly
wide limits to decide for themselves how to solve the problems
they face. Some managers keep out of operations on principle,
and others know that skilled employees are best suited to solve
problems that arise.

Solving all the problems that management lays on employees' shoulders isn't easy. Some try to reorganize the workplace
or modify systems of operation; many join or create new working relationships with other employees. In offices especially, they
form huge informal networks to get things done.

In such cases, working people develop abilities that grow with
time and work into powerful gifts for organization. When they
work for large employers, they can form even larger social units
and forge working relationships with many people and groups.

Those relationships are shaped by the overriding demands of
production. People who work together can't all go their separate
ways. They can't allow petty differences to interfere with doing
the work. They have to find ways to cooperate, communicate,
and respect the abilities and leadership of the best and most ex-

perienced. When problems arise, ideas must be expressed, compromises must be worked out, and the best ways must be found to get the job done.

As people work, they discover that contrary to ethnic jokes or racial slurs, a Pole can be intelligent. An Italian can be brave. A Jew can be generous. A woman can be strong. And a black person can be intelligent, brave, generous, and hardworking. In the process, they bridge racial, cultural, religious, and even language barriers that keep so many other people in distrustful separation. Then, once the barriers are bridged, people begin to work together in progressively larger and more powerful groups.

In unions, employees create highly integrated, vibrant organizations. People who have never taken part in such organizations may take them for granted, as if workers were mindless lemmings who stupidly follow union "bosses." But creating and keeping alive a union is far from easy, and employees are far from being naturally predisposed to joining together against their employer.

In most cases, job applicants come to employers individually and mentally make contracts with their employer long before they meet their fellow employees. Employers keep their special one-to-one relationship with employees by giving them orders and paying them individually.

Employers have many tools such as fear and firings, promises of promotion, and small favors to keep employees separated on the job. People can be separated too by being scattered among offices, cities, and nations; speaking different languages; having different cultural and social practices; and harboring racial or religious prejudices. Far from clan-like cohesion among employees, the natural initial state of employees is isolated separation among themselves and fawning dependency on employers.

To an isolated, perhaps intimidated individual, the idea of organizing an office, factory, company, or government service employing thousands or tens of thousands of unknown people, where no workers' organization exists, and where management has total power and uses it, seems a wildly impossible dream. Most intellectuals, artists, bureaucrats, and "rugged individuals" neither imagine nor want to organize people and join unions for their common welfare. They lack confidence in themselves or others and feel threatened by groups.

It takes extraordinary conditions and enormous character and ability for workers to organize unions of millions of members against employers' efforts to divide and conquer. But industrialized employees—treated as replaceable cogs by large or tough employers— are so accustomed, able, willing, and driven by their work experiences to organize and act within large organizations that they unite on enormous scales.

In the 1930s in America, no big union existed and none was thought possible in the mass-production industries making automobiles, steel, rubber, and electrical equipment. Yet workers did organize. They organized Ford and General Motors with their hundreds of thousands of employees. They won strikes and recognition. They created the Congress of Industrial Organizations (CIO) and its many large unions. Since World War II, millions of government, office, and service employees have also fought and protected themselves by organizing large, democratic, racially integrated unions.

Around the world, workers have organized unions in huge factories with thousands of employees. Time after time in Europe, industrial workers organized and conducted strikes of tens of thousands to millions of workers within five to ten years of being brought together in industrial production, even when they came from ignorant, suspicious, and poor peasant upbringings. Recently, industrial workers in Brazil, South Africa, and Korea have organized unions and have conducted strikes against companies backed by brutal, oppressive government dictatorships.

In 1981, another "unthinkable" happened—in Poland. Industrial workers organized 10 million working people into one union, Solidarity, comprising all kinds of working people, including blue-collar and white-collar, manual and mental, foundry worker and intellectual. They won just as the CIO unions had won half a century earlier, with sit-down strikes.

Organizing unions is incredibly difficult, but industrialized workers organize so well they make it look easy. They make it look so easy that it is easily taken for granted, much as air and gravity are taken so much for granted that we rarely think about them. Many working people themselves think little of their special gifts because they are surrounded by other people who are just as gifted or more gifted, making their own gifts seem commonplace or inferior. In addition, to keep employees submissive, many bosses routinely denigrate what they do. The news and entertainment media hardly portray workers at all, and then rarely in a favorable light.

One has to step back and look at what industrialized workers have accomplished. They are the great organizers of our time.

Union Organization Requires and Builds Peaceful, Democratic Freedoms

How can workers organize so successfully? On a personal level, by work-proven merit; on a large scale, democratically.

On the job, employees are perpetually struggling and organizing in a suppressed state. They have to organize their jobs and they have to organize defenses that are secret from their bosses. All this can go on for a long time before unions form; but when unions do form, or when new energy renews them, they and their gifted leaders often seem to outside observers to come from nowhere. It's no miracle, but it is an incredible achievement.

Not all employees have equal gifts for organization of course. The less-organized, less-disciplined employees are less respected because they cannot work as well; the least able do not last long on the job. The most organized and disciplined workers demonstrate their ability and assert their leadership by doing their jobs well. Other employees come to look up to them about matters on the job and matters in the rest of life too. As a matter of course, the best workers develop a work-proven, earned authority of leadership. This production-based leadership can be so commanding that even arrogant bosses will show it respect. When employees do organize, they have a recognized reservoir of great talent, and they turn quickly to their most able people for leadership.

A whole body of management theory has grown up that recognizes these powers and attempts to keep employees separated and broken up so they can't organize unions. Unfortunately, as we have seen, that has a terrible effect on productivity. Whether management seeks to eliminate or control labor, it cannot weaken employees' organizations without weakening productivity and competitiveness too.

On a large scale, employees are successful only when they organize democratically. And they know it. When they organize, they demand freedoms of speech, assembly, religion, and of the press and media. They want freedom to act within their union, and they know they need freedom in the rest of society to preserve their own union organizations.

Anyone who believes that workers are a mob, a bunch of thugs, mindless followers of union "bosses," or would-be dictators who would trample the Bill of Rights probably can't believe the high level of democracy that Polish workers fought for and practiced when they had the opportunity in 1980–81. But it happened.

In the summer of 1981, Solidarity conducted nationwide elections among nearly 10 million members to elect a representative governing body. Prior to Solidarity, there had been no machinery for open elections at all in Poland. Throughout Solidarity's life, the communist government fought everything Solidarity did. And ordinary life was so difficult that buying virtually any consumer item— even such a simple thing as soap—required waiting in long lines, often exceeding four hours per item. Yet Solidarity went immediately, easily, and naturally to the most advanced form of freedom and democracy yet achieved in America—representative democracy through elections. There have been larger elections in the world, but none has been so large with such a high involvement of voters, simultaneously coming from so inexperienced a base, with so little guidance, and under so difficult and hostile conditions.

Given Solidarity's unpreparedness to defend itself against the government's subsequent attack, we may seriously question the wisdom of its expending precious time and energy at that particular time on those elections while the larger job of survival was not being attended to. Democracy could have been advanced effectively through the ongoing meetings, demonstrations, and debates in the newly freed print and broadcast media. Instead, intellectuals, the Church, and Lech Walesa and his supporters all told workers to go home, stop demonstrating, and leave the job to the new organization. According to the *New York Times*, Janusz Onyszkiewicz, a principal Solidarity spokesman, even said—just days before Solidarity was crushed—that it could safely "ignore" whatever attack might come (12–1–81).

It's incredible. While on the one hand saying that they were defending Solidarity and its members, the people who headed Solidarity practiced "self-limitation" that prevented the new organization from doing anything to defend workers. "Don't provoke'' the communists was the general line—as if the Russians and Polish communists weren't already mortally provoked and just waiting for the best time to counterattack. It's clear that the massive formal election effort diverted workers from defending themselves. We must wonder if that was the idea all along. It put at the head of Solidarity the very people whose policies bound Solidarity hand and foot and demoralized workers before the attack ever came. No wonder Solidarity was crushed so easily. So those particular elections in the summer of 1981 may have been the wrong thing to do. Nevertheless, the fact remains that the workers carried out an awesome feat of peaceful democratic organization on an unprecedented mass scale.

Solidarity's commitment to democracy was not peculiarly Polish. America's industrial, office, and service workers also created large democratic unions. In the 1930s, American workers won for the American people improvements in pay and job conditions that the New Deal only promised. They helped save American democracy by distributing wealth to consumers and small businesses so they could generate new employment and new business. And in the 1980s, as black South African unions form and struggle for their rights, they practice a democracy so vibrant that elected officials of some unions reportedly remain on the job to stay among the people they represent.

These widely separated unions and workers behaved in similar ways, both to organize and to organize democratically, because they developed out of surviving and working for a living every day of their lives in industrialized work. Since industrialized work is much the same around the world, it shapes workers in similar ways despite local variations. Democracy is *typical* of workers' organizations around the world.

Wartime Democracy. Unions' commitments to democracy are all the more impressive because unions come under intense pressure from employers and governments. Employers use money, law, psychology, misinformation, and armed weapons when backed by the government to fight or corrupt unions every chance they get. Opposed by employers, unions are in a perpetual state of war.

During wartime democratic governments often suspend democratic rights in the name of patriotism and national security. Citizens accept curtailments of their liberties because the need for unified action precludes the luxury of divided actions and dissent. In wartime the need to "rally round the flag" puts severe limits on what opponents to the government can do. Yet unions routinely carry on elections of officers and debate policies despite being in a state of war with employers.

The wartime status of unions usually means that the official hierarchy gets elected and stays in office a long time, much as Franklin Roosevelt was elected President four times and the Democratic Party dominated American politics from 1932 to 1952. The reason is the same: "Don't change horses in midstream." Turmoil within an organization can give a hostile outside force the opportunity for a fatal attack.

Union officials' sometimes-long tenures, and the bureaucratic powers of self-perpetuation the hierarchy acquires, tend to give union officials the negative image of undemocratic bosses. That image obscures a much more profound democratic vitality that goes on beneath the surface. It keeps even the most entrenched bureaucrats hopping to serve their members' interests.

Direct Democracy. The simple fact is that if unions don't deliver something of value to members, the members will withdraw their support and the union will collapse. Even in closed shops, where new employees are obligated by union contract to join the union, a disenchanted membership will mean the union has little ability to win a strike and the union will eventually be broken.

Despite the great importance of electing union officials democratically, the heart and mainstay of democracy in unions is not election of top officials, it is voting directly on contracts. That's because if the membership accepts the contract, the union lives; if the membership rejects the contract, the union had better change the contract or risk losing its membership.

Even the union most accused of corruption, the Teamsters, delivers valuable wages and benefits to its members and keeps their loyalty. Despite the closed, often corrupt nature of the top echelons of the Teamsters union, it submits contracts to membership votes. Although a two-thirds vote is needed to reject a contract, it's a real vote.

In 1983, truckers voted down a national contract by a margin of better than 7 to 1, rejecting a recommendation to accept the contract by Teamsters President Jackie Presser, who negotiated the contract (*Business Week,* 10–3–83, 43). Two years later, Teamster carhaulers rejected another Presser-negotiated contract by a 4-to-1 margin (*Labor Notes,* August 1985, 5).

In both cases, opposition to the contracts was led by a rank-and-file group called Teamsters for a Democratic Union. TDU has had some success electing its candidates to the heads of local Teamsters unions. And many Teamster local unions have escaped entirely any charges of corruption. *Forbes* in fact says most of the 685 locals are "clean" (3–25–85, 62). No one says the Teamsters is an ideal union, and making it more democratic isn't easy, especially at its top levels, but it is compelled to seek the approval of its members through elections. And Teamster members are quick to put democratic pressure on their "leaders." As the worst-case example, it shows by exception how democratic unions really are. If only many governments and public agencies such as New York City's Transit Authority were held as accountable!

When union members vote on contracts, there is no more advanced form of democracy practiced in America. It is as if the American people were to vote in public referenda on each budget that the Congress passed and the President signed. By voting on contracts, unions practice the highest form of direct democracy on a mass scale yet known. And they do it while in a state of war. It is extraordinary. It demonstrates the great gifts that organized workers could bring to big business and government if they were allowed to.

Large-Scale Union Democracy. Large size is no impediment to union democracy. Rather, large size makes democracy all that more necessary for unions to survive. Without democracy, a large union will lose contact with its members, will be resented as a costly and unwanted second boss, and will repel nonmembers from ever joining. Just as every union needs the voluntary participation of its members in strikes, larger unions need more participation to connect widely scattered workers and locals. Without hearing members' thoughts, higher union officials will not learn what members want and will not be able to negotiate acceptable contracts. Finally, large size can strengthen union democracy if it gives the union more power to bargain. A strong, secure union can afford more freedoms.

Although many American unions show the same bureaucratic deterioration among their officials that corporations and government show, the largest unions except for the Teamsters are untainted by corruption, vote on contracts, deliver outstanding wages and benefits to their members, and can act decisively and effectively.

Friendly Criticism. It has become fashionable for one-time friends of unions to complain about unions' many faults, acting like the objects of Christ's criticism who saw the splinter in their brother's eye but never saw the plank in their own. Today the rest of society's faults are like planks compared to unions' splinters.

Of course unions have troubles. They need friendly, constructive criticism to adjust to today's new attacks on working people. Their problems shouldn't be made to obscure or diminish what good unions have done, what good they still do, and how they can yet protect all working people against those who would try to take advantage of working people.

If unions don't always live up to the high standards they need to remain healthy, then they are weaker for it. Would-be friends should warn of the dangers unions are exposed to rather than blaming unions—erroneously—for being too big, too strong, too fat. It is not strength but weakness that goes hand in hand with corruption and bureaucratic inertia. Workers are the principal victims and the union itself suffers as dues go higher, the ability to negotiate or strike declines, working conditions get worse, wages and benefits suffer, solidarity breaks up, and unions lose the ability to attract new members or even hold the members they have.

Unions are essentially voluntary organizations. Freedoms of speech, expression, information gathering, communication, and travel are absolutely vital for unions' survival. Members need to discuss and work out common interests, values, expectations, forms of administration, and hypothetical actions their organizations will take. Members need to debate what is best for them, what is needed of them, and how they can contribute. Above all, members need to agree to these things and to commit themselves to these things. They can do this only when they participate themselves, convince others of their ideas, or be convinced by others of different ideas.

As workers' organizations spring up, grow, or respond to challenges, workers need a broad, widely perceived and accepted, and workable set of expectations to agree to follow. A lot of talk, reading, writing, travel, and meeting are necessary to create a workable vision and achieve a consensus for action. Channels of communication, command, and response must be kept open indefinitely in all directions—up, down, and in between—to keep administration and members in tune with each other and in tune with reality, or else the union's actions will fail and members will suffer and withdraw.

In the process of discussion and debate, it is vital that people be kept informed about what is happening elsewhere in the country and around the world. It is often important to know what happened in the past too, to learn what worked, to avoid mistakes, and to speed progress. For these reasons, freedoms to travel and gather information, and freedoms of speech, press, assembly, and academic study develop naturally out of workers' needs for self-organization. And the larger the organization, the greater is the need for formal democratic structures to keep communication and expression working.

Democratic Leadership. Unions cannot survive without these freedoms. To get them, they fight for laws and social practices that defend and expand freedom for everyone.

By providing a national framework for action and protecting individuals who acted within that framework, Poland's industrial workers captured the allegiance of the great majority of white-collar workers and intellectuals in Poland. They showed they could lead, defend, and employ a nation if they had been allowed the chance.

In the ongoing struggle in South Africa, black unions have been a major power defending black workers from police harassment and fighting peacefully against apartheid. When, for example, several shop stewards at a Volkswagen auto factory in Uitenhage were arrested for union activities, 3,000 black workers at the plant went on strike and demanded they be freed. Six hours later, after Volkswagen executives had talked to the police, the union officials were released (Roger Kerson, *In These Times,* Oct. 16–22, 1985, 5).

The black Congress of South African Trade Unions (COSATU) demanded the abolition of hated laws requiring blacks to carry passes (*Newsweek,* 12–16–85, 40), and the government changed the laws soon thereafter. On May Day, 1986, 1.5 million black workers staged a "massive absence from work in almost all urban centers" to press demands for freedom (*New York Times,* 5–2–86, A1). A black union (unnamed in the report!) went to court and got annulled some of the government's most repressive "emergency" measures (*New York Times,* 7–17–86, A6). Black unions also took active roles in organizing and leading consumer boycotts and other protests to oppose apartheid and struggle for democratic rights.

In a series of articles that appeared periodically in 1985, *Business Week* kept reminding the business reader that the unions were the most significant force capable of changing apartheid. The *Economist* said, "The trade union provides the most structured form of organization for black political activity" (5–31–86, 68). The CBS Evening News used almost the exact same words on May 1, 1986. A year later NBC said, "As police crack down on political protest, it is becoming increasingly apparent that black unions are becoming the new tool for protest against apartheid" (Nightly News, 4–16–87). And in mid-1987, the *New York Times* added that COSATU had "emerged as the major vehicle in the black struggle to end apartheid and win political rights for the black majority" (7–19–87, 5). Even in the racist South African dictatorship, industrial workers have such an organic connection to getting work done, and they can be so numerous, that they acquire a genuine power to impose limits on what the dictatorship can do.

Under the leadership of such large-scale union actions, there can be a place and a reward for everyone who supports workers' actions and aids workers' organizations. In solving today's problems with the help or leadership of organized workers, many tasks would naturally arise that would employ scholars, writers, historians, scientists, engineers, doctors, artists, musicians, lawyers, computer programmers, accountants, managers, and businesses of all kinds.

In short, when unions organize, they not only support and defend democracy; they create it. And when unions seek to create new freedoms for their members, they create new freedoms for every individual in society to pursue his or her own interests and desires.

Organization: The Key to Workers' Leadership

The ability to organize is the most powerful quality for leadership. Without organization, there can be no effective social action; and without effective social action, there can be no effective leadership.

Intellectuals, artists, and other people who work alone usually lack the experience, inclination, and confidence to work with groups of people. They certainly don't create large organizations of themselves or anyone else.

Successful entrepreneurs may be better organizers than intellectuals, but they usually organize only their own lives and businesses. They rarely are able to run large organizations. In fact, individuals who start successful companies often sell out or are kicked out by the managements they create, such as the painful exits of Steve Jobs and Steve Wozniak from Apple Computer. Even bureaucrats who do run large organizations rarely can run them efficiently or effectively; they certainly don't cooperate well with other bureaucrats and other organizations— except to build their own personal empires.

In contrast, employed working people, including technical staffs and working managers, work with people and have developed strong powers of organization in doing their jobs. Moreover, industrialized workers have developed the strongest gifts for organization. Their hard jobs weed out the disorganized and weak, then refine and temper the greatest talents for organization among the survivors. And they are grouped together by employment into numbers large enough to form mass organizations.

In the context of great organization, workers' outstanding personal qualities of strength, intelligence, flexibility, patience, courage, discipline, and decisiveness all achieve their greatest expression and result.

Organized workers are a great pool of talent and ability for society to draw on, because large-scale production in big business and government is their singular responsibility. They should get much more credit and authority to apply their abilities more fully, and not just to rescue dying companies where management has already failed and leaves a dying hulk to resuscitate.

─── 12 ───

How to Make Management Listen and Respond to Employees

Making Effective Managements Even Better

Even good managements cannot do their best jobs without strong employee involvement and participation. An enlightened management still remains autocratic and self-serving—it is the sole boss. It cannot avoid using fear and restrictive rules to discipline employees and keep them in their place. And it will always try to pay itself out of what might better go to employees or stockholders.

The best of autocratic managements still lack the finer forms of feedback—internal information about its own performance and internal compulsions to respond to that information. Management needs feedback to regulate its own behavior before external forces compel it, usually painfully and dangerously, to change. To get feedback and encourage initiative among employees, Japanese companies and such American firms as IBM and Ford Motor reportedly seek out employees' involvement in highly diverse union and nonunion environments. Those actions are superior to blind autocracy, but they are not as good as they could be.

To achieve maximum efficiency, large organizations need to have systems of feedback that have equal importance with centralized command in managing operations. Whatever system upgrades feedback from employees to at least equal importance with centralized management will generally be superior and triumph in the long run in open and free-market competition.

Employee groups and union-like organizations are in an ideal position to help bring employees' intelligence into the process of management throughout the economy. If employee contributions are to be maximized, employees must feel free to be forthcoming with ideas and initiatives. Employees must feel that management will not punish them for coming forward, or at least that it will not retaliate in punitive ways, such as changes in work assignments, job status, or pay. Employees must also expect that management will respond to their suggestions, and that it will take them seriously, even if it chooses not to follow them.

Because managements don't always listen and respond even when they make an effort to do so, unions can help supply employees' information and release their initiatives. Unions frequently provide protections that allow working people the freedom to speak their peace. Any open-minded management must benefit from hearing what employees have to say, since that free expression can bring new information, new ideas, and closer contact with business realities. Without their own independent organizations, employees will always have information and initiatives that are suppressed and that never get expressed or tried.

Providing Feedback

In any organization, from publicly owned "private" corporations to government departments and agencies, organized workers and employee groups can act independently to improve feedback without fundamentally challenging the rights of owners or the public interest. It is not necessarily a fundamental challenge of owners' or the public's rights to collect, publish, and analyze information about what *management* is doing. Nor is it a challenge of such rights to formulate plans and recommendations for what management *should* be doing. Stockholders, taxpayers, voters, and all citizens have the right to learn what employees and their organizations know about operations and about management actions.

Stockholders, taxpayers, and voters also have a responsibility—an obligation—to themselves and to the nation to oversee management, keep it efficient and obedient, and prevent management failures from doing great damage. They need what employees can tell them to keep management honest. But employees can help only if they have the right and power to say openly, without reprisals, what happens on the job; and only if employees' information is collected, organized, analyzed, and communicated to stockholders, taxpayers, voters, and citizens.

To date, only unions have provided employees with strong freedoms of expression within big businesses and government. Only unions or independent associations of employees have the potential resources and long-term commitment, through their members' personal attachments to their jobs, to question and pursue major management issues, create honest collections of employees' information, and formulate proposals for better long-term management.

If unions and other employee groups attempt to gather and analyze information independently of management, and if they win the freedom to suggest changes to management, they can become a vital force to improve even the best corporate and government organizations. Further, union protections of free expression, and resulting improvements in managerial quality, could easily spread to companies or government units that are not unionized. Many managements already try to treat their people better to forestall the threat of unionization. If independent employee groups, including nonunion professional associations, were to formulate and present productive new ideas to management, those ideas too could spread to the rest of the economy.

Even if employee organizations lack authority to pick managers and set policy, they can independently participate in the process of management by commenting on what management does, praising good management, and proposing alternatives to bad management. A good management will then consult these organizations, get information, receive voluntary cooperation and freely forthcoming initiatives, minimize friction, and improve operations. A bad management will find itself exposed and bad managers will be replaced or redirected far earlier and long before bankruptcy threatens.

Independent Involvement in the Process of Management

Many employees have significant responsibilities and implicit degrees of freedom to act on their own initiatives, but they have no formal authority or rights. Such employees are dependent explicitly on management for information and to make decisions. They are extremely limited in what they can try, say, or do independently of management.

To improve productivity, employees must be freed of at least some of that dependence. They must have genuine authority to make and enforce decisions on the job; the more their authority to make and enforce decisions, the greater their independence. Perhaps the most basic and important freedoms are access to important information and the right to discuss that information openly, since there can be no intelligent decisions and actions without informed thoughts and discussions.

The most basic operational question in utilizing more of employees' distributed intelligence is what constraints will be put on individual employees and on employee groups to communicate and process information in the course of their jobs. And to act most effectively on that information, employees need some command or control over their own jobs that cannot be arbitrarily vetoed or countermanded by management.

At a minimum, employees and their groups must control some information about their jobs. Even if they get no information from management, they must be free to talk openly about the job without reprisals. In that way they can provide feedback without necessarily challenging a manager's right to issue specific orders. The degree of control of information that employee groups attain about internal operations, investment decisions, and external conditions will determine how independent employees' participation in management really can be.

Even the most militant American unions today, which are clearly independent in their representative and financial structures, are utterly dependent on management for what economic actions it takes and the jobs it provides. The more that those unions guard the purity of their independence by shunning any participation in the process of management, the more that management can find ways to do business without them. Already managements export jobs, restructure into new businesses, get nonunion labor, and automate humans out of production.

Independence is not an all-or-nothing condition; neither are control and command. Independent participation does not mean that employees would have command over management; it should not mean that individual employees can veto or issue orders to individual managers. That way lies chaos.

"Top-down" authority and command structures in management may be wrong when they shut out employees' intelligence, but they are necessary in any large organization to execute coherent actions. Management has a necessary executive role in any large organization to plan operations, issue orders in accordance with plans, see that specific tasks are carried out in accordance with plans and orders, and attend to all other details of operations. If management performed its executive role well in all cases, employee participation in the process of management would not be necessary or justifiable on economic grounds.

The executive role of management must be enhanced to improve large organizations' sensitivity, flexibility, and responsiveness to external events. Achieving such improvements is exactly why independent participation of employees is called for. Managers must have better information to make plans and issue orders, and managers must be more effective in carrying out necessary tasks and attending to operational details. Management's executive authority can be enhanced by any form of employee participation that increases voluntary cooperation among employees and allows them to carry out orders more effectively on their own. Far from being an obstacle to good management, independent employee participation in management has the potential to be the best single tool to raise management's effectiveness.

In a well-working system, employee groups or unions could participate independently with management at the ends of management's chain of command. They could negotiate policies that all of management would be charged to execute. They would not then be interfering at all with management's internal operations and would not necessarily be disobeying any individual manager's orders or challenging his authority. They could also negotiate limits beyond which managers could not go in executing policy— such as breaking the law or endangering human health.

Since many chains of command begin or end within management, information should enter management at every level through every manager. Organized workers and employee groups could work with middle and lower managers when the chains of command begin or end with them, and whenever information is needed. Employees could provide information to management about how well individual managers are carrying out policy or conforming to acceptable rules of operation.

Independent participation in management by organized workers and employees doesn't necessarily mean that unions or other groups of employees would dictate to management. The role of unions in particular will depend very much on what management, unions, and employees want to do and on what they are capable of adding to the management process. Unions may continue to operate in their traditional collective-bargaining role with simply the added activity of protecting employees who come forward with information. Some unions may go further to collect that information, analyze it, and put forward proposals concerning operations or policy. And perhaps in some complicated cases, such as where employees buy into a bankrupt operation, two or more separate organizations of employees may emerge, each representing the same employees, but each charged with different responsibilities. One might concentrate on protecting the employee-as-worker, a union-like responsibility; another might assume a director-like responsibility of selecting management, setting policy, putting limits on management, rewarding management, and replacing bad managers.

Self-Management

The most independent and powerful form employee participation could take would be self-management. That is, setting policy, judging or voting on management's performance, choosing managers, and replacing managers who fail or disobey.

Self-management could happen in two basic ways. Employees could own a business themselves: employee ownership. Or the public or stockholders and lenders could allow employees to manage themselves. The latter case is far more general and could be applied in any business or government service. Employees would need only the permission of stockholders or voters to do it.

Both forms of self-management could be mixed in a situation where the government lends money or buys into a company, such as the bailouts of Lockheed, Chrysler, Conrail, and Continental

Illinois Bank. Employees would then manage the enterprises themselves and perhaps have partial ownership.

Employees who manage themselves would have a very close commonality of interests. They might differ about specific policies or tactics, but they would all depend heavily on their common enterprise to succeed. They already are accustomed to talking among themselves, and they should do better when they don't have to worry about management reprisals.

In some circumstances, knowledge about general operations is as important as knowledge of a particular job or command of a particular skill. Then, under self-management, managerial functions would merge with employee functions. No one need acquire command of, or dependence on, a given job. Jobs could be redefined as operations change. And displaced employees could fit into other jobs more easily. Similarly, the distinction between manager and employee would blur, and the importance of that distinction would diminish. Management could be elected and the elected representatives need not acquire a permanent superiority. Elected managers could be kept responsive to the membership by having only short terms and being subject to recall. But at the same time, managers who leave office would have the job security of returning to operations they had never really left. And job operations for ex-managers would be more attractive or higher paid as employees tried to equalize the overall effects of pay, skill, and working conditions.

Employee Ownership. The terms and conditions of employee ownership as applied in America today are mostly a mockery of true ownership. With few exceptions, employees have been allowed to get only the dregs of bankrupt companies. Large corporations have blackmailed workers into borrowing huge sums of money to buy factories that the corporations said couldn't make a profit and must be closed down. According to the *Wall Street Journal*, "In the past, union buyouts have often been doomed to failure, largely because workers usually acquired companies nobody else wanted" (4–17–87, 7).

Unions and factory workers are not the only ones getting dregs. According to the *New York Times*, Hospital Corporation of America announced a plan "to divest itself of underperforming assets" by selling 104 hospitals to an employee stock ownership plan (6–4–87, D2). The ESOP would borrow $1.8 billion and would get hospitals that "are, on average, smaller and less well equipped... [and] spread across the country." Success of the ESOP "is no sure thing" and "it will be years before the debt is paid off and the employee owners can breathe easier."

Business Week characterized HCA's plan as an example of "unloading lackluster operations on employee-owned companies that begin life burdened with huge debt" and suggested that if HCA could pull it off, "other large public companies are likely to follow in its footsteps" (6–15–87, 94). The article concluded by calling the ESOP "a fragile child indeed" because, "with a projected annual cash flow of $250 million to $300 million, the new company will be hard-pressed to pay off its onerous debts. Annual debt service should reach $200 million at a time when hospital margins are under pressure from federal and private medical cost-containment efforts."

As the HCA ESOP clearly shows, the debts many employee "owners" have had to shoulder make their enterprises shaky from the start. Yet the employees still cannot act as owners.

When they borrow money for buyouts, employees have to cede most of the powers of ownership to creditors—usually financial managers of institutional investors—most of whom have no faith in workers and who see traditional American management as the creditors' sole guarantors and representatives. Employees have paid hundreds of millions of dollars in these buyouts merely for the right to exchange bosses and to work for lower wages in businesses that are struggling with bankruptcy! They deserve better fates than workers suffered at Hyatt Clark and Eastern Airlines, and some cases may just prove successful despite the obstacles.

Advocates of employee ownership such as Corey Rosen and Louis Kelso say employee owners generally do as well as or better than their previous managements. These successes show the superiority of involving employees in management, but the widely known failures have nothing to do with true employees' ownership or self-management: The employees were not truly independent to run the business themselves.

Employees who truly own their businesses would not need to

set up elaborate checks and balances to accommodate the interests of an independent management and stockholders or the public. A single pyramidal structure of elective bodies could allow all members to debate and vote on policies, then elect representatives to execute those policies. The body of representatives could also have its own organizations for specialized work or centralized coordination and administration.

Such a single structure could formally combine "legislative," "executive," and perhaps "judicial" functions. With the support and pressure of its members that come from working closely on the job, the structure could function coherently and intelligently. Operations would be subject to continuing scrutiny and reorganization as needed. Then many smaller difficulties or disagreements would be resolved organically among members themselves long before they would have to be raised to organizational conflicts and schisms.

Employee ownership can create a very powerful form of self-management, but it is much more difficult to start up and keep going. It is not likely to be widely applicable to the American economy today.

To own a business, employees would have to raise considerable capital and be hemmed in on many sides by heavy debt, doubtful business prospects, hostile creditors, and leftover managers, who basically would work for the creditors. If an employee-owned business succeeds, employee-owners could sell out quickly as individuals or as a group, just as the employees of *U.S. News & World Report* sold out to Mortimer Zuckerman. Employees could also just quit. In these ways the quality of ownership would be diluted and loyalties would be divided.

This is not to say that employee ownership can't work. It is only in its infancy and several imaginative variations are currently being tried to preserve a high quality of ownership. Still, they are not widely known or studied, and they are not being generally tried.

When Bankruptcy Threatens. Bankrupt or failing businesses are a special case. Where viable economic potential still exists and mismanagement has been the problem, voters and taxpayers or stockholders have usually failed to do their jobs of keeping management honest, are unlikely to do any better in the future, and have little to lose in ceding many management powers directly to unions or new employees' elected organizations. Then employees deserve a full chance to reorganize and revitalize the ailing business. And stockholders and the public will get an added chance to avoid bankruptcy or to recoup part of their investments.

To get a fair chance, employees will have to seek allies among stockholders and creditors who would otherwise see their investments go down the drain. And employees will have to seek allies among taxpayers and voters who may be asked to bail out a failing corporation or who are compelled to pay higher taxes for deteriorating services.

Some important allies may be found within management too, for many managers would lose their jobs in bankruptcy. Some managers value a cooperative work force, do good jobs, and are frustrated with bureaucracy and professional nay-sayers. Working managers need to be convinced that management-by-employees would be more intelligent, objective, and successful than management-by-bureaucrats. Good managers need to feel that they would be rewarded more for their efforts by a knowledgeable and appreciative work force than by their present bosses. Many technical, middle, and lower managers might be won over and support employees' efforts to revitalize failing enterprises.

Employee self-management of a bankrupt business would be less independent than true employee ownership. Employees would organize and direct failing businesses by themselves with the form of management they chose for themselves. But they would be constrained by difficult economics and hard market competition, at least at the start. And they would be subject to agreements they made to stockholders or lenders, or subject to voter and taxpayer approval, in exchange for managing themselves.

If the enterprise is to work, at a minimum the new employee managers would need relief from old debts and creditors and perhaps would need new capital too, like any other newborn organization after bankruptcy. The capital could come from many sources.

If a factory or company is bankrupt due to bad management, then it ought to be sold at salvage rates—just land and scrap metal, for example—to employees or to the public, and public loans could be set aside for such purchases. At a minimum, employees deserve the opportunity to manage an enterprise themselves during the process of bankruptcy if they are willing and able to try. But currently when a company or government goes bankrupt, frequently the same management that presided over the trouble is left in charge, and it is allowed to blame all its problems on unions, workers, government regulations, or foreign competition. That is ludicrous.

If a management is going to close down a factory or business, then it shouldn't get tax breaks for doing so, unless management first offers control free to workers and they reject it. Workers shouldn't have to pay extortion rates to buy a factory or business that was going to be shut down and couldn't be sold to anyone, as auto workers and steelworkers have been forced to do to ransom their jobs and livelihoods.

Even at salvage rates, some businesses may be expensive to buy, perhaps because the land or other assets have appreciated greatly. Without government subsidies, which incidentally *are* given to private corporations when the national interest is said to be involved, it may appear that employees can't put up the capital to buy a business for themselves. Just such a charge was raised to oppose efforts by the unions and workers of Conrail to buy the railroad. Putting aside, for the moment, the unions' claim that they acquired a form of equity in the hundreds of millions of dollars of wages they gave back to management, market mechanisms exist even in the present economy without government subsidy to finance employee buyouts, but they aren't called employee buyouts.

One mechanism is called "leveraged buyouts." Managements of companies or operating units within conglomerates have been doing the buying out. And management may be allowed to put up as little as 1 percent of the capital ("Where the Smart Money Wants to Go," *Forbes*, 12–19–83). The rest comes from lenders and investors who anticipate greater profits with a more involved and entrepreneurial management. This is of course not the ideal way to salvage a bankrupt enterprise, because bankrupt managers and stockholders shouldn't be rewarded for their failures; but it shows an already existing, working market mechanism that could be adapted to finance employee buyouts.

Where would the money come from if banks and other creditors refused to finance employee buyouts? Time after time already, employees have given back substantial wage cuts, benefits, and jobs in return for shares in the business.

A far larger source of capital exists in the hundreds of billions of dollars of employee pension funds. However, those funds are currently managed by money managers, banks, and other representatives of corporate management who certainly would resist investing in employee self-management. But if pension money doesn't belong to the employees who are vested in it, who does it belong to? No one is saying that that money should be invested foolishly, but the short-term, money-chasing preoccupation of pension-fund managers proves that that money is not being wisely invested now.

Given the potential employees have to improve management, careful investments in employee self-management would seem to be the most prudent growth investments possible. Organized workers and nonunion employees will have to fight to get control of their pension funds, but they have a right to decide how to invest that money, and they couldn't do better than to invest in well-thought-out plans for self-management.

Another source of capital might be the government. Government funds could be used directly to invest in employee self-management. Contrary to current loud voices among right-wing politicians and economists, many government investments have worked excellently. Lockheed and Chrysler were bailed out and became solvent again. The GI bill after World War II gave millions of people the opportunity to gain educations, buy homes, and go into business. It gave postwar America a skilled and educated work force and generated purchasing power to support many an entrepreneur.

The entire agricultural power of this nation, and all the industries that do business in agriculture, are built on large and far-ranging agricultural subsidies for growers. The entire home-building industry, and all the lenders and suppliers to home builders and homeowners, are built on tax subsidies that builders and homeowners get when they deduct interest payments from income taxes. That subsidy long supported the auto industry, the banking industry, and every business that made substantial sales on credit. Large government subsidies go to the medical industry in the form of medicare and medicaid.

The biggest government subsidy of all goes to the military industrial complex. Military spending is largely a subsidy because the instant that it is seriously questioned for being more than the nation needs to defend itself, its defenders loudly claim that it creates jobs and employs people. In other words, military spending is justified (and disputed by many others) as a stimulus—a subsidy—to the whole economy.

It is ludicrous to say that government spending never works. The people who repeat and shout that charge are engaging in the same type of "big-lie" tactics that Hitler used. The fact is that government spending, subsidies, and regulation often work excellently and the American economy would collapse or go into convulsions without them.

Judicious government investment in employee self-management could work just as well as other subsidies of market operations. No one is asking for welfare. The investments should be made on sound economic grounds. But those grounds should include what employee self-management can add to an enterprise in lower costs and higher productivity. Unless attitudes are changed in America toward government involvement, however, government investments will probably come only later, after employee self-management has proven itself. Perhaps, too, the people best suited and most willing to invest government funds may very well be employees from enterprises that have learned to manage themselves successfully.

For Viable Businesses. All these sources of financing could just as easily, and more securely, go to buy into corporations that are not bankrupt but merely lackluster or slipping. And why not buy into good companies just as other companies merge and acquire among themselves?

If unions and employee groups are allowed to make their case, and if they present credible cases for self-management, they ought to be able to win broad public support. Then, assuming democracy is allowed to operate, huge amounts of public and private funds could be made available and productively employed for employee self-management. If management can borrow 99 percent to buy out a company, so, too, should employees. The borrowed funds would be employed just as productively, or more productively, than they are at present. Clearly the problem is not economic. The problem is resistance to the idea that employees can or should manage for themselves.

Part of that resistance comes from powerful managing bureaucrats in big business and government who don't want competition from employees. And resistance comes from rich individuals who fear that their property will be expropriated. But this entire book shows how market mechanisms can be modified—and improved—to protect private property and open opportunities for organized workers and employees to manage themselves.

In fact, foreign competition and American management's own actions have already effectively "expropriated" many a stockholder's wealth by sending a business toward bankruptcy or draining the economy of funds needed for growth. And billions of taxpayers' dollars have similarly been expropriated by mis-management in government. Ironically, employee self-management may be the sole or best means to prevent such "expropriations" and preserve investors' and taxpayers' capital.

Most people would agree that a healthy economy is preferable to a sick economy. Many stockholders and creditors may agree that any share, even a minority share, in a self-managed enterprise is better than full shares in a nonexistent business. And if they allow a business to go bankrupt or a factory to be closed down, then they don't deserve to stand in the way of others who want the chance to make it succeed.

In these ways employees would not have to mortgage their lives to buy out—and reward—managements or stockholders who have bankrupted their businesses or ruined their producing units, as in milking businesses and failing to modernize factories or stores. Clearly, this form of employee self-management could work even in solvent companies or governments where organizations of employees could convince stockholders or the public that they can do a better job than the existing management. Then the employees would be responsible to stockholders, the market, or the public, as appropriate, for overall performance of the organization. They would either manage day-to-day operations for themselves or elect or work with management in setting policy and making managerial decisions.

For Government Service. Government workers face no financial difficulty in compensating private investors. Since government management is usually less efficient than business management, government workers should have many opportunities to expose failures and offer alternatives. With pertinent information and realistic proposals, organized workers and employee groups could appeal directly to the public for support, bargaining over the heads of management and hostile politicians.

Government employees desperately need to increase their public support. Currently, striking government employees run increasingly into public apathy, resentment, or opposition which enables the government to break their strikes. Increasingly, their strikes are viewed as an economic burden and a public menace, and they are opposed with the same justifications. Then the government feels free to write antistrike laws, use court orders, and send out police and the National Guard to break strikes and defeat or destroy government unions.

However, if government employees demonstrate to the public—which is composed of working people too—that they are ready, willing, and able to assume managerial responsibilities and improve government operations, then they will win important public support and give the public a strong incentive to fight for them. Government employees could be the first to win self-management or extensive independent participation in management. Otherwise, their future is clouded in the long term. Regardless of short-term success, they are perilously vulnerable to budget cutbacks, deteriorating job conditions, no-strike laws, and police-state tactics when necessary to break strikes.

Surprisingly Little Need Be Changed

All these possible forms of independent employee participation in management can be implemented entirely within the American system, comprising a mixture of market and government forces, small and big businesses, and a democratic form of government. In fact, some forms of independent participation make economic sense in *any* economy with large employers and a skilled or industrialized work force, especially where state employers or multinational corporations dominate the economy.

With widespread employee participation in management, companies will still have to make a profit—or at least not lose money—to stay in business. Stockholders will still have the rights they currently have but do not effectively use. Voters will decide through their representatives and public referendums, as they already do today, on budgets and payrolls for government employees and on what constitutes acceptable behavior for business and government operations. Government is not needed in any additional way to replace or regulate private business, except to provide the laws and mechanisms to incorporate employees' independent participation into the economy. Employees will still be disciplined to work hard and effectively. And individuals will still have all their present opportunities for private enterprise and self-employment.

The difference will be in improvements in living standards and how the economy operates. Working conditions will improve as employees' interests are better taken care of. Productivity will rise from higher employee satisfaction, greater commitment, and better overall organizational effectiveness. The people who set and administer policy in big business and government will be closer to, or at least be much more familiar with, the average person—meaning closer to the market, the consumer, the producing employee, the community, and the national interest.

Government services will improve from more efficient operations and from more humane relations between government employees and the general public. Bureaucracies will be trimmed. More effective governments will lower taxes or increase services for small businesses and private entrepreneurs, as for all citizens and businesses. More efficient big businesses will generate more opportunities for smaller suppliers and distributors, as well as for their own employees.

Better marketing will produce more successful investments, more investments in small business, and more products that raise consumers' standards of living. All the employees of government and business will have more purchasing power to support professionals and other individually operated businesses. And countless professionals who work in big business and government will get more professional opportunities as their employers use them more effectively, more confidently, and toward more productive ends.

Employees' organized participation in all aspects of production, marketing, and consuming will create larger amounts of higher-quality economic information. That information will aid business and government in planning for the future. And *every* business makes plans. No business can get a loan without presenting a plan to lenders. The point is not to eliminate but to improve planning.

Higher qualities of economic information would also aid job seekers, youths, and students of all ages to prepare themselves and find employment. And better information would also aid prospective students and educational institutions in formulating, choosing, and judging educational programs.

Demonstrate Leadership; Earn Respect; Win Authority

Organized workers and employees will have to work hard to prove they are ready, willing, and able to participate independently in management or to manage themselves. They will need to acquire new outlooks and deeper information about the American and world economies. They will also need new managerial and technical skills to cope with those parts of business and government from which they are presently excluded and about which they know little. Above all, they will need to convince themselves, significant parts of management, and the public that including them in the process of management is both necessary and desirable. Otherwise they will never get the chance to contribute their full potential or to share in what they could have produced. And we will all suffer from bad management and mounting failures in big business and government.

To work toward independence, even on the minimal level of free speech, organized workers and employee groups must collect specific examples and communicate their information to all appropriate parties. They must attempt to influence management and win support from the public, stockholders, the press, and government. But this is nothing new. Unions already do this, albeit mostly in an extremely limited way.

For example, the head of New York City's Transport Workers Union charged on WCBS TV (7–12–81) that transport workers in repair shops could make a machine part for $21 that the Transit Authority had purchased for $100. The charge was effective and believable in light of similar charges of bad management by the city and state controllers, as well as the TA's terrible record of buying buses, subway cars, and trucks that broke down soon after being put into use. Nevertheless, despite being revealing and convincing, that charge and similar charges were neither voiced loudly nor repeated often enough to convince the public that the union's participation really could improve operations or that the union really wanted to do so.

The AFL-CIO's Solidarity Day demonstration on September 19, 1981, was much more effective. Following soon after the brutal crushing of the air traffic controllers' strike, a reported half-million "middle-class" working people traveled to Washington, D.C., from all over the country and peacefully marched to protest the Reagan Administration policies. Commentators were shaken by the immense degree of dissatisfaction the demonstration represented. James Reston, for instance, worried about an "Impotent Presidency" and "the union of the nation" being "wrecked by reckless opposition" of unions "going into the streets" (*New York Times*, 9–20–81). Thereafter, the previously common expression "Reagan steamroller" disappeared from use. Unfortunately, Solidarity Day was not followed up and its impact died away.

In 1986 and 1987, several unions began to take advantage of management incompetence in a novel, in-plant strategy: workers do exactly what management tells them to do—and nothing else. Apparently in these cases, the strategy disrupted production and was more effective than strikes in the long run (*Wall Street Journal*, 5–22–87, 1). Consequently, the AFL-CIO published and distributed an in-plant strategy manual, *The Inside Game*. Also at this time, New York City's Transport Workers Union and the city's American Federation of State, County & Municipal Employees (AFSCME) District Council 37 took out advertisements showing how transit officials were failing. And management problems were the wedge that got the United Steelworkers and the Air Line Pilots Association involved in their management teams and buyouts. Still, much more could and needs to be done.

Working people have much to offer a management that respectfully seeks them out. There is no lack of information for employees to use in self-defense and in the public interest to offer alternatives to management's faulty practices in big business and government. There is no lack of suggestions, voiced mostly in the form of pithy complaints, coming from working people about how to work better. There is no lack of desire among working people to fight back when they feel abused. Many employees know from long years of experience what needs to be done on the job, and they know how to do it.

But so far, with precious few exceptions, there is only uncertainty or fear among union officials that paralyzes union actions and stifles individual actions within unions. Intellectuals and technical experts who could facilitate communication and perform technical analyses have doubts, hostility, or lack of faith in workers and unions. Political "leftists" have betrayed workers so often that any union activist can be effectively smeared, and often rightfully distrusted, as being linked to the discredited "left." A strong, well-financed "right-wing" political campaign is supplementing the worldwide squeeze on working people to attack, discredit, and isolate unions and organized workers in every conceivable way. Many individuals and union leaders don't know what can be done in full detail and feel helpless about their stifled organizations, impotent isolation, and partial ignorance. And most important, there is no organization yet dedicated to tying together all employees' information and desires with ideas, discussions, and frameworks for action. Without an effective organization, even employees' vast potential resources cannot be developed into effective defenses and productive actions.

Union officials must consider this very carefully: The trend that began in the mid-1970s of stopping and then pushing back unions entered a new stage in the early 1980s: union busting. First, public unions had to "give back" to save bankrupt local governments. Then PATCO was broken and the National Guard was called out in Arizona to break a copper workers' picket line at Phelps Dodge. Every employer seems to be demanding givebacks, and the bankruptcy laws have been used to take back what isn't given back. Japanese auto makers are building in America, but many are keeping out unions. And American manufacturers, led by the auto makers, are rapidly removing office and industrial jobs via robotic automation and foreign production.

How long will it be until industrial production is as automated as the oil and phone companies, with "manless factories" that wipe out the industrial work force? How long until "tele-scabbing" (performing office work during strikes at distant locations and then transmitting it via computers and telephone lines), "privatization," budget cutbacks, and harsh laws decimate service and public unions? And the more that production is automated, exported, or farmed out, the more that strikes will teach management how to do away with union jobs. What power will unions have left when they can't stop production? What will be left of many unions when they have no jobs to organize and no money to win from employers?

Without dramatic new policies that promise leadership to improve the economy, unions will continue to be falsely charged with causing inflation, lowering productivity, lowering competitiveness in the private sector, and raising taxes to pay for union wages in government services. Unions could be crushed with the public's mistaken blessing as a too-costly burden on the economy and on the average, nonunion person's pocketbook.

If union officials do nothing, their unions and their own jobs and pensions will be wiped out by computers, robots, recessionary budget cuts, big business's successful exporting of jobs to countries that offer the lowest-wage labor on earth, and by the growing use within the U.S. of no-strike laws, police, and the military to break strikes and bankrupt union treasuries.

Without the involvement of unions or other employee groups that bargain collectively to protect employees, management will be much slower to listen and respond to employees. The process of bringing employees' intelligence into management will be much more difficult, take much longer, and be much less successful. America just doesn't have that much time and luxury left to respond to foreign competition.

——13——

What Managers and Employee Groups Could Do Together

Joining Entrepreneurial Spirit with Democracy

When management fails, either through incompetence or through professional mis-management, and stockholders and voters cannot improve management, democratic means of internal debate and election must be found to improve the way management operates. Many unionized workers in offices and factories are already accustomed to working in large, democratic organizations. If anything, they want their unions to be more democratic. Judiciously adding their democratic experience to management would not result in anarchy, although it would change normal operating procedures considerably.

Union workers understand more than anyone that they are producers of wealth. They know that they can't have more collectively if they don't produce more. They just want more of a say in what they produce, how they produce it, and how their production will be used. They want a more equal share with management in enjoying what they produce, and they are prepared to work hard for their share.

What they and many other employees want may be thought of as the entrepreneurial spirit applied to *themselves*. Everyone works harder for himself or herself. It is hope for material gain, and more: It is freedom to employ oneself at what is most satisfying. Wealth may be the goal of entrepreneurs, but everyday on-the-job satisfaction is the sustaining force. When employees have a meaningful say in production, and when they share in the benefits of production, they always work harder and better. Is that so surprising or unreasonable?

Adversarial Cooperation. Although management and labor are often adversaries, they cooperate much more than they fight to get work done. What's more, so do all Americans. The U.S. is built on many systems of cooperation among adversaries. The Democratic and Republican political parties fight yet work together; so do Congress, the President, and the Supreme Court; so do lawyers and prosecutors in a court of law; and even consumers and producers. Seeking such a civilized "adversarial cooperation" between organized employees and management, where each can oppose but each has clear limits also, would be an ideal way to keep their mutual, "employing" organization viable.

Within such a system of adversarial cooperation, employee groups must still have the freedom to express their thoughts and demonstrate the strength and importance of their convictions. Unions and similar employee bargaining groups must also have legal freedoms to strike when they feel strongly enough that they have not been treated fairly. There is no serious danger, however, that their strikes would lead to economic or social collapse. They must keep working to support themselves. So they may struggle, and the struggles may appear chaotic to outside observers. But all the noise and apparent confusion will be hiding some real sorting and reasoning going on among individuals and groups. Quickly enough, organized workers arrive at conclusions and unite for action, or they do nothing. This can happen among unions too. If a union does not convince other unions of its case, it finds itself isolated, abandoned, and has little power left to disrupt much of anything for long.

A Bill of Rights for Employees

Strikes would be highly unlikely with cooperative managements, but all too often management seeks absolute power and doesn't cooperate at all, or else it is too inept to cooperate effectively even if it wants to.

Where management won't or can't cooperate and its failures are hurting a business or government, employees must be free to scrutinize operations, evaluate what management does, and look into everything that is made, served, or purchased.

If employees can conduct widespread discussions about operations and policies, with voting on occasion to determine if there is widespread support for particular actions, then recommendations for setting policy or starting remedial actions can evolve with the broad support and intelligent cooperation of the work force. These activities should involve as many working people as possible, for they have information, much to lose when management fails, and much to gain if they share the rewards of improving management. On occasion, it may be necessary for employees to do to management what the free press does—or at least claims to do—to government.

The managements in most need of improvement will also be the most resistant to employee scrutiny. Opposition to free speech will come from managements and representatives of management who claim the rights and powers of private ownership, as if *they* owned big business and government! They use corporate and government information and money for their own private enjoyment and enrichment, yet they claim that employees have no right to use such "private" information or to give it to the public. Against bureaucratic managements' false and self-serving claims, employees will have to fight for the First Amendment freedoms of speech and assembly, in the name of freedom, in the name of stockholders, and in the name of the public welfare and national security. With wit and spirit, they can make it a patriotic duty to improve the economy. They must make it a constitutional duty to defend First Amendment rights for working people on the job.

Incentives for Involvement, Rewards for Loyalty, and Pay for Value Added

Before employee groups and organized workers can carry the economy forward, they must surmount many obstacles that are more immediate than creating a new Bill of Rights for working people. Presently, many working people feel unions have become obstacles to progress. And many employees have been betrayed so often by management that they distrust what management says, resist what management wants to do, and fear that union cooperation with management can be nothing but a trap or sell-out. They think management is trying to abuse them, and often they are right. Many times management only "cries wolf," but sometimes management really needs help.

If employees had valid reasons to believe management, if employees had publicly participated in collecting data and debating and deciding policy, then they would be much more able and willing to cooperate and do whatever is necessary. And if employees could share equitably and honestly with management in the ups and downs of a business's or government's budget, then they would feel much more commitment and incentives for efficiency, growth, and innovation.

Employees already get modest degrees of commitment from employers in some highly successful companies. In their early years, American high-tech companies and start-up service companies have found it necessary to give their employees extensive profit-sharing or stock-sharing rights, and they sometimes get astronomical results. Japanese companies promised lifetime employment to a substantial number of skilled workers, and Japanese managements are not as fat as American managements or as distant as American managements from their employees. As a result, Japanese employees reportedly identify more closely with their employers, and management gets extensive employee-inspired contributions to raise productivity. Unfortunately, the Japanese example is not a model of independent employee involvement because Japanese employees and their unions are not really independent of management. They have little or no real say in higher management decisions, and union officials may even be paid or appointed by management.

Organized workers and employee groups must get something in return for their contributions to better management. Their rewards would be the right to bargain for the pay, benefits, profit incentives, and authority that their new positions and higher-quality labor would deserve.

Working Together

Even modest employee involvement in the rewards, authority, and responsibilities of management gives working people patience and a long-term outlook. Extensive involvement and sharing would introduce and stimulate new sources of innovation in big business and government. It would also enable and encourage employees to use their knowledge to make valuable suggestions and cooperate with good managers.

Employee groups and organized workers could then go beyond the confrontational, "free-press" role to suggest plans, formulate policies, implement plans and policy, and propose or choose people for all these activities. In particular, they could fight *for* good managers while criticizing bad ones; promote good managers; place people where they are best suited; reduce the friction of competing bureaucracies; reduce the stress of unsuitable jobs; and propose new people for managerial jobs based on demonstrated ability. Alternatively, they could propose whole teams, or "slates," for election of managers to new or reorganized projects. In a larger sphere, they could suggest new ways to organize production, provide services, and get other things done.

As noted in an earlier chapter, it is tragic that working managers cannot be better recognized and more appreciated in the bureaucratic management system. They usually are respected, however, by the people who work under them. Working people recognize and respect people who do good work. Such respect goes with the responsibilities and pressures of production. Anyone who can get a job done automatically rises in esteem. Were working people to have authority as well as responsibility for their jobs, they would often choose as managers, especially as executives, the same working managers they already know and respect. That would mean greater satisfaction, recognition, rewards, security, and career advancement for deserving managers.

This does not confuse respect with friendship, although the two are not entirely separate either. A hard-driving manager who gets results may not be liked, but he or she will be respected. And a hard-driving manager will be liked if the results mean that a factory does not shut down, or jobs are expanded, or employees can get higher pay for greater productivity. Unfortunately, many hard-driving managers do not get results because they substitute pressure for intelligence, as if many kinds of work can be *pushed* rather than *crafted,* and because they do not pay for more productive workers. Then a brutal manager will create resentment, resistance, and conflict. To assume that employees have an instinctual antagonism toward hard-driving managers is to confuse the substance of hard work with the form of pushing to produce work. The pushing can be both brutal and counterproductive when performed by management-by-bureaucracy and when enforced by the blind, insatiable, and knee-jerk version of the profit motive.

Not all good managers are hard-driving or unattractive to work for. A competent manager in a smoothly running organization can manage with a light touch. Employees are then protected from needless problems and freed to turn out superior work. They prefer bosses who create such good working conditions and would choose them as managers if they had the right to do so.

Good managers usually also provide employees with opportunities for advancement. The experience of doing good work is itself a valuable job qualification. Good managers provide education, training, or wider experience to keep or upgrade good employees. In many office organizations, good managers bring promotions through their own advancement, pulling subordinates along, or through expansions in their own organizations if they are successful and grow. And since truly competent people are more likely to be confident too, good managers are less likely to be afraid of competent employees and are more likely to promote them or find them promotions in other departments or organizations. It is also very shrewd: Well-placed friends are the best security.

Good managers wouldn't find their jobs changed drastically in substance, except mostly for the better, if employees organized the workplace. In most big businesses and government organizations, every manager must report to somebody anyway, and sometimes to several people. In fact, lines of responsibility and authority often get so tangled and compromised that they make many actions impossible and all actions painful for a manager who wants to get things done.

The whole concept of management could be rewritten to free managers of their distasteful and corrupting burden of being policemen. When the responsibility for production is openly accepted and enforced by every employee, then managers don't have to dissipate their energy fighting their own employees. When plans are formulated, agreed to, and enforced by the entire work force, managers don't have to waste energy keeping secrets from employees and tiptoeing around their own bosses. When information is transmitted freely and validated by open discussion, managers have much better chances to make high-quality decisions and to see those decisions carried out rapidly and intelligently. Then managers can be freed to be executives.

Good managers will be perceived and rewarded rapidly for their superior performance. And management as a whole will become far less bureaucratic, less insensitive, less heavy-handed, and much less fearful of the consequences of its own actions.

Smoothing Market Extremes and Clumsy Lurches

Involving employees in managerial decisions may create an internal oversight system that is far more rational, sensitive, flexible, and manageable than the present system of quarterly market reviews that compel managers to think "short-term" and sacrifice future growth for the sake of immediate gain.

Financial analysts who currently review a management's performance know little about running a business, have no loyalty to the business, and manipulate stock prices like yo-yos every three months to make their own fund's performance look good to their own shareholders. And funds in the capital markets flow strictly to wherever seems to be the *most* profitable investment at the *present moment*. In their pursuit of momentary, monetary profits, both financial analysts and markets show little loyalty to an individual business or even to their own country. First they shove capital into something and inflate it beyond all workable size. Then they deflate it just when it needs help or blow it to smithereens in a crisis.

IBM. There was nothing rational in the way IBM stock went from almost 48 on October 29, 1981, to 115 in the spring of 1983. Its business certainly hadn't doubled. Indeed, there had been nothing rational in IBM's having dropped to around 48 in the first place. Or at least the "rationality" had much more to do with the ebbs and flows of capital, as well as the fads and panicky misperceptions of Wall Street analysts, than it did with basic business fundamentals.

Even the phenomenal success of IBM's Personal Computer added only a reported 5 percent to IBM's sales in 1983. Business reports didn't say what profits—if any—IBM was making on it. And the PC was in a volatile market. After exploding in 1983–84, personal computer sales slowed drastically and profits plummeted in 1985. Many high-flying high-tech stocks took nosedives. Many other companies went out of business. Indeed, all computer companies and related companies took beatings in 1985. IBM itself shocked the market with actual earnings drops. It seems that the analysts' infatuation with IBM in 1982–83 shared an ominous similarity with their 1983 infatuation with Texas Instruments: They just didn't understand computer products and what makes or breaks computer products.

Many reports in business and computer magazines in 1983 said openly or implied that IBM's name was magic. Why? Some analysts and writers seemed to think that the IBM Personal Computer was mediocre or overpriced, and others had too little experience with the product to judge its appeal at all. Not understanding what made the PC successful, they thought that only a "magic" name was selling it. To be sure, a good reputation helps—at first. And if the product bears out the reputation, then the name should sell the product, but that doesn't mean the name could indefinitely, magically sell a bad product.

Writers in computer magazines which weren't geared specifically for the IBM PC either ignored the IBM PC or belittled it far into 1983. They said it was technologically inferior and had less software programs than other computers. Or else they said that the older, "8-bit" computers could do more than almost anyone would want done, so that most people didn't need to spend several thousand dollars more on the IBM PC. Some said it was both too new and too old at the same time! These ideas carried well into 1986 and were still being repeated by *Business Week* (7–28–86, 62) and the *New York Times* (4–22–86, C5).

What these writers failed to say was that computers that had more advanced technology than the IBM PC had much less software; therefore, they were much less useful. And the computers with more software were older machines that handled much less data and were much more awkward to use.

The IBM PC was special and advanced: It was the first major entry in the more powerful, higher-tech "16-bit" computer market.

While not using the most advanced technology even at its birth, it was advanced. While lacking the most extensive software, it rapidly acquired extensive and growing software support when IBM encouraged non-IBM, independent programmers, so-called third-party sources, to write software for it. And its monochrome display (the video screen, which people must use for many hours per day and which makes or breaks personal acceptance, not to mention vision and health problems) set new standards in the personal computer industry for being easy, comfortable, and attractive to use for hours at a stretch. IBM's PC worked without major problems, just as IBM's name implied. And IBM's financial muscle enabled it to produce large quantities of computers and distribute them widely among carefully selected retailers.

In other words, when the IBM PC was introduced in 1981, and carrying well into 1983, it was the only well-working advanced machine from a major company smack in the middle of the biggest market—business and professional users. IBM did it more through marketing power with financial support than through technology, but its marketing coup didn't use the wizardry of a "magic" logo. IBM just saw the market for what it would be and tailored existing technology into the most suitable product to sell in that market. Then it jumped into that market wholeheartedly well before anyone else. And even it underestimated how large and how quickly the market would grow. So it prospered for a while, and its stock soared.

There was, however, no guarantee that other computer makers would not blow IBM's PC out of the water with more powerful, cheaper, or better-designed computers; nor even that IBM wouldn't undercut its PC itself to stay competitive. Indeed, IBM stumbled badly with just this problem. It introduced a home computer, PCjr, in January 1984, that was a more limited version of the PC. Apparently, it didn't want to undercut its mainline PC by introducing a computer that would be as useful but would be less than half the price. As a result, the PCjr was too limited and failed to sell well. By 1985, it was discontinued. The IBM portable PC suffered the same fate. Those failures to keep introducing better products helped open the door to a host of companies that imitated the PC, cheapened things like the screen and keyboard, and sold such so-called clones for lower prices.

Reports as early as 1983 show that IBM also failed to attack the copiers for infringing its copyrights when they got started ("PC Piracy," *PC Magazine*, 1–24–84, 188). Consequently, the clone industry got a free ride, and analysts should have known that too.

That is why in 1986 the analysts who previously banked on the letters "IBM" to sell a product were wrong, were rudely shocked, and pummeled IBM's stock. At one point in 1986, it sold for $116, $2 less than in late 1984, while the Dow Jones Industrial Index had gone from 1,100-plus to nearly 1,900. If soaring interest rates or recession return, or if IBM makes marketing mistakes as it did in 1979 in mainframes ("Why IBM Reversed Itself on Computer Pricing," *Business Week*, 1–28–80), or if IBM just fails to live up to analysts' expectations, IBM's stock may suffer again as it did in 1981 and 1986.

Financial Follies. Many companies cannot survive that kind of treatment and so desperately try to keep in the markets' good graces. Yet, while the financial markets strongly influence what management does, they do little to improve the quality of management's internal operations, and they do much to disturb that quality with frequent and wrenching changes.

The strongest influence of the financial markets on management comes from the largest lenders and stockholders. They may try to dictate policy or hire and fire top managers. Market evaluations will of course affect these lenders and stockholders, but many markets are dominated by the same lenders and stockholders—banks, mutual and pension funds, and other financial institutions. Their money managers are active in financial markets and help create financial evaluations. Yet they still cannot summarily replace management, nor do they want to. So they cannot step in to remake bad managements. But their endless ebbs and flows of opinions and capital can wreak havoc if they lead to frequent changes in business policy or management personnel.

Financial markets pressure management in more subtle ways too. A low rating by analysts causes a rise in the interest rates that a company or public agency must pay on the money it borrows. That raises costs, hurts operations, and perhaps pushes management to go uncertainly in some new direction that it thinks analysts want it to go. But if markets were clear about their intentions, then playing stocks and interest rates wouldn't be the biggest gamble in town.

A low or falling stock price hits management at least three ways. First, it makes capital more scarce or expensive. Either a company can't sell stock at all or it must pay out a high dividend rate. That is like paying higher interest rates or not being able to borrow at all. Second, many executives are paid in stock, so a lower stock price takes money out of an executive's pocket— sometimes big money. Third, a cheap stock may tempt some outside buyer to try to buy the company and replace or eliminate the existing management.

For example, when oil prices declined or barely stabilized in 1982 and 1983, the stock of some large "integrated" oil companies, notably Gulf Oil, had prices that made their total stock market value less than 40 percent of their book value. That means that the theoretical value of their assets would far exceed their stock market value if the companies were broken up and sold outright. So, "rather than wait for oil company managements to improve," *Business Week* reported in 1983, "the investment community is calling for the immediate breakup of some companies" (11–14–83, 138).

In the years that followed, that's exactly what happened, not only to Gulf, and not only in oil. Many companies were bought at stock prices that were depressed by high interest rates and recession, then sold off piecemeal at higher prices as interest rates fell and the economy recovered. The movers in these financial maneuvers, by the way, took no risk at all and got multimillion-dollar gains. That's exactly the opposite of what they would have us believe: that they deserve their millions because they took risks to build prosperity.

Whether a management deserves it or not, whether it is in the national interest or not, a low stock price is a powerful stimulus to management to increase earnings, and it is almost always a short-term stimulus because stockholders usually want immediate results.

Keeping Jobs in America Isn't Allowed. Take the case of Burlington Industries Inc., the nation's largest textile company in 1986, based in Greensboro, North Carolina. While J.P. Stevens & Co. and other textile companies gave up trying to compete with imported fabrics, Burlington's former chairman, William A. Klopman, invested $2 billion over 11 years on state-of-the-art machinery and plants (*Business Week,* 5–11–87, 50). And he succeeded. While less profitable than other apparel makers, Burlington made a profit of $56.5 million in 1986. In the process, Burlington kept many jobs in the U.S. that would have gone overseas otherwise.

And with the dollar falling in 1987, promising to make foreign producers less competitive, Burlington's investment begins to look considerably better. Other companies in many industries that invested heavily in foreign production or came to depend on foreign suppliers, such as Caterpillar Inc., suffered as the dollar dropped (*Fortune,* 10–27–86, 91).

So what was Burlington's reward for being competitive and keeping jobs in the U.S.? With low earnings, its stock languished and the company became the takeover target of Asher B. Adelman and Montreal-based Dominion Textile Inc. Speculation ran that the raiders thought they could break up the company and make a profit selling the parts, which included several highly regarded divisions making denim, carpets, industrial materials, and worsted fabrics.

Adding insult to injury, *Business Week,* reflecting analysts' opinions, wrote, "Burlington can blame itself for becoming a takeover target."

Burlington's fate is a telling example of how America has lost international competitiveness. The super-liquid financial markets simply won't allow a company to be competitive if, by doing so, it stays in low-profit markets or makes heavy investments in the future that detract from current earnings. Notably, the very Japanese companies that have taken markets away from American companies also take much lower profits. If they were American, they would have been liquidated long ago.

Burlington may have been victimized in another way too: by the antilabor bias that created the super-liquidity trap. Two billion dollars is a lot of money to spend on automation. Since the machinery and plants it bought were state-of-the-art, they sound suspiciously like the ultra-expensive, trouble-prone labor-eliminating variety that hurt GM and many of America's biggest companies. More, the push for automation was enforced by the financial markets. In the early 1980s, market analysts and leading companies like GE were telling the rest of American business to "automate, emigrate, or evaporate." So, apparently, Burlington automated, and it got clobbered by both automation and fickle markets.

Yet while market pressures hit some companies hard, the managements of many others still have enormous freedoms and protections. "Raids" from "sharks" were frequently deflected by paying "greenmail" (special premium stock prices) to the raiders. And management erected so many obstacles to hostile takeovers that by 1987, raids were much more difficult and infrequent (*Business Week,* 5–4–87, 35).

Equally bad, the market raiders themselves are often other bureaucratic managements—with all their faults—such as when U.S. Steel bought Marathon Oil, Du Pont bought Conoco, and Occidental Petroleum bought Cities Service. So as more and more layers are added, bureaucracies become more top-heavy than ever.

Those oil acquisitions, by the way, highlight another market flip-flop. After OPEC and the oil companies profited hugely from ratcheting up oil prices, oil company stocks were hot stuff. But only a few years later, in 1983, the market was dumping or trying to break up big oil companies. And the companies that had bought oil companies were sweating heavily to shed the big debts they incurred to do the buying. Tomorrow? Who knows? It may depend on the Ayatollah again.

The way that the financial markets "regulate" management performance can undermine or ruin a manager's ability to look years ahead and rationally oversee investment and growth. The miracle is that managements that dance wildly at the end of short-term, market-jerked strings could ever achieve long-term profitability.

Independent employee involvement in management could add a longer-term viewpoint, plus a commitment to continuing employment, that would stabilize management decisions against the flip-flops of market fads and humanize management decisions against ruthless demands for profits.

For example, dangerous substances that poison employees on the job, such as vinyl chloride, PCBs, dioxin, pesticides, and asbestos, later pop up to poison entire communities, from Love Canal in New York State and Times Beach, Missouri, to schoolrooms around the nation, millions of people's underground water supplies, and the food we eat. No one can totally escape these substances once unscrupulous companies handle them without regard to the human beings who must work with them.

When employees raise questions about their own safety and demand open information about what they are working with, they automatically benefit a much larger community. By helping to prevent the irresponsible use of toxic substances, they benefit countless people and generations who are not poisoned, sickened, deformed, or bankrupted. Even in a market economy that would demand quick and immediate profits, employees' personal involvement in their businesses can create safeguards for the general community. In addition, they would greatly reduce the need for expensive or inefficient government bureaucracies to regulate industry.

More generally, steelworkers would not invest in foreign steel mills, miners would not invest in foreign mines, and employees would support managers who kept jobs in the U.S. Employees would not abandon a line of business in which they worked just because it was going through a predictable trough in a business cycle. They would stick with a strategy if they felt it was good until it had time to work. They would support academic studies and government regulations to inhibit predatory financial manipulations and embarrass the managers who made such manipulations. They would encourage business schools to develop models of management that teach managers how to make profits from long-term investments. They would support the development of management techniques to employ experienced people more productively, and they would pay more for that experience. Employees themselves could develop new techniques of production and spread them to the rest of the economy. Perhaps most simply and profoundly, employees would increase the intelligence of management decisions so that they could make profits by producing "real things well."

Better Information for Meeting Market Demand

A most important part of producing real things well is targeting production to satisfy market (or public) demand: marketing. This includes creating ideas for new products, designing and tailoring products to consumer tastes, estimating how a product will be accepted by buyers, and everything to do with selling.

The information that employees could provide could increase management's ability to foresee and take advantage of disruptive market changes, such as consumers' sharp and erratic changes of buying patterns in autos, personal computers, and consumer electronics.

For example, suppose Texas Instruments had test-marketed its personal computers first on loyal and cooperative employees and production workers, who would be precisely the people most likely to buy the low-priced computer. Suppose too that the employees had had the courage to speak up about TI's low-ball strategy, and suppose further that TI had listened to their opinions. It might have avoided its costly blunder. Those are a lot of big supposes for TI's former management, as they are for many other managements as well, but they shouldn't be. Any company that sells to the public, even high-tech leaders, can learn a lot from its employees, including its hourly workers, precisely because they are part of its market as well as its work force.

In all the many areas of marketing, the quality of "intelligence" about the real world that an organization has will make or break that organization. Companies can't sell or serve what people don't want—no matter how well it is made or how low the price is. Anything that can markedly raise the quality and increase the quantity of information that a business or government organization has in marketing will dramatically increase that organization's effectiveness. Organized workers already have enormous resources in union members, their families and friends, and internal union communications to bring new and valuable marketing information to big businesses and government agencies. And other employee groups that might form could add still more.

Aiding marketing is a particularly fertile ground for unions to plow in struggling industries, such as the garment and service industries, that are full of small employers or that are labor-intensive and employ many people of foreign origin. Small employers often lack the energy, knowledge, and resources to conduct market surveys or distribute, advertise, and sell their products widely. A national or international union could conceivably create and sell marketing services to small businesses, or bargain to exchange marketing services for higher pay and better working conditions.

Small employers are not well-equipped to export their products. Selling in foreign countries is both expensive to start and hard to learn how to do correctly. International unions with a broad international membership might gather and offer information about many countries, or even provide agents who come from those countries, speak the language, know the customs, and generally fit in better than a small company's representative. The international diversity of the American work force gives American unions an opportunity to help their members, countless small businesses, and the American economy with exports.

Currently, Japan leads world trade with its giant and highly capable trading companies. America has no comparable trading companies. If unions with multinational memberships could create or support effective international trading companies, they could perform a great service to small businesses. We would all benefit from the increased employment and economic vigor that would result. And if union-based trading companies could create greater understandings and economic benefits among peoples and governments, then international tensions might be reduced and the world might become safer and more peaceful.

However, all these changes and benefits will not come easily. To strengthen their case against what will be extremely difficult resistance, employees will have to show it is absurd to exclude tens of millions of working people from exploring what the market wants.

By organizing what employees collectively want and know into a valuable pool of marketing information, unions and employee groups could lay the basis for directing production more accurately and compassionately toward human needs in government and industry and small businesses. Then some market excesses could be tamed with less need for cumbersome or narrow-interest regulations and inefficient, expensive, and corrupt government bureaucracies. Then profits could be made to serve human needs much better than profits serve at present, and profits could be increased at the same time through selling more desirable products.

It is a short step from organizing market information of employees in a business or government to organizing market information for all consumers (working people are consumers too). That means helping consumers by creating clearinghouses of information about product safety, product usefulness, comparative testing, and industrial safety (including environmental pollution).

Organizing market information also means offering consumers

political and legal organizations for redress of costs and damages arising from faulty products or misleading claims. Why should producers and consumers cooperate? Because they need each other. Together, they make a market. Each can benefit from sharing information to improve investment and marketing decisions in industry, government, and small businesses.

Once the expression of consumer preferences is more highly organized, then all businesses and government units—large and small—will have much better information themselves to make their plans. They will be able to offer consumers more products and services that are better suited to consumers' needs, tastes, and desires. That means more successful business and government, better allocation of capital, and more employment. The public availability of organized consumer information would especially help small businesses. And since small businesses create many more jobs per sales dollar than big business or government, helping them will be a special tonic for employment. It will also mean higher profits and wages for all concerned.

Along with all these changes and improvements in economic information for producers and consumers, employment and educational markets may be improved dramatically too. Then young people may have a better idea how to invest their time and energy for future work; universities may learn better how to combine higher education with employable skills; and all people looking for jobs, and jobs looking for people, may be matched more closely, quickly, and effectively than they are now.

Unfortunately at present, bureaucracies in business and government are so unaccountable that rather than serving us better, they are rapidly growing into burdensome rulers of us all. The true danger of "socialism" or dictatorship is not from organized workers but from bureaucrats taking over corporate and state powers. They already rule in communist countries and many Third World countries spanning the extremes of the political right and left. The more the American economy fails under their mis-management, the more they will impose police-state tactics right here in America to enforce their rule and preserve their privileges.

Organizations of workers and employees have the potential to introduce competition within management and be a democratic alternative—an antidote—to rule by bureaucracy. They are the only democratic alternative that has a chance to improve the system of management, raise the vitality of the American economy, and simultaneously serve more of the needs of the American people. They deserve the chance to apply their full personal and organizational abilities to organize production, manage their jobs, and formulate social policies instead of submissively taking orders from managements that often are irresponsible, unaccountable, inept, wasteful, and corrupt.

14

Organizing for a Full-Employment Economy

Using Computers to Create Employment

Historically, management has used computers to eliminate jobs, but computers could very easily be used to help create new organizations for workers, consumers, and people looking for jobs. That would create new jobs in itself, and it would create many more new jobs as people use the collected information to find new things to make and do.

The effectiveness of computer systems boils down to the effectiveness of the human organizations that use the computers. Disorganized efforts produce low-quality information and result in colossal wastes. Badly run organizations typically require more and more office work, more staff, higher overhead, and rising costs and mistakes. That is why management problems can be so costly. Through "computer errors"—which most often are errors in the human system that uses the computers—small mistakes can be turned into million-dollar losses. High-quality information, communication, and organization are vital to operate computers profitably.

This "garbage in, garbage out" principle helps explain a peculiar mystery of American business. In the early to mid-1980s, businesses invested heavily in computer products, especially personal computers, but suddenly that investment slumped and many high-tech businesses collapsed. At the same time, productivity growth slowed dramatically in nonmanufacturing businesses, where "80 percent of all high-tech capital goods" went, according to economist

Stephen S. Roach of Morgan Stanley & Co. (*Business Week,* 6–1–87, 32). Worse, the industries that moved most rapidly into high tech experienced no productivity growth at all during the present decade. A similar story is told in a *New York Times* report entitled "Services Hurt by Technology" (6–29–87, D1). "The sophisticated machines in many cases have been hampering [executives' and employees'] work." This high-tech debacle appears to be the office counterpart of efforts to raise manufacturing productivity by excessive automation.

Where can problems arise in the use of computers and other high-tech devices? High tech has high information needs. It requires close and effective cooperation among employees and departments to be learned, implemented, and used well. Negative management attitudes toward employees degrade information and explain a considerable part of America's inability to use high tech well. In addition, the incessant mergers, selloffs, and acquisitions of companies in America in the 1980s, and the simultaneous growth in temporary employment, which are all consequences of the super-liquidity trap, have no doubt added greatly to the problem. They have disrupted employees and degraded still more the quality of information available to management.

The failure to use high tech widely and effectively, in consumer products as well as in offices and factories, hurts many more industries than the computer industry. It hurts the vital semiconductor industry by needlessly limiting its market, reducing its growth opportunities, and losing important economies of scale. Partly as a result, Japan reportedly emerged in 1987 with the world's largest domestic semiconductor market and growing dominance of the world markets in many semiconductor specialties. More generally, every company and government agency suffers, along with consumers and taxpayers, who might benefit from the more effective use of computers to provide better products and services.

Since management must function as an information processing system, if garbage goes into management, tons of garbage will come out. But if quality goes into management, tons of quality will come out. The dismal failure to use high tech well suggests that American management generally is badly equipped to handle information in any form, whether it be in computers or employees.

Computers are typically introduced by employers to do the labor of existing operations and replace the employees in them. That eliminates jobs rapidly. But gradually computers come to enable higher volumes of work to get done, and at faster rates. Eventually, computers enable many operations to expand, or they make whole new activities possible and desirable. All these activities create new jobs. That's why experts say that computers create new jobs. But they often omit that the new jobs don't go to the displaced employees. The new jobs come too late, or require different education, experience, and skills—or so it seems to employers who value formal qualifications over living experience and abilities. And most managements discard rather than keep and upgrade displaced employees.

To create new jobs for people who are displaced, ways must be created to find as rapidly as possible the new economic activities that computers can support, get displaced working people into those activities, and support them while they make the transition.

Some employees who now are displaced should get promotions instead of pink slips. That's because computers just do many of the old things in new ways, or do new things that we always wanted to do but couldn't do before. Employers would be wise to retain many employees who are replaced by computers precisely because they know a lot that no one else knows about operations. In that way, experienced—and especially older—working people can add wisdom to computer systems and lead rather than be whipped around by the computer revolution.

Most people who use computers don't have to become computer experts. Each computer application must ideally be tailored to each person's or business's individual needs. Each person using a computer must become an independent and world's leading expert in his or her own individual situation to use computers most wisely and productively. That is not as forbidding as it sounds; but it's much more difficult for organizations than for people, because then goals, needs, resources, and operating information are often unclear or even unknown, and certainly not widely or easily shared.

Computers are tools of the mind. They multiply the penalties of incorrect data and sloppy or lazy thinking. And they multiply the rewards of high-quality information and thought. If clear, rigorous, and realistic thinking go into the business or government organization that uses computers, and if accurate and reliable facts go into computer programs and into the data that computer programs process, then highly useful and valuable new information will come out. Management badly needs the free and independent participation of employees to use information better in office and service operations.

Organizing Information to Expand Employment

When references are made to increasing production or raising productivity, one usually thinks of increasing the output of manufacturing and office work. But marketing is not manufacturing, and yet it is a productive activity. Much of marketing uses information: information about human tastes and preferences, which is applied by skilled human labor to fashion products, create advertisements, and sell to buyers. Such information is highly accessible to average working people because they are important consumers in many markets. They can be employed in collecting, analyzing, creating, and applying marketing information. And the more that is produced by computers and robots, the greater are the need and value for timely, accurate, and complete marketing information.

Services too are not manufacturing in the traditional sense. Like marketing, they involve many kinds of information ranging from high technology to countless specialized market niches. Many kinds of labor and jobs are involved in creating, communicating, teaching, analyzing, selling, and using that information.

The challenge in creating a full-employment economy is to employ the great majority of people who are not super-technical specialists yet who create the purchasing power to support those specialists and their products. New organizations and market processes must be created that reward people for their mental labor, possession of unique information, and marketing and service abilities. But that of course requires a greater commitment to employees, which requires sharing more with them and involving them more equitably in management. That is something prevailing management systems simply won't do.

The independent participation in management of employee groups and organized workers fulfills all the above requirements for a full-employment economy. It:

- Adds organization to large-scale production.
- Creates and uses whole new forms of information.
- Creates and supports many new market activities.
- Directs this information and activity toward the interests and needs of the average working person.

And organized workers are extremely skilled and committed to democratic forms of large-scale organization. Consequently, organized workers' independent participation in management shows enormous potential to create many new jobs in information and service industries, which are growing rapidly. That potential could upgrade the quality of information of products and services and use computers to employ people rather than unemploy them. It could support a much more prosperous and peaceful world.

With the aid of their own computer systems and communications, organizations of employees could build mass organizations of working people and consumers, offer services to them, and offer services to countless small businesses too. They would have massive amounts of information to construct realistic economic models for specific businesses and the general economy. They could go on to create laws, guide investment of public and private funds, and found new social organizations to underwrite their proposals for the American economy.

Organize, Lead, Prosper with Better Information

A full-employment economy needs wide, deep, and open democratic institutions. When ruling elite minorities suppress the population, they destroy information and undermine every economic activity based on information; information is a social creation that is stunted, degraded, or destroyed when it is kept private. Information, education, and communication must be publicly used to be productive. They cannot be locked up by privileged elites and minority ruling circles without being impaired or destroyed.

Information needs to flow freely, but dictatorships suppress it. That's why dictatorship is so inferior to democracy, and why communist dictatorships simply cannot raise their economies to high levels of quality production. The superiority of democracy for creating high-quality information is why employee participation in management is necessary and desirable in modern economies that are increasingly based on information. It also explains why capitalist managements that attempt to have any employee involvement—however rudimentary—produce higher-quality products than managements that exercise power arrogantly and share nothing with employees.

If the present world competition does not result in global cartels, whoever makes the best use of information and organization will come to dominate the economy and lead the world.

Thanks to the freest and most democratic society on earth, despite all its imperfections, American capitalism presently has superior innovation in business and technology. Unfortunately, creativity and innovation in America are sadly lacking in big business and government; they are found most often among individuals and small businesses. At the same time, Japanese capitalism—especially big Japanese businesses and government—quickly copies American products, creatively exploits faster the potential of American discoveries, develops early American technological products faster into mass consumer products, and provides superior organization in large industries to surpass American production once products become big business. Japan is also pursuing independent research of its own and may yet emerge as a major leader in creating and developing totally new technologies.

The competition between America and Japan is dangerously unstable. In the short run, it aids both systems; it encourages change and breaks down old monopolies. But in the long run, no one can win that kind of competition. It leads to accelerating change, social disruption, and bankruptcy as investments become obsolete before they become profitable. America cannot escape Japan, and Japan can win only if the American economy is crippled—which will hurt Japan perhaps more than it will hurt America. Japan and the U.S. are running on a treadmill. Eventually their race will lead either to collapse in exhaustion of capital or to domination of the world economy by the particular corporations or cartels that win the present competition. In either case, extreme and rapid changes will occur that will create desperate, displaced peoples who will turn peace into war and life into hell. There has to be a better way. And there is.

There is no mystery or secret that American management must

be improved and that working people have information that management needs. More and more people are recognizing that the strength and brains behind Japan's superior productivity is something that most commonly is vaguely referred to as "worker participation" or "employee involvement"—which includes extensive participation by middle management in making consensus-like decisions. The only real questions in the current debate for many American companies and government operations are: How will employee participation be implemented? And, what role—if any—will unions or other independent employee organizations play in it?

Will "employee involvement" be the modern descendant of company unions or paternalism that managements institute to control employees and keep out unions? Will employees and unions continue to be dependent on management, with little or no freedom to speak up about operations, few opportunities or incentives to share, and no added authority to affect management decisions or policy?

Or will unions and employee groups be free and independent enough to provide new information, make substantive decisions, create new organizations, and enforce their organization and decisions about the workplace, field, investments, and marketplace?

Independent employee participation in management is the best hope to save many industries and revitalize the entire economy. Without unions and similarly independent employee associations, who will supply, protect, and enforce feedback? Who will protect outspoken employees from vengeful or petty or corrupt individual bosses? Who will light a fire under lazy, corrupt, or complacent bureaucratic managements *before* their businesses or government services begin to collapse? And who will protect employees—and the contributions that are wanted of them—from short-sighted demands to make employees pay for everyone else's greed or incompetence? The answer is that to date, without unions, no one has done these things. Only unions or other democratic organizations of working people have the potential ability and motivation to do them.

America desperately needs to have organized workers and employees actively and independently involved in making management decisions. Some parts of American management now have or are trying their own versions of employee participation. They may keep trying as long as they are under pressure from the Japanese, or until they go bankrupt or abandon that line of business. They may partially succeed in introducing some limited form of employee participation. But they can only scratch the surface of the enormous potential that working people have.

Most managements are shackled by inherent weaknesses in the management-by-bureaucracy system and the super-liquidity trap they have created. Ideally they want to keep employees utterly dependent on management. That creates fears that deny valuable information and intelligence to management. And it leads to confrontational attitudes that degrade performance, preclude cooperation, lower quality, and raise costs as employees demand higher wages to compensate for their poor job conditions and slavish dependency. In addition, managers' executive performance is corrupted by their freedom to act as self-serving bureaucrats. And executive performance is further degraded by the brutality of having to act as policemen and jailers to push and suppress working people.

If independent employee involvement in management can introduce higher quality information and greater organization with less conflict, then it can improve the effectiveness of the very large American corporate and government bureaucracies that are most uncompetitive or deficient. It is the right direction to take, and organized employee groups will have to be deeply and independently involved in it to provide the impetus, resources, and protective, "lubricating" environment to release employees' full potential. Otherwise, many managements will fail and drag the American economy—meaning all Americans—down with it.

If independent employee participation in management receives public support to create new organizations for production, marketing, small businesses, consumers, and all working people, then America could become the leader once more instead of continuing to sink into industrial inferiority and economic decline.

To release employees' untapped potential, organized workers and employees need to get recognition and compensation for the value they can add. And they need to get the authority and responsibility to do what is necessary to achieve that added value. Then employees and unions may be much more willing to take risks along with management, instead of against management. And management can be freed of its confrontational policeman role to concentrate on analyzing information and making executive decisions.

With proper compensation and authority, independent employee participation with management would combine the traditional American incentives of risk and reward with the awesome organizing ability that organized workers demonstrate every time they form unions and win strikes. They could incorporate the unique, often suppressed or ignored knowledge that employees everywhere have about the factory floor, the office routine, and field conditions, where bureaucrats rarely venture. They could combine America's unrivaled entrepreneurial creativity and technological inventiveness with the superior organizational productivity and high quality that Japanese management currently demonstrates in large-scale industrial production.

The key to justifying independent employee involvement in management is the information and practical skills that working people possess collectively and uniquely about production and marketing.

The key to using employees' information and skills is the organizational abilities that organized workers possess.

And the key to implementing employee involvement is the power that unions and other possible employee organizations—professional associations, political parties, consumer unions—can use to protect individuals who speak up, democratically debate employee ideas, negotiate for job security, and independently fight for employee goals.

The tasks for organized workers and employees in all cases, from cooperating with effective managements to improving or running businesses and government operations and running candidates for political office, are the same:

- Employees must collect operational information and demonstrate by logic, fact, and example that improvements can be made, especially in production, marketing, and product development.

- Organized workers and employee groups must formulate proposals for improvements and present them to management, stockholders, and the public.

- At the same time, they must develop the union and political organizations to protect, aid, and support the working people who gather the information and make the proposals.

- And unions and employee groups must reach out for allies to all the segments of the public, including consumers, taxpayers, stockholders, small businesses, and everyone who stands to gain from better management in big business and government. They must exchange information and organize for actions in their mutual benefit.

These tasks require an attitude that is far more independently minded than the usual employee's. Employees must approach problems as if they were working for *themselves*; as if they were owners or stockholders—but certainly not subordinates—and stood to gain personally from any improvements that were gained. Employees must not think about what management will allow or approve; rather, they need to think about what exactly they want management to do, and how to do it. They must think as if they were attending to their own interests in improving the overall organization; for on average, in most cases, they are. And, of course, they must simultaneously bear in mind that they will work within the organization that they create and will have to obey its rules of operation.

At first, thinking out a boss's role will feel like a thankless task, but it is an investment in the future. It creates new abilities, and those abilities are precisely the ones necessary to win support for change.

These are immense tasks and won't be easy to do, but industrialized workers have equally immense abilities and an awesome record of achievement. And the penalties they would suffer for failure in these tasks would be horrendous.

Whoever leads in employee involvement will lead the world economy. If organized workers' independent participation in management is allowed to turn the tables of operations in production, marketing, and product development, it promises to sweep American production and revitalize the American economy. If not, then Japan or some other large country or economic bloc that involves its employees more will be the winner. Or worse, all employers will seek the lowest-wage-labor-in-the-world option, resort to ruinous dictatorships to suppress the people who protest being enslaved and impoverished, and sink the world into barbarism. The world may not survive an economically weak or dangerously dictatorial America. America and the world need organized employees' independent involvement in management as much as employees themselves need it to avoid the dangers of runaway inflation or depression, dictatorship, and nuclear war.

As in the 1930s in America and in 1981 in Poland, when workers fought for and won rights that no outside observers thought possible, American working people today are much more eager to take bold initiatives than most "expert observers" may admit to or imagine.

Complaints about bad management are commonplace. Contempt for incompetent managers is widespread. Working people are increasingly hurting, are becoming aware of what is hurting them, and are fighting mad about what is happening to them. But it is not in their nature to engage in empty symbolism or waste their precious time and energy and meager individual finances in vain gestures following self-proclaimed radicals, opportunists, sectarians, or loudmouths to defeat and oblivion. Isolated and alone, individual working people can do nothing of lasting value, except to risk great harm to themselves, and they know it. They won't act without out a chance to win. Without a working people's organization that presents practical and realistic proposals to fight for, and which projects a larger, hopeful vision of a better world, working people in general, and industrialized workers in particular, will not be mobilized in their great strength. But they are not content and they are not asleep, despite their low public profile and their lack of coverage in the general news media. They are just waiting for an organization that will serve them and offer programs that they are convinced will work.

All that needs to be done is for an organization to talk openly, honestly, loudly, courageously, and above all *realistically* and concretely, without wild rhetoric and empty slogans, about independent employee participation in management. Then millions of hopeful working people will pick up the charge, work together, and fight to remake and uplift the world.

If organized workers and employee groups show that they can improve the economy and thereby expand freedoms of opportunity and enterprise for all people, they would appeal to countless millions of working people and would-be working people. They could lead the nation and the world toward stable economic growth, social harmony, and personal fulfillment. They could make the future worth working for.

Index

About the Author

Ernest D. Lieberman is a writer with a special interest in business and technology. As a computer programmer and analyst, he worked with corporate, divisional, and plant-level managers for Western Electric in the manufacturing area and for American Cyanamid Co. in business administration and research and development.

Mr. Lieberman is a magna cum laude graduate of the University of Pennsylvania with a B.A. and honors in physics. At Penn he was elected to Phi Beta Kappa, earned two varsity letters in track, and received the Frazier prize for scholar-athlete. He has an M.A. degree from Princeton University's Aerospace and Mechanical Sciences Department. For his degree, he performed research on liquid crystals, which was published in *Applied Physics Letters*.

He currently lives in New York City. *Unfit to Manage!* is his first book.